THE RESURGENCE OF ANTI-SEMITISM

Jews, Israel, and Liberal Opinion

BERNARD HARRISON

D1225956

ROWMAN & LITTLEFIELD PUBLISHERS, INC.
Lanham • Boulder • New York • Toronto • Plymouth, UK

ROWMAN & LITTLEFIELD PUBLISHERS, INC.

Published in the United States of America
by Rowman & Littlefield Publishers, Inc.
A wholly owned subsidary of The Rowman & Littlefield Publishing Group, Inc.
4501 Forbes Boulevard, Suite 200, Lanham, Maryland 20706
www.rowmanlittlefield.com

Estover Road
Plymouth PL6 7PY
United Kingdom

British Library Cataloging in Publication Information Available

Library of Congress Cataloging-in-Publication Data

Harrison, Bernard, 1933–
    The resurgence of anti-Semitism : Jews, Israel, and liberal opinion / Bernard
Harrison.
      p.   cm. — (Philosophy and the global context)
    Includes bibliographical references and index.
    ISBN-13: 978-0-7425-5226-5 (cloth : alk. paper)
    ISBN-10: 0-7425-5226-8 (cloth : alk. paper)
    ISBN-13: 978-0-7425-5227-2 (pbk. : alk. paper)
    ISBN-10: 0-7425-5227-6 (pbk. : alk. paper)
    1. Antisemitism—History—21st century. 2. Right and left (Political science) 3.
Arab-Israeli conflict—Influence. I. Title. II. Series.
DS145.H377 2006
305.892'4—dc22   2006014650

Printed in the United States of America

∞™ The paper used in this publication meets the minimum requirements of
American National Standard for Information Sciences—Permanence of Paper for
Printed Library Materials, ANSI/NISO Z39.48-1992.

THE RESURGENCE
OF ANTI-SEMITISM

Philosophy and the Global Context

Series Editor: Michael Krausz, Bryn Mawr College

This series addresses a range of emerging global concerns. It situates philosophical efforts in their global and cultural contexts, and it offers works from thinkers whose cultures are challenged by globalizing movements. Comparative and intercultural studies address such social and political issues as the environment, poverty, consumerism, civil society, tolerance, colonialism, global ethics, and community in cyberspace. They also address related methodological issues of translation and cross-cultural understanding.

TABLE OF CONTENTS

FOREWORD

Had a book entitled *The Resurgence of Anti-Semitism* been published six or seven years ago, it almost certainly would have been met with surprise, if not outright skepticism. Today, it is a welcome, even necessary, text. What has changed to make it so? Simply put, since the collapse of the Oslo peace accords and the launching of a low-intensity but deadly war against Israel by the Palestinians, hostility to Jews and, especially, the Jewish state has escalated in ways almost no one foresaw just a half-dozen years ago. The resurgence of anti-Semitism may not have been caused directly by these developments, but it has accompanied them. Moreover, it has intensified in the wake of the 9/11 terror strikes in New York and Washington, D.C., and the wars that have followed in Afghanistan and Iraq. In a climate marked by political turmoil and ongoing violence of this kind, aggressive passions, including those that fuel anti-Semitism, gain a license to thrive. And, beginning in 2000 and continuing up to today, anti-Semitism has not only been thriving but proliferating in sundry ways.

Few people expected this return to anti-Semitism, though looking back it was unrealistic to believe that this most ancient of hatreds would become a thing of the past; after all, ideologies and social pathologies that date back over many centuries are not likely to disappear all at once. Nevertheless, until recently anti-Semitism seemed to be more or less quiescent, and there was little serious talk of its resurgence. No doubt some people may have continued privately to harbor negative feelings about Judaism and the Jews; but it has been widely assumed, after the Holocaust, the overt expression of such sentiments, let alone their return in the form of aggressive actions, was simply unthinkable. Residual passions of this ugly sort might linger for awhile on the fringes of society, but within mainstream Western opinion anti-Semitism has long been regarded as morally and politically discredited—a spent force largely without personal or cultural appeal.

By and large, at least within enlightened circles, it remains so to this day. And yet, as Bernard Harrison demonstrates on virtually every page of this book, anti-Semitism has not only returned but has taken up residence within some of these very same circles. How it has come to do so and what its reappearance portends are questions at the core of this probing study.

If serious attention is once again being paid to anti-Semitism—and too little yet is—it is owing to several factors that most analysts of contemporary affairs could not have anticipated as recently as a decade ago: across the European continent, a series of violent assaults against Jews and Jewish institutions on a scale not seen since the end of World War II; within Israel, dozens of lethal suicide bombings unleashed by Palestinian terrorists against the country's civilian population; within the Muslim world, the rise of a militant or jihadist version of Islam that inscribes hostility to Jews at the very heart of its ideological mission; and, within segments of the political left in Europe and, to some degree, America, the emergence of a fierce anti-Zionism that often resembles traditional anti-Semitism at its worst. It is this last phenomenon that Bernard Harrison finds particularly offensive and that draws his critical scrutiny in the chapters of this book.

Living, as he does, in the United Kingdom, the author has not had to look very far for his materials. Amongst European countries, Britain today has the unenviable distinction of being second only to France as the site of the most numerous and serious anti-Semitic incidents. Now numbering in the hundreds each year, these include violent assaults on individual Jews, arson attacks against synagogues and other Jewish institutions, the defacement of Jewish schools, and the desecration of Jewish cemeteries. Over the past several years, Jewish students at British universities have felt marginalized and pressured by the aggressive activities of anti-Zionist groups on campuses. Britain has also seen calls from the country's largest teachers' union for an academic boycott of Israeli universities; from its trade unions for a boycott of their Israeli counterparts; from the Church of England for divestment from select companies doing business in Israel; from segments of the country's Muslim communities for the cancellation of Holocaust Memorial Day on the grounds that such a national commemorative service might give offense to Muslims; and more. When, in 2005, Michael Howard, the Jewish leader of the Conservative Party, ran for national election, he was greeted by posters from the governing Labor Party portraying him against images of Shylock and Fagin—literary England's most resonant stereotypes of the avaricious and cunning Jew. Other public servants identified as being of Jewish origin—Peter Mandelson, Jack Straw—have been similarly maligned. When the political climate turns this ugly, it is clear that matters have gotten out of hand. Most Jews continue to live well in Great Britain, but as the country's Chief Rabbi, Sir Jonathan Sacks, has noted, they do so with a degree of unease not experienced for decades. "For the first time in my memory," Rabbi Sacks has declared, "it has become uncomfortable to be a Jew in Britain."

A considerable part of this discomfort is owing to biases present within institutions led or otherwise served by people who make up the country's "left-wing cognitive elite," as Rabbi Sacks refers to them. With embarrassing regularity, leading figures in British politics, journalism, academia, and the arts have taken to speaking and writing about Jews and the Jewish state in hostile ways, sometimes subtly, sometimes exuberantly. The current mayor of London, Ken Livingston, for instance, has an obvious fondness for making grossly insulting statements—some of them linking Jews to Nazis—that seem calculated to be offensive. The fact that he has been censured and even suspended from office for such outrageous behavior seems not to bother him at all. And Livingston is hardly alone. In May 2006, Chris Davies, the leader of the Liberal Democrats in the European parliament, embarrassed his colleagues and was forced to resign after making similarly crude and hateful remarks. Two years earlier, another British parliamentarian, Jenny Tonge, was sacked after publicly expressing sympathy for Palestinian suicide bombers. Readers of Britain's leading liberal newspapers and periodicals—*The Guardian, The Independent, The London Review of Books*—are regularly treated to the same display of bias, as are listeners to news programs and special features on British radio and television that focus on the alleged sins of Israel and the machinations of "the Zionist lobby."

An especially egregious example of the latter was the January 14, 2002 issue of *The New Statesman*. With a cover that depicted a large, gold Star of David piercing a supine Union Jack and feature stories on what was not-so-playfully called "A Kosher Conspiracy?," *The New Statesman* was blatant in alleging a sinister Jewish presence within the borders of Great Britain. Not surprisingly, the issue was met with angry responses, and before long the journal's editor, Peter Wilby, issued a formal "Apology." Yet this gesture was as flawed in its formulations as were the ill-conceived stories and visuals that gave rise to it in the first place, and it probably set few minds to rest over what *The New Statesman* was really up to.

In an exceptionally well-wrought analysis, Bernard Harrison dissects the words and images that constituted this nasty affair and exposes "A Kosher Conspiracy?" for what it is: a near-classic instance of rhetorical anti-Semitism newly dressed up as anti-Zionism. Moreover, he probes well beyond this sordid case to argue convincingly that "the new anti-Semitism has spread to infect 'left-liberal' discourse at all levels." "How has it come about," he properly asks, "that the 'anti-racist' liberal-left finds itself up to its neck in the oldest form of racism?" And why should the old lies about the Jews "be making a reappearance just now and from such an apparently unlikely segment of the Western political spectrum?" Answers to these troubling questions are not easy to come by, for Peter Wilby and countless others like him in Britain's liberal media are not anti-Semitic in the traditional mold. In fact, as Harrison acknowledges, it is unlikely that they are anti-Semitic at all in any clearly defined or programmatic way. Nevertheless, they are involved in fostering attitudes that are deeply, if often unintentionally, inimical to Jews and the Jewish state. In exploring the climate of opinion that houses and encourages these attitudes, Harrison is able to clarify the links between anti-Zionism and anti-Semitism in ways that make his book indispensable to anyone who wishes to understand the resurgence of anti-Jewish animosities today.

Harrison is not the first to investigate this complex of questions, but few have brought to the task personal commitments and scholarly credentials equal to his—a searching and capacious mind, unusually well-developed interpretive skills, a rare degree of analytical rigor, and an informed historical sense. Drawing on all of these, as well as a healthy dose of good sense, he offers incisive commentary on a range of false charges against Jews and the Jewish state, exposing in the process the bogus nature of the accusatory rhetoric now commonly employed against Israel and its supporters. As he makes clear, honest criticism of discrete Israeli policies or actions that are deemed injurious or even illegal is perfectly appropriate, and such criticism is not in itself anti-Semitic. What is at issue here is something else entirely: "Coupling the Star of David with the swastika, and Israel with the Nazis . . . is not to engage in 'criticism of Israel'; it is rather to engage in political anti-Semitism in its most traditional form."

Uncovering the inconsistencies and incoherences inherent to the arguments that support such prejudice is a large part of the author's aim, and he fulfils it brilliantly time and again. Thus, if they have not already figured it out on their own, readers of this book accustomed to hearing about Israeli "apartheid," "racism," "colonialism," "fascism," "genocide," and "nazism" will come to see how meaningless these charges are and how inapplicable to the actual situation on the ground in today's Middle East. They will also come to understand the intellectual poverty of that strain of left-wing messianism that depends on such hollow accusations for its raison d'etre and political future. As Harrison lucidly reveals, the theoretical foundations on which such politics rest have virtually collapsed with the defeat of the socialist vision of proletarian internationalism and the reversal of the promise of historical materialism, leaving behind little more than a highly moralized world-view unsupported by developments in the real world. The adherents of this failed world-view, passionate to retain moral and political certitudes now seriously at odds with reality, have improbably, yet tenaciously, taken hold of the most irrational and ruinous of fictions—that of anti-Semitism—and mistaken it for truth. Harrison writes about their drift into delusion with a palpable sadness, for he is fully aware of those on the left who have been principled opponents of anti-Semitism and in the past fought against it determinedly. Today, however, "sections of the British left are currently gripped by a fit of anti-Semitic paranoia," which, in the form of anti-Zionism, they are prone to pass off as moral virtue itself. As this book shows in clear and convincing ways, if the left remains wedded to this state of mind and wins numbers of others to its side, the social and political consequences within Europe could become even more serious than they are at the moment, and also more dangerous. And not only for the Jews.

—Alvin H. Rosenfeld, Indiana University

PREFACE

A good deal of attention has been focused, over the past few years, on whether Europe and America are witnessing the rise of a new version of anti-Semitism, coming this time from the left and left-influenced sections of the media and "cognitive elites" in the universities and elsewhere, for the most part presenting itself as political opposition to Israel.[1]

What has been written so far, almost entirely by Jews, are books that document "the new anti-Semitism" and, of course, protest against it. Rather predictably, the response in non-Jewish circles opposed to Israel has not been receptive. As a non-Jew, I have found, on the whole, my fellow non-Jews altogether too prone to pooh-pooh these Jewish attempts to sound the alarm. The counterarguments customarily heard are that there is, on the one hand, a vast difference between hostility to Israel and hostility to Jews *as such*; and on the other that Jews are in the habit of raising the cry of anti-Semitism solely and wholly with a view to discrediting all and any criticism of Israel.

That response immediately raises the issue of how anti-Semitism should be defined. Without such a definition in mind, it is hardly possible to discuss the question of whether, and if so at what points, contemporary debate about the Middle East might take on an anti-Semitic edge.

The existing literature does not always offer a great deal of help at this point. Iganski and Kosmin, indeed, in their introduction to their anthology, suggest that Jewish opinion should be regarded as endowed with something approaching papal infallibility on this crucial preliminary question.

"Anti-Semitism is not a Jewish problem per se: it is a societal issue. However, judging whether or not it is present and how serious it is, is very much for Jews to decide. To do this most Jews arguably bring much more sensitive antennae, an understanding rooted in painful memory, and a greater historical awareness than do most gentiles."[2]

Morally, psychologically, and historically speaking this stance is understandable and must at the very least evoke some sympathy. Epistemically and forensically, however, it cuts no ice. On the one hand, an injury, though it may in the first instance be brought by the injured to the attention of others, cannot, if it is to be adjudged an injury and remedied, be apprehensible, qua injury, only to those suffering it. On the other hand, to complain of anti-Semitism and then suggest that both its nature and its occurrence must be occult to all except Jews can only play into the hands of those who see in such accusations a dishonest attempt to silence criticism of Israel.

The entry of this blocking move into the discussion sets the stage, in short, for a dialogue of the deaf; one as interminable, futile, and acrimonious as these things usually are. There can, in other words, be no serious hope of establishing the truth or falsity of *Jewish* accusations of anti-Semitism while those accused dispose of such a neatly forensic way of undercutting the credentials of accusations *precisely to the extent that they come from Jews*.

It seemed to me, therefore, that there might be room for a short book, one that might usefully be written by a philosopher, and even more usefully by a non-Jewish one such as myself, that would take hold of this thorny issue at precisely that point of dialectical *impasse*: a book that would attempt to define a clear boundary between anti-Semitism and legitimate criticism of Israel, and to inquire in some detail whether and how that boundary is being crossed in current public debate; and that would also address the salient question how, if we are indeed in the historically unprecedented situation of confronting anti-Semitism situating itself on the left of politics, such a situation could have arisen?

This book is the result. I am conscious that it is very much a sequence of personal reflections, by a writer with little or no previous presence in the field or history of writing about public affairs. For that reason I am more than usually grateful to friends who were kind enough to read and comment extensively on earlier drafts of the manuscript. They include Leona Toker, Michael Krausz, Gabriel Josipovici, Thomas Mautner, Frederic Reynold Q.C., Walter Harris, Eve DeVaro Fowler, Patricia Hanna, and my wife, Dorothy Harrison, in addition to the three anonymous readers, all of them conscientious and helpful in their often telling criticisms, who reviewed an earlier draft of the manuscript for my publisher. I owe a particular debt of gratitude to Alvin Rosenfeld, who, besides reading and commenting on the manuscript with very great kindness, agreed to provide a Foreword. It goes without saying that none of these people necessarily agree with everything in the book, and that none of them are to be blamed for any errors of fact or reasoning remaining in the present version, for which I remain wholly responsible.

NOTES

1. Recent books devoted to this question include Paul Iganski and Barry Kosmin, *A New Anti-Semitism? Debating Judeophobia in the 21st Century* (London: Profile Books, 2003), and Phyllis Chesler, *The New Anti-Semitism: The Current Crisis and What We Must Do About It* (San Francisco: Jossey-Bass, 2003).

2. Iganski and Kosmin, *A New Anti-Semitism?,* Editors' Introduction, p. 5.

1

A NEW ANTI-SEMITISM?

A CERTAIN CLIMATE OF OPINION

An intellectual hatred is the worst.

—W. B. Yeats, "A Prayer for My Daughter"[1]

According to a number of recent books, and a larger number of news-paper and magazine articles, a new wave of anti-Semitism "is said to be sweeping Europe."[2] In Britain, "a rise in manifestations of anti-Semitism on the streets has allegedly been accompanied by an 'elite', or salon, anti-Semitism, manifest in the print and broadcast media, university common rooms and at the dinner parties of the chattering classes."[3] The chief rabbi of the United Hebrew Congregations of the Commonwealth, Jonathan Sacks, shares this depressing diagnosis:

> [The new anti-Semitism] is coming simultaneously from three different directions: first, a radicalized Islamist youth inflamed by extremist rheto-ric; second a left-wing anti-American cognitive élite with strong repre-sentation in the European media; third, a resurgent far right, as anti-Muslim as it is anti-Jewish.[4]

There is no doubt that the number and scale of anti-Semitic incidents, in-cluding the defacing of Jewish cemeteries and monuments, arson attacks on synagogues, and insult or physical violence toward individual Jews, has increased in Europe since the start of the 1990s. But neither the nature nor the motivation of that kind of anti-Semitism is "new." It is entirely continuous with the long tradition of European anti-Semitism, and the vast majority of it comes from two of the three sources identified by Sacks: "radicalized Islamist youth" and the extreme Right.

It is the third element in Sacks's diagnosis that interests me, and it is the subject of this book: the alleged anti-Semitism of "a left-wing anti-American cognitive elite with strong representation in the European media."

Certainly "the Left" has received a great many accusations of anti-Semitism in recent years, the vast majority coming, it must be said, from Jews. If these accusations are sound, then the political phenomenon they claim to detect is indeed new. For the past century and more, the Left has been the main reservoir of principled opposition to anti-Semitism. If that were to change, or worse, if a change were to be already in train, the consequences for European politics could be serious, and conceivably as disastrous as those of the 1930s.

It is not entirely obvious, however, what is meant by "the Left" in this context. Normally such a phrase might be viewed as singling out either organizations or individuals. But are we supposed to possess evidence that any important organized parties or groupings on the European or American left are at present in any important way anti-Semitic, or even infiltrated by anti-Semitism? One needs a criterion, of course, for what is to be taken to constitute anti-Semitism. I shall argue here that there is good reason to consider willingness to advocate or acquiesce in the dismantling of Jewish majority rule in Israel an anti-Semitic stance. But even if one were to grant that, how widespread is such a stance on the *organized* Left? As an American critic of an earlier draft of this book put it: "I certainly know of one or two fringe groups on the left that advocate the dismantling of Israel. It is simply false to claim that such a goal is the agreed upon goal of the left." Quite so; and I am sure the same could be said of mainstream parties and organizations on the left in Britain.

There is a further reason why, if any rational discussion of "the new anti-Semitism" is to proceed, the institutions of organized politics should not be placed center stage. The new anti-Semitism is evidently felt, by those who feel its presence, to be an altogether more diffuse phenomenon; something, as the journalist Petronella Wyatt, quoted above, stated, "manifest in the print and broadcast media, university common rooms and at the dinner parties of the chattering classes." In short, a phenomenon involving considerable numbers of educated people, many of whom, no doubt, would describe themselves as "liberals" or "liberal-minded" or "on the left," but comparatively few of whom would be members of organized political groupings.

Are we then to take "the new anti-Semitism" to be the manifestation of a diffuse collection of anti-Semitic *individuals*; a new class of Jew-haters suddenly, and most surprisingly, raising its head in just those corners of liberal England and liberal America where until very recently any open expression of anti-Semitism would have resulted in the exclusion of the culprit from the very common rooms and dinner parties now asserted to be epicenters of the new version?

There are difficulties with this proposal too. The most obvious one is that when a specific accusation is made with a view to demonstrating an instance of the new anti-Semitism, the person accused will almost always reply that he or she is hostile to *Israel*, or to the actions of one or another Israeli government; but not in the least hostile toward *Jews as such*. It is also very common on such occasions for the accused to remark with considerable irritation that these accusations always seem to come from Jews, and that Jews seem either to be unable to distinguish between opposition to Israel and anti-Semitism or else to display a discreditable willingness to use accusations of anti-Semitism to deflect all and any criticism of Israel.

Whatever one makes of the justice of this last suggestion, the fact that it is so readily resorted to should in itself make us doubt whether, insofar as "the new anti-Semitism" is "manifest," its manifestations can seriously be taken to argue the presence, in hitherto unsuspected quarters, of large numbers of seriously anti-Semitic individuals. Serious anti-Semites, after all, have never been backward in openly avowing that *Jews*, and the harm they supposedly do, are hateful *in themselves*. Someone who claimed that *Jews, in themselves*, enjoyed his warmest sympathy, and that his objections were merely to the activities of certain organizations that happened to be run by Jews, would hardly have been welcomed with open arms, for example, in the German National Socialist Party in 1933, though he might, of course, have been treated as a useful pawn. If we are dealing here with anything deserving the name of anti-Semitism at all, one would be inclined to say, it is at the very least an anti-Semitism which dare not speak its name. One might try arguing, of course, that the universities, the media, and the "chattering classes" are suddenly awash with people who *would* come out in their true colors as virulent anti-Semites of the old type *if it were not for the sympathy for Jews still arising from the Holocaust*. But that argument defeats itself: a sincere, virulent anti-Semite will not stop short at Holocaust-denial, and if the universities, the chattering classes, and so on were awash with such people, their very numbers would surely give individuals enough courage to express their views honestly.

So should we simply conclude, as some commentators have done, that the whole issue is a red herring; that there are not only no, or very few, "new anti-Semites" to be found in liberal-left circles, but no "new anti-Semitism" either? I fear not. A multiplicity of instances cited in Iganski and Kosmin, as well as in other recent books listed in the Appendix, suggests that expressed attitudes toward Jews have hardened and darkened in recent years, in university and media circles, to an extent that should cause anyone, Jew or non-Jew, some disquiet.

So what is going on? I would suggest that we are not dealing here with a conscious turn to anti-Semitism among either educated individuals or organized political groups, at least those in the mainstream of politics. We are dealing with something quite different, though perhaps as dangerous; namely, the recent growth and establishment of a certain climate of opinion. The other day I happened to run into a friend of mine whom I had not seen for some time; a figurative painter whose strong radical sympathies derive in part, I suppose, from membership of a distinguished family, known in England, for several generations, for the strongly liberal views and considerable literary celebrity of many of its members. He asked me what I was up to, and I told him I was trying to finish a book on what I saw as a worrying tendency for anti-Semitic attitudes to infect left-wing writing and talk about Israel. "You're absolutely right," he said. "It frightens me—*and I say that from a position of solidarity with the Palestinians*. And the worst of it is, I don't think it's conscious. I don't think people understand the implications of what they are saying."

It will be my contention—or one of them—in this book that my friend's analysis is broadly correct. But how can that be? We are dealing surely, with people—academics, writers, journalists, lawyers, politicians at all levels—professionally accustomed to assess the implications of what they are saying; people, moreover, apt to adopt consciously "anti-racist" attitudes in all they say and do. It is possible, I suggest, because the capacity of powerful currents of opinion to grip and polarize societies, and in that process to set limits to the powers of conscious reflection and self-criticism retained by individuals who understand themselves as belonging to one "side" or the other, is a matter of record.

A climate of opinion is not, after all, the work of an individual mind. It is something formed out of a multitude of spoken and written items—books, articles, news items, pronouncements by television pundits and news anchormen, lectures, stories, in-jokes, stray remarks—of equally multitudinous authorship. Individuals do not invent it for themselves, they, as we say, "buy into it." When enough people in a given social circle have "bought into" a given climate of opinion, that climate of opinion becomes dominant in that circle. And when that happens it can become quite difficult for individuals in that circle to think outside its terms. For one thing, the dissenter risks making a fool of him- or herself: after all, some very formidable people may have bought into the collection of views in question. For another, climates of opinion are slippery things to take hold of by rational means. Their very multiplicity supplies them with a multitude of escape clauses: refuges to which anyone threatened with defeat in an argument can retreat with a happy conviction of forensic invulnerability. By the same token their protean multiplicity makes their full implications very difficult to unravel, unless one happens to be, for some reason, sensitive to one or another set of them.

The power of these features to mislead and evade the ordinary resources of rational inquiry is multiplied many times when a climate of opinion recommends itself to its adherents on what they consider to be overwhelming moral grounds. That seems to be abundantly the case with the climate of opinion which at the moment tends to dominate any discussion of Israel and the world situation in left-liberal circles.

Any political constituency is defined by certain presiding moral and emotional responses. The presiding response of left-liberal politics for the past two centuries has been generous moral indignation at the sufferings of oppressed classes and peoples. Such responses appear to the liberal mind all the more compelling when the sufferings in question can plausibly be represented as arising from the conduct of the very nation, or bloc of nations to which such minds belong. In such cases the liberal mind is apt to see itself not (in the spirit, say, of John Stewart Mill's defense of the nineteenth-century British Empire) as the representative of a broadly progressive and civilizing mission on the part of the nation to which it belongs; but rather (in the spirit of a much older, religious, and specifically Protestant outlook) as representing the voice of national conscience, called to redeem a wicked society by bringing it, if possible, to repentance and restitution to those it has wronged.

Strong moral convictions, convictions not only of the overriding moral rightness of one's cause, but of the general wickedness of the society to which one belongs, a wickedness made manifest precisely by its failure to recognize and embrace the justice of one's accusations against it, are seldom conducive, in political debate, either to common fairness or to scrupulous attention to what may seem, in the heat of the moment, the more remote implications of what one is saying. A person so motivated will often feel that the very moral urgency of what he has to say compels him to cleave to the central substance of his message and not to waste time quibbling or entering caveats concerning interpretations of his words which distort what he perceives as their intention; interpretations which will no doubt strike him, if he considers them at all, as willful, strained, or "merely theoretical."

To certain of his hearers, however, who may feel themselves, just as urgently, attainted by those implications, which to them, therefore, appear neither particularly remote nor in the least theoretical, his remarks may take on a tone and character which the writer or speaker may neither intend nor be prepared to recognize as his.

It is very tempting for a speaker or writer so accused to take refuge in the notion of authorial intention: to argue that his words cannot bear the interpretation put on them because "that was not what he intended to say." Alas, it will not do. One of the glories of French literary theory over the past thirty years has been to arrive by great labor at a conclusion apparent to English-speaking philosophy for a great deal longer, namely, that what one's words, as uttered, imply or entail, and what one may have intended to assert or imply in uttering them, are two quite different things. A man or woman may well not be an anti-Semite; the sentences he or she utters, on the other hand, in their implications, their entailments, their silences, their evasions, may well be anti-Semitic in character.

It seems to me likely, therefore, that what Jonathan Sacks identifies as a new anti-Semitism coming from a "left-wing, anti-American cognitive elite with strong representation in the European media" is, indeed, objectively speaking, anti-Semitism; but that it is not, or not as yet, a clearly developed and consciously espoused anti-Semitism on the part either of individuals or organized political groups or parties, but rather the floating, impalpable anti-Semitism of a certain climate of opinion.

The conflict between Israel and the Palestinians is one of the most serious of the many international problems affecting the world today. In particular, the plight and sufferings of that part of the Palestinian population which has remained in the refugee camps formed after the war of 1947–48, which resulted in the foundation of the State of Israel, merit sympathy and arouse considerable, and justified, international disquiet, as well, it must be said, as an equivalent disquiet and sympathy on the part of the Israeli left. An entirely admirable moral indignation on behalf of the Palestinians, and a desire to see their sufferings brought to an end, forms the basis of the widespread support for the Palestinian cause among educated people on the left in Europe, Britain, and America.

It is this moral indignation which fuels much of the "elite" media and academic comment currently accused by Jews of anti-Semitism. What is actually happening, it seems to me, is that the very force of the moral indignation felt on the left on behalf of the Palestinians and frustration at the lack of interest shown by large sections of the population compel some of their more committed supporters and publicists on the left to feel themselves not merely tempted, but morally obliged, to present the situation in progressively more extreme and emotionally heightened terms in an effort to capture the attention of affluent Western audiences sated with endless television "news" and adversarial politics to the point, very often, of nausea and indifference.

In this process, people who consider themselves, for the most part with perfectly good reason, to be committed anti-racists, find themselves led, under the stress of what seems to them overriding moral imperatives, to commit themselves to pronouncements and stances which mimic in disquieting ways the claims and motifs of traditional anti-Semitism. Some of the more extreme suggestions which have come to the surface in this way and show signs of establishing themselves almost as *idées reçues* among educated people in the universities and elsewhere are: that the Israeli-Palestinian conflict is the most important international issue facing the world today; that the problem is wholly the fault of Israel, and that no responsibility whatsoever attaches either to the Palestinians themselves or to the Arab states; that Israel is by its nature a "racist" or "apartheid" state; that the crimes committed by the Israelis against the Palestinians far exceed the crimes committed by the Nazis against the Jews; that although the Israelis use the sympathy generated by the Holocaust both to justify the existence of Israel and to blind people to the iniquity of their treatment of the Palestinians, they have not only "learned nothing from" the Holocaust, but have become Nazis, or worse than Nazis, in their turn, and have turned Israel into a Nazi state; that all Jews are alike in supporting Israel and being ready to justify any act of any Israeli government; and that "the Jews" are either plotting, or are in the process of carrying out, a "Holocaust"—that is to say, genocide—against the Palestinians.

Almost any committed Western defender of the Palestinian cause will, in conversation with an uncommitted and skeptical opponent, draw back from defending some, or sometimes all, of these claims. None of them are, as we shall see, particularly rationally defensible. Nevertheless such claims are made, and made very publicly: they stand in print, are repeated endlessly in interviews and in conversation with more sympathetic interlocutors, and, in short, make their way in the world. Taken collectively they imply something very close to the most central and damaging contention of traditional anti-Semitism: the idea that one can speak intelligibly of "the Jews," meaning to denote by that phrase a diffuse but unified polity extending across national boundaries and pursuing essentially malign ends, ends deeply deleterious to the health and prosperity of nations which harbor them, or, in this case, to the peace of the world.[5]

Having said that, one faces an obvious question: Does it matter? How important politically is a vein of largely rhetorical anti-Semitism, confined to the discourse of a "cognitive elite" in the universities, the arts, and the media, central contentions of which are liable on occasion to be tactically disowned by the very people engaged in creating the climate of opinion from which it emanates? As Richard Bolchover notes, out of a survey of three thousand Jewish respondents in London, conducted in 2002 by the Institute for Jewish Policy Research in collaboration with the National Centre for Social Research, only thirty-four reported any experiences with business orders or contacts which might "definitely" or "probably" be put down to anti-Jewish feeling.[6] "The business world," says Bolchover, "is a friendlier environment for Jews and other minorities now than it has ever been." For "the business world," read the economy, and the workplace at large. If the workplace, the main theater of daily life is relatively free of anti-Semitism, should one worry if some of the transient skeins of talk that fill the daily newspapers, resound from television screens, and float around dinner tables sometimes mimic, intentionally or unintentionally, the darker voices of the 1930s?

I think we should, for a number of reasons. For a start, although the utterances, the newspaper articles, the stray remarks which sustain and generate a climate of opinion are indeed transient, are *flatus vocis*, the climate of opinion they sustain need not be. The durability of climates of opinion resembles that of biological species, which are at any given time composed of transient individuals, but fail to die with them because new individuals bearing the characteristics of the species are continually being born. Climates of opinion extend and perpetuate themselves as people buy into them, and in so doing, come to say and believe the same sorts of thing, talk the same language.

The engendering of a climate of opinion, whatever its social constituency, which casts Jews as latter-day Nazis and endangerers of world peace, seems to me to pose a number of threats, to non-Jews as much as to Jews. First, although anti-Semitism in Europe is not, as it was in the 1930s, exploited as a populist rallying cry by any major political party, there remain a number of parties of the extreme Right, such as the French *Front National*, whose candidate came in second at one stage of a recent presidential election, in which it is still very much alive. Street attacks on Jews and on Jewish institutions, coming mainly from small groups on the Right and from young Islamists have greatly increased in number lately. Again, rightly or wrongly, even in England, though less powerfully, it must be admitted, than in France, the views of those perceived as "educated" carry weight with the less educated, certainly more weight than the views of those in the commercial and business worlds. To have it constantly suggested, by mainstream intellectuals, academics, politicians, writers, and political commentators, that Israel, and by extension, "the Jews," are, to a quite extraordinary and terminal extent, corrupt and wicked in their political proceedings, cannot but smooth the path, for organizations which not only every sane anti-racist but every sane democrat should wish to see kept out of power, in propagating their—in their case, straightforwardly racist—outlook. There is, in short, every reason to concur with Jonathan Sacks when he says, "Anti-Semitism begins with Jews but never ends with Jews. Now is the time for those who care about humanity to join the defence of humanity, by protesting this newest manifestation of the world's oldest hate."[7]

In the 1930s the main bulwark in Europe against Right-wing anti-Semitism, weak though it ultimately proved, was provided by the anti-fascist Left. What is truly disturbing about the present state of left-wing opinion on Israel is that it largely disables the Left from focusing on the equally pressing issue, for anti-racists, of anti-Semitism, whether in its own ranks or in those of a resurgent Right. I shall have, in this book, many sharp things to say about the Left: or rather about some individuals and institutions *on* the left, since the expression "the left" is as defective as the expression "the Jews" and for the same reasons; ones ably stated by the philosopher Berel Lang in the essay cited earlier. But I would be very unhappy if that sharpness were to make my readers conclude that I am engaged in a partisan polemic against "the Left" on behalf of "the Right." My purpose is quite the reverse of that. What I would hope to do is simply make people on the left—non-Jews and Jews alike, for there are plenty of Jewish opponents of Israel on the left at present, and some of their pronouncements are quite as extreme as those of some of their non-Jewish comrades[8]—think twice about some of the things being said at the moment, to draw back a little, and, I hope, without giving up their espousal of the Palestinian cause, to couple it with an anti-racism a little wider in scope and more in tune with the outlook of the anti-fascist left of my youth.

There are also reasons closer to the Middle East than to Europe for regarding the present climate of strident denunciation of Israel and "the Jews" by parts of the European and American left as unhelpful. One of the saddest things about the Israeli-Arab conflict is the extent to which it has prevented Israel from serving, as it might and should have served, as an economic locomotive capable of raising, in the long term, the standard of living of the whole region. Within the framework of a secure federal structure analogous, say, to that of Switzerland, which might guarantee religious diversity and tolerance, allowing Jews to live at peace in Muslim or Christian cantons, as Muslim and Christian Arabs live at present, largely unmolested, within the Jewish polity of Israel, the condition of the bulk of Palestinians might at last improve. Indeed it is not easy to see what else, besides the final dawning of peace on some such basis, could improve their condition in any fundamental, structural way. Necessary, although doubtless not sufficient, conditions for that outcome, are, on the one hand, the evolution of Palestinian politics to the point of admitting the possibility of a permanent, self-governing Jewish population in the area; and, on the other hand, the development of a sufficient sense of security on the part of Israeli Jews to permit them to envisage relationships with the surrounding Arab world different from those of an armed fortress with its besiegers. It does not help the latter project that a climate of opinion not only exists in Europe and America, but is widely and insistently disseminated in university and media circles, according to which Israel is a Nazi state whose departure, even whose bloody departure, from the world stage would give cause for the kind of moral rejoicing which accompanied the fall of the Third Reich. What is needed, in short, to serve the needs of a region whose prospects have been wrecked for almost a century, since the fall of the Ottoman Empire, by rabid nationalism on the part of ethnic factional groupings—for the conflicts in the region include, after all, not only that between Jew and Arab, but those between Christian and Muslim Arabs, and, among Muslims, the extraordinarily bitter conflict between Sunni and Shi'a—is not yet more factional moral ranting, but, surely, some attempt to lower the moral and emotional temperature.

My object in this book, beyond the simple desire of the skeptical philosopher to expose manifest and dangerous nonsense, is to pursue that aim. My interests in writing this book are not, in other words, those of the historian, the sociologist, or the professional student of politics. While aiming at factual accuracy, this book contributes nothing original to the sociology, history, or politics of the Jews, of Israel, or of "the new anti-Semitism." A number of excellent books by writers far better qualified in those areas exist, and where I have needed to base my arguments on matters of fact, I have relied entirely on such authorities, citing them in notes or in the Appendix.

In professional terms I am an analytic philosopher, though one, unusually, with a foothold in literary studies. Philosophers and literary critics share an interest in the close analysis of texts, the unraveling of the meanings of words and sentences, their implications, their entailments, their suggestions, as well as those less apparent meanings inscribed, as the late Jacques Derrida liked to put it, in "the margins" of discourse: its silences, its evasions, its carefully concealed founding incoherences.

To these concerns philosophers add their own overriding interest in truth and logical consequence, in the question whether what is said is true, or even makes sense (is even a candidate for truth or falsity), and in whether an argument actually demonstrates what those who rely on it believe it to establish. It is in terms of those modest concerns and capacities that I have chosen to approach the issue of "the new anti-Semitism." This book belongs, in short, to the essentially philosophical genre that used at one time to produce titles of the form: "An Examination of Mr. So-and-So's Philosophy." It sets out to examine the credentials, both moral and intellectual, of the climate of opinion I have so far been discussing, basing that examination in part on close textual scrutiny of some of the writings which have given rise to the accusation of a new anti-Semitism on the left.

Because the book's aims are analytic and critical rather than descriptive, I have resisted suggestions by readers of earlier drafts that I include more illustrative material. There exist, as I have noted already, a number of books and articles in which the sociological and literary evidence for the new anti-Semitism is abundantly documented, and I have listed a selection of these in the Appendix. To have inserted more sociological reportage in the body of the text would have done little, it seemed to me, to help the argument forward and much to obscure its structure and content. Given the urgency of the topic I wanted the book, in any case, to be as short and as readable as possible; something more in the nature of a popular essay than an academic tome.

I begin with a discussion of a single instance of the sort of writing on the left which has provoked accusations of anti-Semitism from Jews—the cover and contents of a certain issue of the venerable British political weekly the *New Statesman*—with a view to showing in detail precisely how, and how easily, an unexceptionable moral indignation felt on behalf of the Palestinians can pass over by insensible degrees into something very hard to distinguish from anti-Semitism of the most traditional kind. Later I pass to the examination of the moral and intellectual bases of some of the more striking and hyperbolic claims made about Israel and Jews in current political polemic. In a concluding section I offer the one very tentative shot at historical explanation that the book contains. I try there to suggest how we might understand, in terms of political disillusion and retrenchment, the strange evolution of political sentiment which has brought us to a situation which fifty years ago would have seemed almost incredible to someone "on the left," as I was then; a situation in which respectable academics and commentators on the left, avowed "anti-racists" to a man, can be found propagating views not all that far from those which, in those days, used to be propagated only in hateful little booklets from the extreme Right. This final chapter (Chapter 9) concludes with a brief discussion of the recent controversy over a paper, "The Israel Lobby" by two senior American academics, John Mearsheimer and Stephen Walt, which serves two purposes in the book. It serves as a further example on which to test both the criteria advanced in the book for distinguishing between anti-Semitism and "legitimate" criticism of Israel, and the suggestions about the causal background of the new anti-Semitism advanced in Chapter 9. And, from the point of view of American readers, it brings the discussion, in a sense, full circle, by concluding with an American instance of putatively, if no doubt unintentionally, anti-Semitic writing which shares many features with the British examples from which the discussion started out.

Before getting to any of that, however, I want to begin, as philosophers so frequently do, by drawing a distinction: in this case a distinction between two forms, one much more dangerous than the other, which anti-Semitism can take.

TWO TYPES OF ANTI-SEMITISM

> To take only the subject of the Jews; it would be difficult to find a form of bad reasoning about them which has not been heard in conversation or admitted to the dignity of print. — George Eliot, "The Modern Hep! Hep! Hep!" *The Impressions of Theophrastus Such*[9]

Before getting down to business I propose to introduce a distinction that I have not found generally marked or observed in discussions of the topic, but which will turn out to be important to what follows: the distinction between what I shall call *social* or *distributive* anti-Semitism and *political* anti-Semitism. Distributive anti-Semitism is contempt visited upon individual Jews for no other reason than that they are Jews. Expressions of it abound in Victorian literature. One can pick up the general tone of the thing from, say, the passage in Surtees's *Mr. Romford's Hounds* in which Lucy Glitters's friend Miss Shannon, pursuing the former's request to find a suitably impressive but cheap and second-hand livery for her mock footman, goes from

"Nathan's to Levy's, and from Abraham's to Solomon's, bartering and bargaining with the hook-nosed *costumiers*."[10] This is *social* anti-Semitism, because the type of tolerant, amused contempt it visits on "hook-nosed costumiers" and their coreligionists is the kind appropriate to *social* inferiors. But for that very reason it is not a very dangerous kind of anti-Semitism. There are two reasons for that. The first is that social contempt of the sort expressed in Surtees's view of Whitechapel Jews in the 1850s was, as more recent forms of it still are, such a central pillar of British, and more specifically English, life, that it in no way singled out Jews as *any more* contemptible than a host of other groups, from Irish immigrants to virtually anybody perceived as "foreign," from young men "in trade" masquerading as gentlemen to the entire working class. The second reason is that one of the characteristics that distributive racism most readily denies to those it despises is *importance.* Surtees's contemporary reader, chuckling over Miss Shannon's pursuit of a bargain in livery, might well subscribe to a stereotype of Jews—which we, from our rather different and far sadder historical perspective, would perceive as anti-Semitic—as shabby little foreign bounders dealing in old clothes in Whitechapel. But, *just in virtue of the dismissive character of that estimate,* such an anti-Semite could hardly see the activities of Jews—any more than those of such other objects of his contempt as dishonest horse copers, cardsharps, or drunken Irish railway workers—as a serious threat to the British Empire. In the ordinary way of things, contempt drives out fear. I am half inclined to think, indeed, that the relative safety and respect in which the Jews have lived in Britain for several centuries is less due to any superior virtue on the part of my countrymen than simply to the fact that the extraordinarily central role played by notions of social class, and the associated modes of contempt and snobbery, in British culture and society, has ensured that the only kind of anti-Semitism which has enjoyed any currency in the culture at large—as distinct from isolated political groupuscules on the Right (and Left), and some individual intellectuals,[11] the latter effectively neutralized by the enduring, and to a certain extent, speaking myself as an intellectual of sorts, endearing, anti-intellectualism of British society[12]—has been the social, distributive kind.

Political anti-Semitism is rather more dangerous. Political anti-Semitism, I want to say, is anti-Semitism directed not at Jews perceived as forming, one by one, as one might put it, a collection of more or less socially unappetizing individuals, but at the *Jewish community* perceived as actively pursuing, *on a collective basis,* goals and policies inimical to non-Jewish individuals or polities. This type of anti-Semitism is remarkable for having produced a specific body of beliefs about Jews, of considerable antiquity, supported by a mass of hate-filled literature, of which the *Protocols of the Elders of Zion* is only the best-known example. The beliefs in question are in one sense protean in character. As they are handed down or disseminate themselves from century to century, new grudges, new accusations, step in to replace older ones which too obviously have had their day. But these represent only the changing content which fills the gaps in a structure of claims or theses which never changes. These "structural" claims invariably include at least the following three:

1. "The Jews" are a mysteriously but totally depraved people, given over unreservedly to wicked and destructive activity aimed at the overthrow or corruption of non-Jewish society.
2. The Jewish people is distinguished from all others by the fact that membership of it is essentially membership of a *conspiracy*.
3. Because of the inimical and conspiratorial nature of Jewish culture, Jews constitute a permanent collective threat to the well-being of any nation which harbors them.

Political anti-Semitism is in principle, and has proved in practice, far more dangerous than the social or distributive kind. For a political movement to turn anti-Semitism into a winning element in its program and propaganda, it is necessary to actively induce fear of Jews, considered as something more than the collection of rather pathetic and contemptible individuals which a merely social or distributive anti-Semitism would make of them: to induce fear of them, that is, *considered as constituting a shadowy but well-organized and infinitely malign political entity*. For genocide to be set in train, in other words, it was necessary for a linkage to be forged between a widespread distributive anti-Semitism and millennial politics. Political anti-Semitism is what has always forged, and continues to forge, that linkage.

Presented with a set of categorical assertions of the type numbered 1–3 above, the temptation is to ask: *Is all this true?* The liberal-minded will respond that it is not true, that it is a monstrous falsehood, perhaps that it is "madness." And their voices, as they say these things, will often betray, to the attentive ear, a certain disquiet occasioned by the consciousness of a repressed, but still audible little voice which murmurs, "But all the same, perhaps there's something to it." Perhaps because it is difficult to prove a negative, perhaps because ingrained cultural attitudes defeat attempts to suppress them by mere acts of will, the effort of denial in this context is likely, often, merely to lead to people being, as the psychoanalysts say, in denial. I once had a very sweet, very liberal American colleague who confided to me that anti-Semitism of this kind had proved so durable, had had such a long and varied history, that there must be at least a grain of truth in it. He didn't wish to think that, of course, but he was too honest to think that the claims of political anti-Semitism could be entirely refuted.

Happily, however, we need not exert ourselves to deny, in the ordinary sense, or in the ordinary sense to refute, the three root propositions of political anti-Semitism. I mean by that that we do not need to hunt for empirical grounds on which to demonstrate their falsehood. They are, of course, in one rather weak sense at least, false. But, contrary to what is often supposed, there is more than one thing that one may have in mind by calling a proposition false. I once knew a linguist who was interested in what he called "dissolving sentences." An example would be: (A) "My wife is three-fifths Cherokee." Compare this with a sentence like: (B) "Gorillas are native to Algeria." Both are false. But the latter might, had the history of the world, in terms of plate tectonics and climate, been different, have expressed a truth. In the case of the former, on the other hand, there are no facts about our world whose failure to obtain could make it true. In a world in which the production of a child required the sexual congress of five, rather than two, individuals of a given species, it might, indeed, stand a chance of expressing a truth. But *our* world is not *that* world. In our world, since the carnal congress of two and only two individuals is required to create a child, the state of affairs expressed by (A) could not express a truth. That being so, two consequences follow. The first is that we need not exert ourselves to discover empirical grounds for asserting it to be false. The second is that in asserting it to be false we, as it were, understate the case. What is wrong with (B) is that, although it might have been true (had the tectonic plate bearing the continent of Africa moved otherwise), it is, in fact, false. What is wrong with (A) is that there is no way of assigning truth-values to propositions characterizing *this* world (as distinct from those characterizing another possible world in which human sexual relations are pentadic rather than dual) which could make it come out true. Not only is it not true, it is not—in this world, anyway—even a candidate for truth. It is not that it says something false; rather, it says nothing; is a failed, misfired, attempt to say something. Ascribing falsehood in the full sense implies the possibility of truth. Dissolving sentences lack that possibility; hence, they are "false" only in the weak and minimal sense that they are not true.

What I suggest is that the sentences which express the concrete claims of political anti-Semitism are one and all akin to my friend the linguist's dissolving sentences. The three numbered propositions listed above outline, if you like, the structural form of a dissolving system of belief. The deeper one inquires into the putatively factual claims with which successive generations of anti–Semites have associated them, the clearer it becomes, not merely that they are in the ordinary, weak, or minimal sense false, but, more seriously, that they are so vaguely formulated, display such a tendency to dissolve in one's hands into wisps of foul-smelling vapor under the least pressure of rational scrutiny, that there is nothing that could possibly count as establishing either the truth *or* the falsity of such "statements"—which in consequence appear not so much *statements* as the stuff of dreams or nightmares: expressions of personal threat or inadequacy cast superficially, but delusively, in the grammatical form of statements.

Take, for instance the celebrated depravity, the intrinsically inimical character of "the Jews." What does it actually come to, this threat that the Jews as a supposedly organized collectivity pose to the non-Jewish world? Take, for example, one of the earliest claims advanced to give substance to it: the so-called Blood Libel, the charge that Jews abduct and kill non-Jewish children in order to mix their blood with the meal from which the Passover matzo is made. Notice—because it is important to the argument—that the substance of the Blood Libel is not that some *individual* Jew, or even that small, crazy groups of Jews, putatively analogous to the Satanists who lurk on the edges of the Christian community, do, or have done, or might have done, such things. The claim is that the *Jewish community* does or has done such things. But it is precisely at this point that the claim begins to dissolve into incoherence. The early medieval Jewish community against whom the Blood Libel was first directed was a profoundly observant one. One of the first things one learns from interaction with actual observant Jews is that Jewish observance is directed by two things. The first is fidelity—to a degree frequently stigmatized by Christians as obsessive—to the Law (*Halakah*) laid down in the first five books of the Bible, known to Jews as Torah and to Christians as the Pentateuch. The second is the interpretation of *Halakah* in concrete cases, where difference of opinion might arise, by an immensely long tradition of rabbinic argument and interpretation, codified in a large number of authoritative texts (where "authoritative" is to be read as "authoritative subject to further rabbinical reasoning"), including not only major texts such as, say, the Mishnah, or the *Pirkhe Avot*, but also a multitude of minor works by individual rabbis respected in their day, such as the early medieval *She'elot U'Teshuvot Min Ha'Shamayim* (*Questions and Answers from the Heavens*) of Jacob of Marvège.[13] Moreover, great tracts of this literature, at any one time, have always circulated among widely separated Jewish communities. We are talking, after all, about the original People of the Book. If one wished, then, to develop the claim that the *Jewish community*, obsessively observant, largely literate, and intricately rabbinically advised as large parts of it have always been and as virtually all parts of it were in the early Middle Ages, employs in the rituals of Passover the blood of Christian children; if one wished to develop that into a serious proposition, capable of being assessed for truth or falsity, the first thing one would have to do is unearth the rabbinic and textual authorities for the use of infant Christian blood in this way. And here one meets with a check. For not only is there no textual authority for such a proceeding, there are very serious and central *Halakhic* considerations which militate against it. A substantial part of *Halakah* is concerned with issues of ritual cleanness (*kashrut*) and uncleanness. The Torah specifically stigmatizes blood as unclean and forbids its consumption. And as anyone can discover by consulting a table of degrees of uncleanness, a gentile, and what a gentile touches, is also unclean. It is difficult to imagine, therefore, anything more revoltingly, blasphemously unclean, to the religious sensibility of an observant Jew, than Passover matzo contaminated with gentile blood. For these reasons, nothing could be more alien to Judaism than the idea that the consumption of blood could have a sacramental significance. The Blood Libel is internally incoherent, in short, falls apart in one's hands, because it accuses observant Jews of doing, *for religious reasons*, something precisely forbidden by the terms of Jewish religious observance. It is as if ecologists, searching for the cause of the sudden disappearance of a particularly large and revolting species of spider, were to suggest that they had all been harvested and eaten raw, as a delicacy, by wicked arachnophobes.

The religion in which the idea of blood as a sacramental substance *is* firmly rooted is, of course, Christianity. Christians symbolically consume the blood of Christ in the form of the wine of the Eucharist, and have always made familiar use of such related phrases as "washed in the blood of the Lamb." To give substance to the Blood Libel, in the sense of making it the sort of thing that *might* be true, one would need such ideas to be common to both Christianity and Judaism. And in another possible world, one as bizarre as the world in which the production of a child requires genetic input from five individuals, they might be. But that world is not our world. Hence, in our world the Blood Libel, considered as an attempt to state something which might be false, but which might, equally, be true, is a nonstarter: a misfire.

A Jewish friend of mine said to me that when he first came across the Blood Libel he was unable to take it seriously, no doubt because all the considerations I have just laboriously exhumed passed rapidly before his mind—but passed so rapidly before it, and seemed so tediously obvious, that he would never have thought of unpacking them in detail in the way I have just done.[14] Yet they need to be unpacked if we are to begin to think rationally about such accusations. One reason is that many of them are utterly unfamiliar to non-Jews. But there is a second, more important, reason. The only way to kill off the Blood Libel is to see that it is not so much a false accusation as a misfired attempt at accusation, on all fours with "The arachnophobes have eaten all the spiders." Someone who did not see that might start looking around for grounds on which to demonstrate its falsehood. He might observe, for instance, that all the Jews he knows seem far too nice to kill babies for their blood. At which point his adversary retorts, "Ah, but how can you be sure of that?" And at once the argument sets off in new directions, with the Blood Libel up and running again as a possible truth, sustained now only by the entirely misplaced attempt to refute it.

All the concrete accusations in the armory of political anti-Semitism share this curious property of dissolving in our hands when we attempt to drag them before the bar of truth and falsity, though not all for the same reason. Take the accusation that "the Jews killed Christ." This rests on a sentence or two in the Gospel of Matthew: rests, as Frank Kermode puts it, on "the horrible success of Matthew's fiction that the Jews, after Pilate washed his hands, voluntarily took upon themselves and their children the blood-guilt of the crucifixion."[15] Suppose we ask now, as we must if we are to take these things seriously, is it true, if what Matthew says is not "a fiction" but as true to the facts as many Christians believe it to be, that the Jews do indeed bear collectively the blood-guilt of the Crucifixion? There are, evidently, cases in which such questions can receive clear answers. If a group of juvenile thugs are seen to pursue a boy and collaborate in throwing him off a bridge into a river, and he dies, then all in the group are collectively guilty of his death; on the other hand, if only one pushes him off the bridge while the others are seen to trail behind shouting to the killer not to go so far, the guilt belongs only to the one who pushed him. But suppose the guilt does belong to the group, what about their descendants? As Sartre puts it, "if one is going to reproach little children for the sins of their grandfathers, one must first of all have a very primitive conception of what constitutes responsibility."[16] Even if, for the sake of argument, we embrace that conception, where does that get us? So "the Jews killed Christ." Who, for the purposes of this claim, are to count, then and now, as "the Jews"? Is there not an evident difficulty in constituting Jews contemporary with the Crucifixion, let alone their descendants, into a single group of persons all prima facie implicated in the Crucifixion? Jews in the period, after all, even before the destruction of the second temple in 73 C.E., were already spread across the known world, with large groups elsewhere in the Roman Empire and even larger groups outside it, most of whom would have had not the slightest knowledge of events in Jerusalem at the time. To raise the question whether group G was guilty of crime C, in other words, one needs grounds on which to assign membership of G to specific individuals, and those grounds can only come from some circumstance establishing that a given individual was prima facie implicated in the commission of the crime. And it seems perfectly clear that the anti-Semite who holds, on the strength of some words in Matthew, that "the Jews killed Christ" has no means of furnishing this necessary preliminary to any inquiry into whether what he says is true or not. Once again we have not so much an accusation, which might be assessed for truth or falsity, but a dreamlike stab at such an accusation, lacking the prerequisites even for the possibility of falsity (in the strong sense), let alone for the possibility of truth.

Or take T. S. Eliot's suggestion, in *After Strange Gods*, that the danger to our civilization does not come from observant Jews, but that the presence "in large numbers" of "free-thinking Jews" is incompatible with the ideal homogeneity of a healthy society.[17] Pursuing as usual the issue of truth versus falsehood, we ask whether it is true that free-thinking Jews, as a group, have this deleterious effect. To get anywhere with this inquiry we need to know, for a start, what common features of thought or commitment unite "free-thinking Jews" into a coherent group, since if there are no such features, any influence such people may have on society, deleterious or otherwise, will be exercised as individuals, not as a group. But, leaving aside the difficulty of separating, in individual cases, the free-thinkers from the observant, it is surely difficult to see what unguessable set of common features could conceivably connect, say, Freud with Georges Perec and Saul Kripke, or K. R. Popper with Jacques Derrida and Daniel Barenboim. Yet without such features what we have in our hands is once again an accusation of group turpitude, which fails not because it is false, but as it were at an earlier stage, because there turns out, given the way in which the accusation is formulated, to be no coherently specifiable group to accuse.

The philosopher Cora Diamond, in an important essay, discusses—for purposes remote from those which engage us here—medieval hagiography as a type of writing which neither aims at realism nor feels its absence as a fault.

We are told that in an ecstasy Brother Pacificus saw the soul of his brother ascend direct to heaven at the moment it left his body. We are told that is what he saw, but we are not told at all what it was like to see such a thing. In fact we do not have any idea what he saw and how he knew it was his brother's soul. But in the context of the narrative, that is not something felt as an omission. I do not mean that there is nothing that we could imagine here if we were asked to fill in the story, but that what we have here is a narrative style, a texture of story, in which such gaps are not felt as gaps.[18]

Diamond proposes that medieval lives of saints may be regarded as "constructions out of . . . 'linguistic surfaces', sentences used independently of the ties to evidence and consequences which characterise the ordinary application of the expressions which they contain."[19] Of course those expressions can still be used with the ordinary ties to reality uncut, and it is this that allows us to draw a distinction between what, in such accounts, plainly issues from the application of conventions of narrative and genre, and what might, conceivably be, in a commonplace, everyday sense, true. But nevertheless in hagiographic narrative many of the ties connecting discourse to "evidence and consequences," and thus to the issue of truth or falsity, are cut. What I have been suggesting, in effect, is that much the same thing is true of the narratives of political anti-Semitism: that we no more know what it would be like to establish the existence of a Jewish conspiracy than we know what it would be like to see a monk's soul fly straight to heaven; and for the same reason: namely, because the terms in which such things are discussed leave it quite unclear what could conceivably *count* as establishing either of these things.

When it ceases to matter, or to be possible even in principle to establish, whether what is said is true or false, the internal consistency of what is said also ceases to matter. The profound internal incoherence of its specific accusations also characterizes political anti-Semitism as a general outlook. As Jonathan Sacks notes: "Anti-Semitism exists and is dangerous whenever two contradictory factors appear in combination: the belief that Jews are so powerful that they are responsible for the evils of the world, and the knowledge that they are so powerless that they can be attacked with impunity."[20] That is both a thumbnail definition of political anti-Semitism and a tacit acknowledgment of its power to derange the heart by deranging the reason of all those who give ear to it.

The question before us, however, is the existence or nonexistence of a new wave of anti-Semitism coming, inter alia, from a "left-wing anti-

American cognitive elite." What is alleged is not, plainly, a new wave of social or distributive anti-Semitism, but a new version of political anti-Semitism in which "the Jews"—not individuals, taken one by one, who happen
to be Jews, that is, but Jews viewed collectively—are seen as constituting a
reactionary conspiracy to promote a range of political developments ob-
noxious to a wide range of people on the liberal left, and in general to constitute, through the existence of the State of Israel, an obstacle, perhaps even
(as a majority of respondents to a poll recently conducted in Europe were
prepared to agree), the main obstacle, to world peace. Given the fairly un-
controversial account of the perennial nature of political anti-Semitism that
I have just offered, we are clearly faced with the question why any "cognitive elite" should be seriously tempted by it. What could induce educated
men and women to take seriously a dreamlike tissue of pseudo-propositions
having not merely no connection, but not even the possibility of a connection, with reality? I think it is beyond question that that is a fair description
of political anti-Semitism. Unfortunately, it is also beyond question that political anti-Semitism has in the past exercised a firm hold over the imagination of a great many momentarily influential European political elites, not
all of them on the right of politics. What could account for this? One clue
no doubt lies in the intensely theoretical cast of European politics over the
past two centuries. One needs to remember here a central thought in the
work of another philosopher, W. V. Quine (one which he derived from the
French philosopher of science Pierre Duhem), namely, that very few sentences in an elaborate structure of theory need to be capable of independent verification for the theory as a whole to pass as descriptive of reality. If
that is true of the theories of natural science, how much more true it is
likely to be of the systems of political and social theorists, constructions
more grandiose, it is true, certainly more seductive to minds in love with
some of the more soaring and specious promises of the Enlightenment, but
also vastly poorer in possibilities of empirical confirmation than those of
physics, chemistry, or molecular biology? Take, for example the following,
from Marx's second essay "on the Jewish Question":

> When society succeeds in transcending the *empirical* essence of Ju-
> daism—bargaining and all its conditions—the Jew becomes *impossible*
> because his consciousness no longer has an object, the subjective basis of
> Judaism—practical need—is humanised, and the conflict between the
> individual sensuous existence of man and his species-existence is tran-
> scended. The *social* emancipation of the Jew is the *emancipation of society
> from Judaism.*[21]

Julius Kovesi says of this, "In this strange last sentence, 'Jew' stands for the actual Jew and 'Judaism' for the universalised egoism that has been universalised in civil society and idealised in Christianity."[22] What is strange about the sentence, and it is surely a strangeness which pervades the entire passage, is the deployment of the terms "Jew" and "Judaism," which have, one would have supposed, a concrete reference very remote indeed from the content and aims of the philosophy of Hegel in its Young Hegelian redaction, *as if they were terms whose meaning could be exhausted by appeal to the conceptual vocabulary of that philosophy*. That is hardly surprising, of course, given the claim of nineteenth-century German historicism, whether in its Idealist or Marxist version—a claim which it shares with all forms of metaphysical philosophy—to offer a "universal" view of the evolution of human society, which by its nature entirely transcends the deliverances of empirical observation. To a mind saturated in *Geistesgeschichte*, or, for that matter, in dialectical materialism, the modest proposal advanced in this book, that one might best seek an understanding of Judaism by looking into the Mishnah or the Book of Leviticus, or of Jews by talking to some, can appear desperately naive: typical in spirit, indeed, of the vulgar and intellectually Philistine empirio-criticism popular among the academic time-servers who have for so long abounded in our universities, whose chief function is to serve as a support of a civil society whose outmoded class relations are already slipping into history under the pressure of the dialectic. From our point of view, however, that response is just what is needed to explain how such a mind can accommodate without strain the prima facie ludicrous pseudo-propositions that Judaism *is in its essence* "universalized egoism" or "practical need." It can do so because the absurdity is required by the structure of the theory, and to a mind dominated by theory of this type, that is enough.

I do not want to suggest that Hegel and his school, or for that matter the Romantic wing of the Enlightenment, represent the only or the main sources of modern intellectual anti-Semitism, though they are certainly important ones.[23] My point is rather that they provide many examples, such as the one above, of how it is possible to assimilate the terms *Jew* and *Judaism* into systems of theory or social criticism, as terms whose meanings in the context are entirely responsive to theoretical demands internal to the system and entirely unresponsive to the empirical nature of either Jews or their religion. Bryan Cheyette provides a further array of illustrations of this phenomenon in the work of a series of British literary worthies of the last quarter of the nineteenth century and the first half of the twentieth, from Kipling to Shaw and from Belloc to James Joyce and T. S. Eliot. As Cheyette engagingly shows, the accounts of "the Jews" obtainable from these sources are almost risibly diverse and contradictory, ranging as they do from the dottily negative to the loopily positive, and have in common only that strong smell of the study which can come only from a blissful—or acrimonious—innocence of the least contact with, or knowledge of, anything so unpleasant as an actual Jew or an authentically Jewish idea.[24]

In France a new wave of political anti-Semitism, accompanied by an increase in attacks on Jewish institutions and individual Jews, has been taking place for a decade or more. Pierre-André Taguieff, of the *Institut d'études politiques de Paris*, has this to say about the continuities and discontinuities linking this new form of the old evil to its earlier manifestations.

> This recent wave of Judeophobia is inseparable from a legitimating and mobilising ideological discourse of worldwide diffusion, in which one recognises a heritage of words and themes deriving from various traditions of anti-Jewish writing, but also new motifs of accusation, centred upon "Israel" and "Zionism" invested with mythic status as synonyms for all that is repulsive.
>
> One can say, to go straight to the heart of the matter, that the general argumentative form of this discourse is as follows: "The Jews are all, openly or covertly, Zionists. Zionism is a form of colonialism, racism and imperialism; thus all Jews are colonialists, imperialists and racists, either openly or covertly." By way of this representation of "Zionism" as the incarnation of absolute evil, we are witnessing the reconstitution of an anti-Jewish vision of the world in the second half of the Twentieth Century. Like the old "anti-Semitism" in the strong sense of the term, it is structured by an absolute hatred of Jews fantasized as the representatives of a single, unified and intrinsically negative entity exerting a vast power for evil: a hatred directed at Jews as such, considered as the bearers of an essentially evil nature or essence.[25]

One might have hoped, perhaps, that Britain, with its long and frequently celebrated, if not always warranted, reputation for reasonableness, common sense, and political moderation, might have escaped this new wave of nonsense-on-stilts, together with the sonorous drivel of its "legitimating and mobilising discourse." One might indeed. But as we shall see, one would have hoped in vain.

NOTES

1. W. B. Yeats, "A Prayer for My Daughter," in A. Norman Jeffares, ed., *W. B. Yeats: Selected Poetry* (London: Macmillan, 1962), p. 102: "An intellectual hatred is the worst / So let her think opinions are accursed."

2. Paul Iganski and Barry Kosmin, eds., *A New Anti-Semitism? Debating Judeophobia in the 21st Century* (London: Profile Books, 2003), p. 1.

3. Petronella Wyatt, "Poisonous Prejudice," *Spectator*, December 8, 2001.

4. Jonathan Sacks, "A New Anti-Semitism?" in Iganski and Kosmin, eds., *A New Anti-Semitism?*, pp. 38–53.

5. On this, see Berel Lang, "On the 'the' in 'the Jews,'" in Ron Rosenbaum, ed., *Those Who Forget the Past: The Question of Anti-Semitism* (New York: Random House, 2004), pp. 63–70.

6. Richard Bolchover, "The Absence of Antisemitism in the Marketplace," in Iganski and Kosmin, eds., *A New Anti-Semitism?*, pp. 267–74.

7. Sacks, "A New Anti-Semitism?" pp. 38–53.

8. See Alvin Rosenfeld, "Modern Jewish Intellectual Failure: A Brief History," in Edward Alexander and Paul Bogdanor, eds., *The Jewish Divide Over Israel: Accusers and Defenders* (New Brunswick and London: Transaction Publishers, 2006), pp. 7–32.

9. George Eliot, *The Impressions of Theophrastus Such,* ed. D. J. Enright (London: J. M. Dent, Everyman Library, 1995), p. 135.

10. R. S. Surtees, *Mr. Romford's Hounds* (London: Bradbury, Agnew & Co., 1865), p. 173.

11. For an insightful discussion of anti-Semitism in intellectual, political, and literary circles, see Bryan Cheyette, *Constructions of "the Jew" in English Literature and Society: Racial Representations. 1875–1945* (Cambridge: Cambridge University Press, 1993).

12. One thinks of Auden: "To the man-in-the-street/ Who, I'm sorry to say, / Is a keen observer of life, / The word *intellectual* suggests right away / A man who's untrue to his wife." W. H. Auden, *Collected Poems*, ed. Edward Mendelson (London: Faber, 1976), p. 232.

13. I found Jacob and his book in Leon Wieseltier's *Kaddish* (New York: Knopf, 1998), a work remarkable among other things for its loving exploration of the by-ways of rabbinic thought and writing.

14. Walter Harris, to whom I am indebted for some very helpful e-mail discussions of the argument of this section.

15. Frank Kermode, *The Genesis of Secrecy: On the Interpretation of Narrative* (Cambridge, Mass.: Harvard University Press, 1979), p. 20.

16. Jean-Paul Sartre, *Antisemite and Jew* (New York: Grove Press, 1962), p. 16.

17. See Cheyette, *Constructions of "the Jew,"* chapter 6, for extensive documentation of Eliot's views on this topic.

18. Cora Diamond, *The Realistic Spirit* (Cambridge/London: MIT Press, 1991), p. 51.

19. Ibid.

20. Iganski and Kosmin, *A New Anti-Semitism?*, p. 40.

21. Karl Marx, *The Writings of the Young Marx*, ed. and trans. Lloyd D. Easton and Kurt H. Guddat (New York: Doubleday Anchor, 1967), p. 248, emphasis in original.

22. Julius Kovesi, "Moses Hess, Marx and Money," in *Values and Evaluations: Essays on Ethics and Ideology*, ed. Alan Tapper (New York: Peter Lang, 1998), p. 180.

23. See, for instance, Berel Lang, *Act and Idea in the Nazi Genocide* (Chicago/London: Chicago University Press, 1990), chapter 7.

24. Compare Sartre, *Antisemite and Jew*: "Facile talkers speak of a Jewish will to dominate the world. Here again, if we do not have the key, the manifestations of this would certainly be unintelligible to us. We are told in almost the same breath that behind the Jew lurks international capitalism and the imperialism of the trusts and the munitions makers, and that he is the front man for piratical Bolshevism with a knife between its teeth. There is no embarrassment or hesitation about imputing responsibility for communism to Jewish bankers, whom it would horrify, or responsibility for capitalist imperialism to the wretched Jews who crowd the rue des Rosiers" (p. 38).

25. Pierre-André Taguieff, *La nouvelle judéophobie* (Paris: Mille et une nuits, 2002), pp. 12–13, my translation.

2

POLITICAL ANTI-SEMITISM AND THE *NEW STATESMAN*

THE COVER

Early in 2002 I picked up the January 14 issue of the *New Statesman*, a weekly which for many decades has been one of the main intellectual organs of the mainstream Left in Britain, and glanced at its cover. The cover illustration on that issue shows a very small Union Jack, placed horizontally, being pierced by the sharp lower apex of a very large, vertically placed Star of David, which appears to be made of, or painted, gold (it shines with the characteristic luster of that metal). Below it, in large black characters, is the legend "A Kosher Conspiracy?"[1]

One thought at once of the cartoons in *Der Stürmer*. The parallel was expressly noted, for that matter, in a letter published in a subsequent issue, by Stefan C. Reif of St. John's, Cambridge.

> Your cover illustration, depicting the Star of David piercing the heart of the Union Jack was in the best traditions of Nazi Germany's Der Stürmer.[2]

Der Stürmer, as those of us over a certain age remember—as, I suspect, a large majority below that age do not—was, in the Germany of the 1930s, an anti-Semitic magazine of National Socialist Party affiliation edited by Julius Streicher. The brand of anti-Semitism it peddled was political in the sense outlined above. Its aim, in other words, was to represent the Jews not merely as a haphazard collection of more or less repulsive, contemptible, and comic individuals, like the stage Irishmen familiar to a bygone age, but as constituting a malign and conspiratorially organized *political entity*: an entity whose nature, once that nature was exposed and understood, must compel the patriotic citizen to combat and expel it, lest the host body politic be irretrievably harmed, corrupted, or both. To compare the cover image of the January 14 issue to *Der Stürmer* is thus to accuse the *New Statesman* of peddling full-blown political anti-Semitism.

That accusation, considered just in terms of the overt content of the image in question, is very hard to rebut. The Union Jack, presumably signifying Britain, is shown as small and prostrate. It is being pierced, or stabbed, by one apex of a very large Star of David, a symbol, not of Israel, but of the Jewish people. The Star of David is golden, gold being a universally understood symbol for money and the power of money. Finally the caption links the idea of conspiracy to the laws of *kashrut*, a symbol, once again, not of Israel but of the Jewish people as a whole. What the image as a whole conveys, at a glance, is that British Jews are lovers of gold who use the power of money to conspire against the interests of Britain, which lie prostrate under the Jewish dagger.

Strong stuff. And stuff of a sort hitherto associated in Britain only with extreme right-wing, neo-Nazi, or, more recently, extreme Islamist groups. In another of the letters of protest published in a later issue David Triesman, the general secretary of the Labour Party, makes precisely that point:

> Your front cover (14 January) showing a gold Star of David impaling a Union Jack and titled "A kosher conspiracy?" must be one of the most offensive images I have seen. It gathers together a symbol of Jewishness (not of Israel), conspiracy and wealth in ways candidly redolent of the extreme right.[3]

It is certainly true that in the past—fifty years ago, at the time of the foundation of Israel, for instance—the publication of such an image by the *New Statesman*, of all papers, would have been simply inconceivable, and had it occurred, would have produced howls of protest from people of all the shades of opinion which then made up the British left. Given that fact, Triesman's letter leaves hanging a number of questions, of which the following are perhaps the most pressing: How has it come to be possible for such an image to be published in a hitherto highly respectable British left-wing weekly? How could its manifestly anti-Semitic character have been invisible to the able and consciously "anti-racist" journalists on the editorial board which must have discussed its publication? How deep does it go, this insensitivity to the distinction between serious left-wing political debate and the sort of thing that in the 1930s used to be called "Jew baiting"? I shall turn to these questions in a moment. Even at this preliminary stage of the discussion, however, we surely have an answer to the question raised in the first part of this chapter, whether what has been perceived, largely by Jews, as a new anti-Semitism abroad in Western cognitive elites is really anti-Semitism, rather than just political opposition to Israel, or to Zionism. Jewish protesters have not misperceived the situation. Mixed in with the fulminations of the Left against Israel there is indeed a vein of—conscious or unconscious—anti-Semitism; and of the most traditional and most dangerous sort: political anti-Semitism. We have yet to inquire how consciously intended, and how committed, this particular vein of political anti-Semitism is. But that it exists there can be no doubt.

THE "APOLOGY"

The January 14 cover, as might have been anticipated, led not only to a brief occupation of the *New Statesman* offices by a group of Jewish young people, from the left of the political spectrum,[4] it appears, but to a storm of protests, including some from people, like Triesman, highly placed in the Labour Party. Some sort of editorial apology was clearly required, and a lengthy statement by the editor, Peter Wilby, duly appeared in the February 11 issue.[5] It is a document worth considering at some length.

For a start it must be said that Wilby is plainly worried by the accusation of anti-Semitism, in a way in which, of course, Streicher would not have been. On the other hand the February 11 statement is far from a simple throwing-in of the towel. Its object is, first, as far as possible, to weaken the force of the accusation, and, second, insofar as it cannot be completely robbed of force, to deflect it from the magazine, and by extension from the Left, first by restricting its application to the *cover*, as distinct from the contents, of the offending issue, and then, honorably enough, transferring responsibility for *that* entirely to the editor, that is to say, to Wilby himself. The arguments set out in pursuit of these ends are a mixed bag. None of them is entirely internally self-consistent, nor are they entirely consistent with one another. It is these inconsistencies which demand scrutiny.

The nearest thing in the statement to an outright apology is the following:

> We (or, more precisely, I) got it wrong. The cover was not intended to be anti-Semitic; the New Statesman is vigorously opposed to racism in all its forms. But it used images and words in such a way as to create unwittingly the impression that the New Statesman was following an

anti-Semitic tradition that sees the Jews as a conspiracy piercing the heart of the nation. I doubt very much that one single person was provoked into hatred of Jews by our cover. But I accept that a few anti-Semites (as some comments on our website, quickly removed, suggested) took aid and comfort when it appeared that their prejudices were shared by a magazine of authority and standing. Moreover the cover upset very many Jews, who are right to feel that, in the fight against anti-Semitism in particular and racism in general, this magazine ought to be on their side.[6]

The opening claim is that "We got it wrong." Fair enough. But this is immediately softened by two caveats. The first proposes that this admitted lapse on the part of a magazine "vigorously opposed to racism in all its forms" was, after all, venial, because *inadvertent*. The cover "used images and words in such a way as to create *unwittingly* the impression . . ." (my italics). But this is a suggestion which strains credulity. We are being asked to believe that, fifty years after the Holocaust, an event which, so far from being of exclusive interest to Jews, has shaped major political aspects of the world in which we now live, and which has been exhaustively documented, the intensely political journalists staffing a leading British journal of the Left carry about with them so little consciousness of all that, that they simply failed to notice, were *unaware of*, the essential continuity between the January 14 cover and the iconography of Nazi political anti-Semitism.

It is a suggestion, in any event, hardly consistent with a remark of Wilby's earlier in the statement, "The purpose of a magazine cover is to attract attention on the news-stands and sometimes to hint that the contents may be daring and unconventional. It became apparent that this cover had done its work all too well."[7]

The attractions of the cover to the editorial team prior to publication were, it appears from this, that it would hint at "daring and unconventional" contents, presumably by appearing "daring and unconventional" itself. But what "conventions," exactly, does it flout? The only one that comes at all easily to mind is the convention which has grown up since the Holocaust that overtly anti-Semitic imagery and language are unacceptable in respectable circles. Not to put too fine a point on it, if the editorial team of the *New Statesman* had simply been *unaware* of the continuity of the cover with "an anti-Semitic tradition that sees the Jews as a conspiracy piercing the heart of the nation" they could hardly have been in a position to perceive it as either "daring" or "unconventional."

The second of Wilby's caveats in the first of the above passages is that, anti-Semitic or not, the cover *did no great harm.*

> I doubt very much that one single person was provoked into hatred of Jews by our cover. But I accept that a few anti-Semites (as some comments on our website, quickly removed, suggested) took aid and comfort when it appeared that their prejudices were shared by a magazine of authority and standing.

There is a certain grisly humor in the image of the staff of a journal "vigorously opposed to racism in all its forms," busily and with prudish horror deleting from its website messages from genuine anti-Semites welcoming their new left-wing friends to the fold, somewhat in the manner of a dowager whose love of the turf has led her into unfortunate company urging the maid to bar the door against the bookies. Humor aside, however, the episode sharply points up what I identified in the previous chapter as two of the main dangers latent in the new anti-Semitism: that the diffusion on the "anti-racist" left of a climate of political hostility and moral condemnation directed against Jews, one sufficiently naive in its moral enthusiasm as to be capable of blundering cheerfully into the employment of elements of the traditional iconography of anti-Semitism, not only gravely diminishes the power of the Left to act as a bulwark against racism, when it happens to be directed against Jews, but gives active aid and comfort to traditional anti-Semites on the Right who have no commitment whatsoever to "anti-racism" in any shape or form. While it is no doubt true, as Wilby says, that such anti-Semites are unlikely to have been made so by reading the *New Statesman*, the point is, surely, that "magazines of authority and standing" should if possible avoid giving such people a helping hand by suggesting that their views have a solid foundation of truth to them.

Let us leave that aside, however, and consider whether something cannot still be made of the claim-in-mitigation before us. Might it not be rephrased as follows: "Our unwitting anti-Semitism was harmless, because it stood little chance of promoting the real (i.e., witting) variety *among the sort of people who normally read the magazine.*" This may be what Wilby intended. Its tendency is plainly to weaken the force of expressed criticism, on the grounds that even if the cover did reiterate the familiar iconography of political anti-Semitism, only a captious and legalistic critic would press the point with the pertinacity of a Reif or a Triesman, since there could be no question of its actually *promoting* political anti-Semitism, at least among the vigorously antiracist readership of the *New Statesman*.

The trouble with this is that the appearance of the cover precisely puts into question the immunity of the *New Statesman's* largely left-wing readership to the appeal of anti-Semitic propaganda. In Wilby's own words, "*the purpose of a magazine cover is to attract attention on the news-stands*" (my emphasis). You do not do that, presumably, or at least, not in a way helpful to your continuing sales, by publishing a cover which will bring the bulk of your weekly readership leaping to their feet with cries of disgust and loathing. To put the point bluntly, you could not hope to sell, *and to continue to sell*, copies by taking a leaf out of Julius Streicher's book, unless the horror and contempt which the appearance of such a cover would have aroused in British left-wing circles in, say, 1950, had, with the passage of the years, largely dissipated. Senior journalists filling major editorial posts do not, presumably, arrive in such positions unless they are very good indeed at estimating the effects likely to be produced among their readership by an article or image. The calculation in this case can only have been that, although such a cover might produce outrage in some Jewish circles, it would nevertheless go down well with at least large sections of the readership.

Putting it that way, of course, makes it look as if I am accusing Peter Wilby of combining a real, if muted, anti-Semitism with a reprehensible willingness to pander to similar tendencies in his readership. The inconsistencies which litter the February 11 statement, of course, give one plenty of ammunition for such a suggestion, and a certain sort of opponent, one anxious to demonize the Left, would, like a certain sort of literary critic, doubtless make a meal of them. But, actually, I don't believe it. Although I have never had the pleasure (and I am not joking, or indulging in heavy sarcasm) of meeting Mr. Wilby, he and I happen to share a mutual friend, another, older, London journalist, in whose judgment long experience has taught me to repose a certain confidence. That person informs me that Wilby is an entirely honest, decent man, who really is "vigorously opposed to racism in all its forms" and who really is most unlikely to have had any idea, when he authorized the publication of the January 14 cover, that he was authorizing the emission of a singularly revolting anti-Semitic libel. Following up that thought, one can see how a responsible editor might, without the least taint of venality, welcome such a cover for its likely appeal to the readership, while at the same time discounting the likelihood of some predictable protest from certain right-wing Jewish circles, *if he thought (a) that the Jews in question would be mistaken in thinking the cover anti-Semitic, and (b) that their protests would therefore be morally unjustifiable.* The interesting question, of course, is by what tortuous processes of thought any honest person in his right mind could conceivably bring himself to the point of

thinking that Jews of any political tendency would *not* be justified in object-
ing, on grounds of anti-Semitism, to such a cover image? It is upon that question that I hope to shed some light in the following pages. It is an interesting,
indeed pressing, question because the processes of thought, and the resulting
state of mind, which allowed Wilby to pass a cover worthy of Streicher are not
confined to him but currently affect, if I am not mistaken, very large sections
of "Left-liberal" opinion, notably in universities, in the print and broadcast media, and in some sectors of public life, throughout Europe and America.

Meanwhile, back to the February 11 statement. Its concluding, and
longest, section addresses the issue which has just engaged us: whether the
Jewish protesters deserved an apology. It does so by way of the question
whether one would feel any obligation to apologize for a cover which reflected unfavorably on Italians or Australians ("A Garlic Conspiracy?" "A
Wallaby Conspiracy?").

If there were really nothing objectionable about the cover, then this
entirely specious objection would be perfectly justified. And one can imagine a less scrupulous journalist than Wilby setting himself to brazen it out
along precisely these lines. To his credit, that is not the line Wilby takes. He
begins by making the obvious point that "Americans, French and Australians (white ones at least) have not suffered centuries of continuous oppression, discrimination and murder."[8]

But then things get murkier. Between this sentence and the next following one, Wilby passes seamlessly from this morally relevant and factually unexceptionable observation to the highly contestable moral claim that "racism
against white people is of no consequence." Here is the whole passage:

> Racism against white people is of no consequence because it has no his-
> torical resonance. To call somebody a "white bastard" is just not the same
> as calling someone a "black bastard", with all its connotations of humil-
> iation and enslavement. Given the distribution of power in our world,
> discrimination by blacks or Asians against white people will almost al-
> ways be trivial.[9]

Two grounds are offered for the extraordinary opening proposition
that racism directed against white people is (morally? legally?) "of no consequence." They are:

1. Discrimination against white people is "of no consequence" ("is
   trivial") because "it has no historical resonance."

2. Discrimination against white people is "of no consequence" ("is trivial") because of "the distribution of power in our world" (the intention here is presumably that, in some global sense, that distribution favors "white people").

For convenience of reference, let's call the principle that racism against white people is morally and/or legally trivial "Wilby's Principle," the first of its author's grounds for it "the Argument from Historical Resonance," and the second, "the Argument from the Distribution of Power." The Principle itself is, surely, not merely counterintuitive but morally incoherent. If there are moral objections to racism, however one chooses to define the term, then they are, presumably, objections to racism per se. The suggestion that the moral force of the objections to racist abuse weaken when the abuse is practiced against members of a particular race is surely itself racist. The two grounds offered fare little better. To suppose that an injustice becomes less of an injustice when committed against someone whose ancestors were guilty of injustice mirrors precisely the reasoning of the traditional anti-Semite who justifies his treatment of Jews on the basis of the claim that their ancestors bore the blood-guilt of the Crucifixion. Similarly, one would have thought, an injustice against someone is not lessened because "the distribution of power in the world" favors the race to which the person concerned belongs.

Still, for the moment, and for the sake of argument, let's let Wilby's Principle and its two supporting contentions stand uncontested. No doubt a majority of Jews, though by no means all, are "white people." Once again, it seems, Wilby has formulated an argument of sufficiently magisterial generality to defeat all objection to the January 14 cover; since it follows trivially that if racism against "white people" is "of no consequence," then racism against Jews—unless they happen to be Yemeni or Iraqi Jews, or Falashas, or Sammy Davis Jr.—is a fortiori "of no consequence" either. But once again Wilby draws aside from the conclusion lying in wait for him. Jews, though white, are "a different case." The long concluding passage which opens with this admission is of some interest here. It begins with the following words:

Jews are a different case. They no longer routinely suffer gross or violent discrimination; indeed, in the US and Europe at least, Jews today are probably safer than most minorities. But the Holocaust remains within living memory, as do the language and the iconography used by the Nazis to prepare the way for it. We have a special duty of care not to revive them.

Having voiced these unexceptionable sentiments, however, Wilby returns to the theme of inequalities of "power" between communities. Earlier, the *New Statesman* had published a cover ("Koran con trick") offensive to Muslims. Should an apology have been published on that occasion too?

> The answer, I think, is that to question a body of belief is not the same as to accuse members of a racial group of conspiracy. Even so, I have to admit that I know many fewer Muslims than I know Jews: the latter have an advantage in making their case to me and to other newspaper editors. . . . This is not a point about Jews; I am not suggesting that their influence in the media is disproportionate. It is a point about Muslims' lack of power and influence in our society.[10]

Despite the suggestion lurking here that Muslims have real problems, whereas Jews merely have influence and use it, the apology to the latter, if that is what it is, is allowed to stand. The article concludes, "Readers should be assured that we shall not censor ourselves; but we shall try to present our views with greater sensitivity."

Two things are going on in this passage. On the one hand, the charge of anti-Semitism is being softened into that of "insensitivity." On the other hand, the suggestion is being floated that Jews are not, in fact, *quite* as legitimately entitled as other ethnic groups to the sympathy of those "vigorously opposed to racism *in all its forms*" (my emphasis). Let's examine the second first, since it provides the rhetorical basis for the first. Wilby's Principle, we recall, denies sympathy to "white" victims of "nonwhite" racism, on the grounds, first, that racism exercised in that direction lacks "historical resonance," and on the second that "the distribution of power in our world" favors whites. The problem for Wilby is that on both the Argument from Historical Resonance and the Argument from the Distribution of Power, Jews wind up profiting rather than losing out under the terms of the Principle. Racism against Jews, after all, disposes of greater "historical resonance" than any other form of racism. And—outside the fetid dreamworld of anti-Semitic conspiracy theory—the distribution of power between Jews and non-Jews remains, one would have thought, as it has always been, weighted overwhelmingly in favor of the latter. It is difficult not to read the concluding passage above as motivated by the desire, perhaps unconscious, to mitigate to some degree the force of these unwelcome facts. Thus, the reader is asked at least to entertain the thought that, although "the Holocaust remains within living memory," "Jews no longer suffer gross or violent discrimination; indeed, in the US and Europe at least, Jews today are probably safer than most minorities." These claims are, factually speaking, less than accurate: attacks, both against Jewish individuals and property such as synagogues, schools, social centers, or cemeteries have continued since World War II to occur in a constant trickle which, over the past few years, particularly in Europe, has swollen considerably, if not, or not yet, to a flood.[11] But no doubt they would carry conviction to readers who had not bothered to inform themselves concerning the real state of affairs. Their effect is (1) to introduce—or rather, not so much to introduce as to imply—an ad hoc adjustment to the Argument from Historical Resonance, to the effect that "historical resonance" only exempts "whites" from the operation of Wilby's Principle if the "historical" persecution continues to this day, and (2) to suggest that in the case of Jews it does not. There remains the Argument from the Distribution of Power and the unfortunate but rather evident fact that that distribution can hardly be said to favor Jews. The tendency of that thought to invoke the sympathy of antiracists is delicately undermined by the suggestion, supported on the one hand by the information Wilby vouchsafes concerning the relative numbers of Jews and Muslims in his circle of acquaintances, and on the other hand by the old journalistic trick of insinuating something by denying that one is insinuating it ("mind you, I don't myself believe it for a moment!"), that "[Jews] have an advantage in making their case to . . . newspaper editors," which makes their "influence in the media" not (of course) "disproportionate," but certainly greater, in proportion, than that of some of those other minorities (Muslims, for instance) who may be—as Wilby has earlier suggested—less safe from racist attack than present-day Jews.

It is easy to see how weakening the claim of Jews to the sympathy of antiracists in these subtle and indirect ways lends credence, at least rhetorically, to the first of the two suggestions we found floating in the cloudy ichor of this passage: the suggestion that the disputed cover was guilty, not of *anti-Semitism*, and political anti-Semitism at that, but merely of *insensitivity*. If the power of "historical resonance" to enlist the sympathies of antiracists lapses in the case of a *merely* historical resonance, if that is the case where the Jews are concerned, and if the overall weakness of Jews with respect to "the distribution of power in our world" turns into a—possibly illegitimate—strength in certain special cases, of which the media may be one, then it will begin to look—at least to those blessed with the capacity to take Wilby's Principle and its supporting arguments seriously—as if anti-Semitism really is, *nowadays* anyway, a "trivial" version of racism, and that Jews who protest it are displaying a purely historically based hypersensitivity toward which "we," meaning presumably the majority of the

European intelligentsia holding "left-liberal" opinions, should no doubt, in view of the enormity of past horrors, display "sensitivity," but which "we" are otherwise justified in treating as entirely irrelevant to serious politics. Moreover, it may seem—the thought is at any rate being insinuated—as if Jews who insist on having mere *sensibilities* pandered to in this respect by hard-hitting investigative journalists, journalists "vigorously opposed to racism in all its forms," may in some cases be attempting, morally quite illegitimately, of course, to use, to manipulate, the sympathies of those fine antiracists in order to distract them from the sufferings of other minority groups with, currently, a far greater right to benefit from those sympathies.

I think we are now getting close to the heart of Wilby's stance, state of mind, whatever you want to call it. It is, I have been trying to show, a very dangerous stance, which among other things is helping to drive not only large segments of the left-wing intelligentsia, and more importantly, perhaps, a much larger number of well-intentioned people of "liberal" or "left-liberal" sentiments, for the second, if not the third time in the past century, into the welcoming arms of a version of fascism. It is at any rate well propounded here. Wilby is a highly skilled journalist, and if it were not for the training in habitual skepticism, bitterly close reading, and aggressive contentiousness contributed by forty years in the amiable shark-pool of analytic philosophy I might have been half-persuaded myself. But that, of course, only makes matters worse. What I have tried to do for the moment is simply to show how systematically beset by internal contradictions and inconsistencies the piece of prose before us is. On the whole its effect is to trivialize the charge of political anti-Semitism into one of mere "insensitivity" and to exclude, by specious reasoning and, in one place, by outright trifling with the facts, Jews from the sympathies of antiracists. But these aims do not seem altogether wholeheartedly pursued. Over and again there surges in Wilby's prose a sense that what he is saying won't quite do, that after all is said and done some sort of enormity has been committed. That sense shows, for instance, in the remark that "to question a body of belief is not the same as to accuse members of a racial group of conspiracy" (I myself would have preferred "one's fellow citizens" to "members of a racial group," possibly because I am actually, no doubt in a tediously naive and old-fashioned sort of way, opposed to racism in *all* its forms, but let that pass). And there are other points in the passage, in which, as here, exoneration and self-accusation do a little dance around one another. One of the things which, I have the impression, most puzzle Jews in the current debate about Israel is the repeated assertion, which I have certainly heard a good many times at dinner parties and so forth, that "anyone who criticizes Israel is automatically accused of anti-Semitism." Alan Dershowitz, the eminent Harvard lawyer, is a case in point. "I have never heard," he says, "a mere critic of Israel called anti-Semitic."[12] And, I must confess, neither have I. What, then, is the source of what would appear to be a quite widespread urban legend? *Who*, exactly, is going about calling mere critics of Israel anti-Semitic? I have a shrewd suspicion that it may be critics of Israel, or some of them, themselves. What makes itself apparent in the stresses and strains of Wilby's prose is an irritated sense that, on the one hand, over Israel "the Jews" are getting away with things that ought to be attacked hip and thigh, and on the other, a nervous sense that to attack "the Jews" at all, about anything, may perhaps, on some level which one cannot quite grasp or clearly conceptualize, amount to aligning oneself with very traditional kinds of anti-Semitism (those National Front messages of congratulation on the *New Statesman* website, for instance). The voice saying "anti-Semite!" may perhaps, in other words, not be a Jewish voice—though the one who hears it in the silence of his thoughts may perhaps, out of a natural desire to preserve peace in the interior of his own head, construe it as somehow coming from the Jewish Other. And perhaps one should not wonder at that. The sleep of reason, after all, is well known to yield nightmares.

We have spent enough time on Wilby. I propose to stay with the *New Statesman's* January 14 issue for a little longer, but to switch my attention now to the articles heralded by the cover and its caption.

THE "CONSPIRACY"

Two articles in the January 14 issue—"A Kosher Conspiracy" by Dennis Sewell, and "Blair Meets with Arafat but Supports Sharon" by John Pilger—are pertinent to its cover. The latter concerns a visit to Downing Street by Yasser Arafat in the aftermath to September 11, 2001. In his statement of February 11, 2002, Peter Wilby shows, as we noted earlier, some concern to exclude these two articles from the charge of anti-Semitism. His suggestion is that only the cover could even conceivably be regarded as anti-Semitic in content, and that he himself is wholly to blame for that.

Honorable as this stance undoubtedly, in one sense at least, is, I find myself unpersuaded by it. Of the two articles Pilger's certainly seems to me the least open to accusations of anti-Semitism. It begins by accusing the

British government of both supplying arms to, and buying them from, Israel; repeats a "disclosure" in *Jane's Foreign Report* to the effect that "Britain and France had given 'the green light' to Sharon to attack Arafat if the Palestinian resistance did not stop"; offers some alarming, but unattributed and contestable (contested, anyway, as one can discover by reading commentators of other political affiliations) statistics concerning the relative numbers of Palestinians and Israelis killed during "the uprising" (no dates given); and concludes by claiming that the assassination by Israel of Hamas leader Abu Humud was expressly designed by Ariel Sharon to destabilize Arafat and the Palestinian Authority by provoking a counterattack by Hamas. All of this, I take it, is the common coin of weekly political journalism nowadays. Whether one takes any of it seriously is up to the reader who has sufficient time to ascertain for himself which of its claims have some substance and which are eyewash; otherwise, one believes what one wishes to believe, or nothing. In any case, the accusations Pilger levels at Sharon, and at the British and Israeli governments, are of types regularly leveled at politicians and nations everywhere in the world: there is nothing specifically anti-Semitic about them.

A tinge of something that might reasonably be termed anti-Semitism enters the article in two passages only, but they are significant ones. The first concerns Tony Blair's appointment of Lord Levy as a special envoy to the Middle East.

> Shortly after his election in 1997, Blair shamelessly appointed a friend, Michael Levy, a wealthy Jewish businessman who had fundraised for new Labour, as his "special envoy" in the Middle East, having first made him Lord Levy. This former chairman of the Jewish Appeal Board and former board member of the Jewish Agency, who has both a business and a house in Israel and has a son working for the Israeli justice minister, was the man assigned by Britain's prime minister to negotiate impartially with Palestinians and Israelis.[13]

There are two ways of construing this. The first, anodyne one, would be to take it as making the point that it might have been wiser for Blair to choose an envoy without personal connections with either side in the Israeli/Palestinian dispute. But one might equally read it as suggesting that Lord Levy was an unsuitable choice for the role assigned to him because no Jew could be expected to conduct even-handed ("impartial") negotiations between non-Jews and his own people. This, of course, is a very serious charge. It amounts to saying that Levy could not be trusted to discharge the duties assigned to him as a representative of the British government because of his Jewish connections. And it would be very difficult to defend that charge on any terms which would not entail assent to the ancient anti-Semitic canard that no Jew can be trusted to serve his adopted country faithfully when contrary Jewish interests are at stake. Equally, under this second interpretation of the drift of the passage, the characterization of Lord Levy as "a wealthy Jewish businessman who had fundraised for new Labour," an irrelevancy under the first interpretation, falls into place as carrying the suggestion that new Labour itself is culpable in having placed the affairs of the country in unreliable Jewish hands in return for Jewish gold. Neither reading is necessary, of course; but equally the passage as it stands is equivocal between the two, and one would expect a journalist of Pilger's experience to insert a clause disclaiming the second. Evidently, no such clause is present.

The second passage about which floats a certain odor of anti-Semitism forms an addendum to one in which Pilger, making a point about the number of arms export licenses to Israel granted by the Blair government, quotes an answer to George Galloway MP by the Foreign Office minister Ben Bradshaw. Pilger adds: "(Bradshaw is an active member of Labour Friends of Israel, which has arranged for 57 Labour MP's to visit Israel, the largest number of MP's from any British government.)"[14]

The tone of this, it seems to me, makes it more than a hard-left smack at Blair's center-left. The remark could only be relevant to what has gone before if, once again, the insinuation is that Bradshaw's discharge of his duties as a Foreign Office minister might be influenced by his membership of Labour Friends of Israel. The suggestion floating here, in other words, is that Bradshaw is a member of a sinister organization, a tool perhaps, possibly even a purchased tool, of the International Jewish Mafia. The actual state of affairs is that Britain is, for the moment at any rate, a free and democratic country whose citizens are free to form whatever political groupings they please, a right which stops short, and should stop short, only at the point of collusion with the nation's enemies. The fact of the matter, moreover, is that there is widespread support and sympathy for Israel in Britain, both among the majority of people with no party affiliation, and in all three main political parties,[15] although it is a fact not easily gathered from the output of British television news services or much of the press. And even on the specific issue of Bradshaw, Pilger's intelligence gathering appears to have let him down. In the January 21, 2002, issue of the *New Statesman* the following letter appeared:

Once again, I'm afraid, John Pilger has got his basic facts wrong: "Bradshaw is an active member of Labour Friends of Israel . . ." I am not and never have been a member of Labour Friends of Israel. The rest of Pilger's customary piece of polemic is not much better for accuracy either.

BEN BRADSHAW
Parliamentary Under-secretary of State,
Foreign and Commonwealth Office, London SW1.

Bearing that in mind, let us turn now to Sewell's article. It is an odd document, not least for the happy-go-lucky cheerfulness it exhibits in embracing its own internal contradictions. Somewhere toward the middle of its first main section it more or less grants as a commonplace fact of life the thesis to which we have been devoting such anguished scrutiny: that sections of the British Left are currently gripped by a fit of anti-Semitic paranoia.

> That there is a Zionist lobby and that it is rich, potent and effective goes largely unquestioned on the left. Big Jewry, like big tobacco, is seen as one of life's givens. According to this view, Israel has the British media pretty well sewn up. Wealthy Jewish business leaders, acting in concert with establishment types and co-ordinated by the Israeli embassy, have supposedly nobbled newspaper editors and proprietors, and ensured that the pro-Palestinian position is marginalised both in news reporting and in the comment pages. As one well-known foreign affairs specialist puts it: "The sheer scale of activity is awesome. It operates at every level. By comparison, the disparate, underfunded and shambolic pro-Palestinian organisations don't stand a chance." He insists that these words remain unattributable because, he claims, "the fact is that journalists put their careers in jeopardy by speaking up for the Palestinians. That's ultimately the Zionist lobby's most powerful weapon."[16]

The sheer number of consistently pro-Palestinian, anti-Israel journalists currently at work in Britain (Robert Fisk at the *Independent* is perhaps the best-known example, but there are many more) makes this a hard proposition to swallow for any reader not already committed to the view of things characteristic of what in Britain is called the "hard left." Reassuringly enough, therefore, the ostensible drift of the article is toward minimizing the power of the "Zionist lobby." Few pro-Israel lobbying organizations in Britain, we are told, are more than a "two-man and a dog" operation.

So what becomes of "Big Jewry" with its battalions of "wealthy Jewish businessmen" and its establishment connections? (Whither is fled the visionary gleam? Back into the twilight regions from which it emerged, one would suppose.) Curiously, though, the article begins with a long passage apparently designed not to debunk the fears thus set at naught, but rather to encourage them. It concerns a Jewish armaments industrialist and Auschwitz survivor, Shlomo Zabludowicz, credited with being an important architect of Israel's armaments industry and with having more recently diversified into domestic appliances and property. The ground for introducing it is that Zabludowicz's son, Poju, is, it is claimed, "the Mr. Moneybags" behind the Britain Israel Communications and Research Centre (Bicom).

The account offered of both father and son is, of course, a demolition job, permeated by the unspoken suggestion that arms, while a very good thing in the hands of agents and movements of whom one or another section of the Left happens to approve this morning, are a very bad thing indeed in the hands of those of whom it happens to disapprove; and that investment companies and arms manufacturers, bad things, no doubt, when run by non-Jews, become altogether intolerable things when run by Jews. We are told that Shlomo, after his release from Auschwitz at the age of thirty, moved first to Sweden, then Finland, where he founded the weapons manufacturer Soltan, "one of the pillars of Tel Aviv's military-industrial complex." The passage goes on to credit the company with a major role in turning the Israeli army into an unstoppable force by the Yom Kippur war of 1973, with the suggestion that unspecified illegalities, hinted at by the phrases "a Finnish passport" and " a knack for skirting arms embargoes," entered into this achievement. The same method of hint and innuendo is then pursued with regard to Shlomo's son, the sinister force behind Bicom, by way of his involvement in the arms manufacturer Pocal and a London property company, Ivory Gate.

The Zabludowiczs, father and son, are presented, in other words, as the very paradigm of the Big Jew who, we have just been told, figures so largely in the current mythology of the Left. Floating around in the passage are a couple of suggestions that echo both ancient and modern themes of anti-Semitic propaganda; the first, that Zabludowicz senior exemplifies the charge of "rootless cosmopolitanism" traditionally leveled against Jews by anti-Semites ("settled first in Sweden and then in Finland"); the second that his experiences in Auschwitz *taught him nothing*, since after his release from that educative establishment, he became, of all things, an *arms manufacturer*. Nothing, it seems, could be more calculated to confirm fears on "the left" of a "Zionist lobby" fueled by the gold of plutocratic, rootless cosmopolitan Jews engaged in sinister commercial enterprises. Yet a page later we learn that Bicom, the engine of their sinister plutocratic efforts to stifle criticism of Israel, is "a two-man and a dog operation."

"ALL JEWS SUPPORT ISRAEL"

In addition to these marginal inconsistencies, there are two general objections, both invoking the issue of anti-Semitism, which can be raised against the editorial stance that provides, as one might put it, the frame for Sewell's piece. Both have to do with the repetition of the query, "A Kosher Conspiracy," together with a smaller version of the cover illustration, at the head of Sewell's article.

The first is the rather evident one that there is no conceivable constitutional, legal, or moral basis for the use of the term "conspiracy" with reference to political pressure groups in Britain using the methods of public relations and press management to advance the concerns of a special interest. The country is awash with such groups, representing every conceivable political, charitable, and local interest, including ones which promote support for the Palestinians. Jews, and non-Jews, have as much right to organize such groups in support of Israel as any other body of citizens has to organize them in support of, say, cerebral palsy, flood relief schemes, comprehensive schools, "real education," or the abolition or preservation of fox hunting. Had the word "kosher" been omitted, in other words, the resulting heading, "A Conspiracy?" over an article about a collection of special-interest pressure groups would have been not merely lame but incomprehensible. The addition of the word "Kosher," in short, is not only what spices the presentation up, but what renders the connection of the heading with the content of the article intelligible—but intelligible only to someone sharing the ancient presuppositions of political anti-Semitism—which are, to spell them out once again, that a group of Jewish Englishmen claiming the right of any Englishman to fight his cause, by forming a political pressure group, for any cause which happens to take his fancy, claim that right illegitimately, since Jewish Englishmen are not really "Englishmen" at all, but members of a foreign Fifth Column whose activities are intrinsically inimical to British interests. Dropping briefly into Derridean mode, one could say that anti-Semitism is inscribed in the margins of this text as an unavowed—and in left-wing circles, of course, unavowable—condition of its intelligibility. It is hardly surprising, under the circumstances, that the *New Statesman* website should have received a flurry of supportive e-mails from members of the various groupuscules making up the extreme nationalist Right.

That the loyalty to their countries of citizenship of Jews qua Jews is suspect, is, of course, a central plank of anti-Semitism. It is this accusation above all others, however, which calls to mind Jonathan Sacks's observation that, though anti-Semitism begins with Jews, it rarely ends with them. The tactic of wrapping oneself in the flag and accusing one's opponents of sedition is, after all, one that any political group can adopt, very often with good reason. Sections of the British Right in the 1930s supported Hitler; sections of the British Left supported the Soviet Union from 1916 to 1989. William Wordsworth and Samuel Coleridge were rather keen, to start with, anyway, on the French Revolution, and because of that were very properly followed about the Chilterns by an incompetent government spy concerned about their possible sympathies with Napoleon.[17] So what is new, then, about Englishmen defending the interests of foreign states? Why pick on the Jews for exercising a right which every non-Jewish inhabitant of these islands appears to assume as an inalienable political perquisite? The noise of thrown stones crashing into the glass houses of their throwers on this issue is so deafening, indeed, that the more intelligent journalists readily admit that accusations of divided loyalties against Jews supportive of Israel need to be handled with tongs. Thus Geoffrey Wheatcroft:

> More than 50 years ago, when Harold Laski demanded more sympathetic treatment for newborn Israel, The Spectator wondered editorially whether he spoke as "a Jew or an Englishman." If, as it appeared, "Mr Laski is a Jew first and an Englishman second", he was perfectly entitled to feel that identity. "But if that is the case, his right place would seem to be Palestine, not England." Despite the mounting accusations of anti-Semitism against media critics of Israel, and although Will Self not long ago baited Melanie Phillips on television by asking her what she would do if England went to war with Israel, it's hard to imagine this or any other respectable British paper putting it like that nowadays.[18]

Wheatcroft's reassurances notwithstanding, however, Will Self (a left-wing journalist) presumably *did* taunt Melanie Phillips in precisely those terms. And is not the *New Statesman* (in Britain the left-wing equivalent of the *Spectator* on the Right) "a respectable British paper"?

The second effect of the inclusion of the word "kosher," a term indelibly associated with Jewishness per se, rather than with Israel, the Israeli Right, or the Right in general, is to insinuate the suggestion, rightly identified by Pierre-André Taguieff (mentioned in Chapter 1) for instance, as a central pillar both of the old and the new anti-Semitism, that *all Jews, and only Jews, find in Israel anything worthy of support.* Since this suggestion opens a further window on the nature of the anti-Semitism implicit in the phrase "kosher conspiracy," it will be worth analyzing it in some detail.

All Jews, and only Jews, support Israel. Both clauses, logically speaking, of this suggestion are, one would have thought, demonstrably false. The second, that *only* Jews find Israel, taking the good with the bad, worthy of support is, so far as the immediate context of Sewell's article goes, contradicted by Pilger's remarks concerning Ben Bradshaw and his—in the event nonexistent—membership of Labour Friends of Israel. Who would have guessed, from listening to BBC coverage of the Middle East or reading the *Guardian* or the *Independent* that such an organization exists? In fact the British Left in its broader reaches is as deeply divided on the rights and wrongs of the Middle East conflict as on much else, including both wars on Saddam Hussein's regime in Iraq; while outside the Left, general support for Israel extends far beyond the small Jewish community. The same divisions cut through British society at every level. Though one body of opinion in the Church of England is broadly pro-Palestinian in outlook, there is another body of opinion which expresses itself, among other ways, through the website "Anglicans for Israel" (see Appendix).

Now for the first half of the claim implicit in the phrase "kosher conspiracy": *all Jews support Israel.* This is as false as the "only" clause, since the Jewish community is demonstrably as divided on the topic of Israel as are non-Jews. Diaspora Jewish opposition, opposition not merely to the policies of the Israeli Right, but at times to the very existence of Israel in its present form, unites the Orthodox of *Neturei Carta* at one, religious, extreme of Jewish life with the writings of Jewish liberals such as Noam Chomsky in America or Daniel Lindenberg in France, at another, secularist, extreme. Fruitfully in between comes the broad range of mostly liberal-to-left-of-center opinion represented in the *Jewish Quarterly*, a British publication worth reading, not merely by those with an interest in Jewish affairs, but by anyone who wishes to rediscover a style of intellectual journalism, sane, deeply informed, and committed to rational coherence in argument, which commercial pressures, no doubt among other things, have made sadly rare in the non-Jewish world. Within Israel itself there is, and has always been, not merely the political liberal-Left personified to the outside world at present by Shimon Peres, but also a multitude of broadly "left" groups working in many fields and on many levels for reconciliation with the Arab population. The strand of "left-liberal" opinion which the *New Statesman* at present represents evidently finds these facts difficult to deal with, a difficulty betrayed by a further tectonic fault in the already somewhat perturbed intellectual geology of Sewell's article.

A FURTHER STEREOTYPE

The facts I have just outlined, not to mention the rather evident presence of large numbers of pro-Arab, anti-Israel, anti-Bush Jews on the British Left, clearly pose a problem for the *New Statesman*'s lead story, not least for its iconography, but also, since iconography and argument cannot be as cleanly separated as Wilby would have us believe, for the content of the articles accompanying the cover and its echoes in the interior of the magazine. How does Sewell deal with this difficulty? By introducing another stereotype of the Jew, not this time—indeed one wildly inconsistent with—that of the sinister figure working behind the scenes in a dreamlike world of resistless power and unquantifiable threat, but the comic/pathetic one of the desperate, desperately argumentative ghetto Jew—"two Jews, three opinions!"—incapable of combining to pose a threat to anything, because incapable of arresting the manic proliferation of arguments for long enough to arrive at any common conclusion.

> When one looks at the array of pro-Israel organisations in Britain, one is struck not so much by their cohesion so much as by their fragmentation. . . . the only Jewish stereotype they reinforce is the one portrayed in Woody Allen films, where a dozen or more members of a family sit around the dinner table, all shouting different things at the same time. Some clearly believe that Ariel Sharon can do no wrong, others that he can do no good. In this, they reflect the pluralist cast of Israel's polity. And that Israel is the only fully functioning democracy in the Middle East is something they constantly invite the rest of us to remember.[19]

One is reminded of Sacks's shrewd remark that anti-Semitism consists in the combined and contradictory beliefs that Jews are so powerful that all the evil in the world can be attributed to them, and yet so powerless that they can be attacked with impunity. Sewell's article has, so far, pursued a looping course from the first of these polar and contradictory stereotypes to the second. Since the second might be seen as more genial than the first, Sewell's essay might be interpreted, despite the opening attack on the Zabludowiczs, as debunking rather than reinforcing the widespread belief in a conspiracy of Big Jews he says is "unquestioned" on the Left: the Big Jews are after all only little Jews. But look a little more closely at the above passage and a subtler and more unpleasant suggestion can be detected. This is the one passage, not merely in Sewell's article, but in the entirety of the issue bearing the disputed cover, in which any mention is made of the fact, so embarrassing for the profitable enterprise of conspiracy mongering, to which that issue is more or less dedicated, that large numbers of Jews, both Orthodox and Left-oriented, sympathize strongly with the plight of the Palestinians. It is a very passing mention indeed, amounting to the words, "others that he [Sharon] can do no good." The ambiguities of the phrase "do no good" leaves open the suggestion that the dissent of the Jews in question from the views of the "Zionist lobby" are purely prudential, or practical in nature (that Sharon can "do no good" because he has *failed to go far enough* in attacking the Palestinians). And the whole phrase is set in a context which serves to ridicule and diminish Jewish dissent. Not only the Big Jews of Left demonology, in other words, but the Jewish *Left* itself is being ridiculed here. The entirety of the *Jewish* debate about Israel, that acutely anguished but also acutely serious array of divisions within the Jewish community, is being presented, contemptibly, as a comic Babel of Woody Allen characters "all shouting different things at the same time." And as the paragraph winds on the scope of the debunking widens. "Israel's polity," with its "pluralist cast," the phrase spat out as if pluralism were a moral defect, and finally democracy itself, are successively brought within the range of the same diminishing image of everyone shouting at once; an image as reminiscent of pre-war fascist attacks on parliamentary democracy as a "talking shop" as the cover image was reminiscent of prewar anti-Semitism. When the final sentence of the paragraph ends it has become unclear whether it is the Jewish debate or debate per se that is being debunked and ridiculed. In Sewell we are dealing, it would appear, with a mind which has very little time for dissenting opinion, whether Jewish or non-Jewish.

But it is no doubt primarily *Jewish* opinion, whether pro- or anti-Palestinian, which the image of the Woody Allen Jewish family works to expel from the debate over Israel. One cannot, after all, debate seriously with people "who all shout different things at the same time." One is reminded of Proust; of the passage in *Côté de Guermantes*, in which the Belgian M. d'Argencourt refuses to debate the Dreyfus case with the French Jew Bloch because "It is an affair which the French must settle among themselves" and because *"c'est une affaire dont j'ai pour principe de ne parler qu'entre Japhétiques."* ["it is an affair which it is a principle of mine to discuss only with non-Jews" (*my translation*)]. D'Argencourt's response to Bloch marks a further point in the corruption of a nation by anti-Semitism, one which falls a little beyond the initial stage of fabricating conspiracy theories. It marks the boundary between liberal and fascist politics, no matter whether the fascism in question is of the Right or the Left, at which Jews are excluded from political activity on a particular wing of politics not because their views align them with a different wing of politics, but simply because they are Jews. Once that boundary in politics is crossed, it is a short step to transgressing other boundaries, both moral and political: to the exclusion of Jews from non-political professional and social groupings, and finally from society altogether. The first of these boundaries, the political one, was crossed in Europe recently, for almost the first time since the 1930s, when young left-wing Jews were abused, beaten, and expelled from marches against the war in Iraq not because they were right-wing supporters of the war, but because they were Jews. It is a boundary with which Sewell's article, and the entire issue of the *New Statesman* to which it belongs, along with much other current "respectable" left-wing journalism in Europe, is flirting in an appalled, not-quite self-deceiving, half-fascinated way. But even to approach that boundary, even to try on for size the idea of crossing it, is to drift, not toward "insensitivity" but toward an admitted and overt anti-Semitism.

IN PRAISE OF IGNORANCE

Bad as this is, worse is to come. Sewell's thesis, of the impotence of the "pro-Israel lobby," requires him to provide evidence of the failure of pro-Israel organizations to influence coverage of Israel in the British media. This he does as follows:

> Read the liberal press almost any day of the week and you will find that Israel comes off worst. Many younger correspondents appear to have forgotten that the UN was instrumental in bringing Israel into existence, that the Israelis have had to fight off three invasions from neighbouring Arab states; and that UN Resolution 242 is a more nuanced document than the reflexive attachment of the epithet "illegal" to the occupation of the West Bank suggests. Palestinian acceptance of Israel's right to exist behind secure borders is often reported uncritically, sometimes im-

plying that this position is shared by Hamas. And a creeping cultural and moral relativism holds Israel to account for every action and reaction while excusing Palestinian excesses on the grounds of poverty and general victim status. I could go on, but only at the risk of being thought to have been nobbled myself.[20]

Is this irony, or just schizophrenia? The issues are so serious, the tone so inanely superior and at the same time so foppishly Woosterish, that I find it very hard to say. My guess is that it is not meant as irony, or at least that only some bits are: in other words, that a hopelessly ramifying bunch of contradictions are supposed to be held under control in ways in which they are not, and could not possibly be. Read straight, it yields the following claims. Liberal "prejudices" about Israel are, after all, not really prejudices because they are "confirmed" by the fact that the operations of one pro-Israel press organization are "greased by the profits made from . . . [the] mortars and bombs" of a man whose chief claims to obloquy appear in context to be that unlike other arms manufacturers, he is a Jew, and that his assistance helped Israel to fight off one of the "three invasions from neighbouring Arab states" (the 1973 Yom Kippur war) Israel has had to face since its foundation. The activities of the "Zionist lobby" *are* intrinsically nefarious, but are also, happily, largely ineffectual, a failure demonstrated by the daily suppression in "the liberal press" of a large number of elementary facts favorable to Israel, a suppression so complete that "many younger correspondents" have forgotten, or are just unaware, that they exist. One may recite these inconvenient facts in a left-wing journal, however, without anyone seriously supposing that one has been "nobbled" by the "Zionist lobby."

I originally thought of titling this section "In the Footsteps of Dr. Goebbels." But on reflection that seemed to me not only over the top, but inadequate to the gravity of the case. The above passage does indeed display a Goebbels-like mood of triumph at the success of propaganda, not only in suppressing the truth but in obliterating all paths of knowledge, memory, or rational reflection that might lead to it. In Goebbels's case such triumphalism is fueled by fascist nationalism and a conscious and deeply felt anti-Semitism. In Sewell's case—for I do not believe for a moment that Sewell, any more than his then editor, is an anti-Semite—it is fueled by left-wing humanitarianism.

I think that makes matters worse, not better. I have already drawn attention to a good many inconsistencies of aim and tone in this short article. The ostensible aim of the piece is to pooh-pooh fears, on what Sewell calls, sweepingly, "the left" of a Jewish "conspiracy" to suppress criticism of Israel in the media. Yet on the one hand the piece begins with a long passage (the one about Zabludowicz) which seems designed to augment such fears, while on the other hand the main issue of whether such a "conspiracy" exists falls between two stools: the "conspiracy" exists all right, but its machinations are not to be feared, because the people running it are incompetent: absurdly comic "little Jews" who cannot agree with one another for long enough to get a decent conspiracy up and running.

In the final passage quoted above, which must strike any reasonable person as briskly probing the frontiers of coherence, three things stand out. The first is that Sewell appears to think that it is a good thing, a matter for congratulation, that "the liberal press almost any day of the week" suppresses facts supportive of Israel, and an even better thing that this suppression often does not even have to be contrived, but arises from the ignorance of the younger correspondents themselves. The second is that these suppressed facts, well enough known to him to be brazenly listed, do not seem to him to possess any power to invalidate, or even disturb "left-liberal prejudices about Israel." The third is the confidence displayed in the passage that one can list these inconvenient facts *entre nous*, as it were, for a left-liberal audience, without being suspected of sympathy for Israel. There is only one underlying conviction that could make the union of this strange collection of beliefs intelligible. It is the conviction that Israel is so evidently the embodiment of evil that the facts in the case do not matter; that they constitute, morally speaking, merely a confusing diversion which, if more widely known, could only confuse decent people and reduce the level of righteous indignation against Israel which it is the duty of every right-thinking journalist to augment, if necessary by suppression of the truth. In Chapter 5 I shall examine that conviction more closely. But before doing that we need to look more closely at the suggestion promoted by the iconography of the issue (despite Sewell's attempt to defuse it by what might in some quarters, I suppose, count as humor): the suggestion that all Jews (*really!*) support Israel; a belief without which, after all, the central contention of both the new and the old anti-Semitism, that "the Jews" constitute a *cohesive and unified* force for evil, in short a "conspiracy," falls to the ground.

NOTES

1. See the article by Charlotte Halle, from the Israeli newspaper *Haaretz*: http://www.haaretzdaily.com/hasen/pages/ShArt.jhtml?itemNo=128266&contrassID=2&subContrassID=1&sbSubContrassID=0&listSrc=Y.

2. Stefan C. Reif, letter to the editor, *New Statesman*, January 21, 2002.

3. David Triesman, letter to the editor, *New Statesman*, January 21, 2002.

4. According to Wilby they were opposed to "the policies of the present Israeli government."

5. Peter Wilby, ed., "The *New Statesman* and anti-Semitism," *New Statesman*, February 11, 2002, pp. 9–10.

6. *New Statesman*, Feb. 11, 2002, p. 10.

7. *New Statesman*, Feb. 11, 2002, p. 9.

8. *New Statesman*, Feb. 11, 2002, p.10.

9. *New Statesman*, Feb. 11, 2002, p. 10.

10. *New Statesman*, Feb. 11, 2002, p. 10.

11. For recent news coverage of specific and typical instances, see "Jews Suffer Surge of Hate on Streets of Belgium," *Daily Telegraph*, May 30, 2002, p. 18; or the harassment currently suffered by some prominent British Jews, including Lord Triesman, the former general secretary of the Labour Party, Barbara Roche, Labour MP for Hornsey and Wood Green. Uri Geller reported for the *Sunday Telegraph*, February 15, 2004, p. 8, under the headline "Prominent Jews Targeted by Muslims and the Far Right." Information on this and a host of other incidents can easily be obtained from a number of websites including that of the Board of Deputies of British Jews.

12. Alan Dershowitz, *The Case for Israel* (Hoboken, N.J.: John Wiley, 2003), p. 208.

13. John Pilger, "Blair Meets with Arafat but Supports Sharon," *New Statesman*, Jan. 14, 2002, p. 17.

14. *New Statesman*, Jan. 14, 2002, p. 17.

15. All three have groups supporting Israel, the web addresses of which are given in the Appendix.

16. Dennis Sewell, "A kosher conspiracy?," *New Statesman*, Jan. 14, 2002, p. 15.

17. The spy in question was gratified to find the two poets deep in conversation about one "Spy Nosey" (the philosopher Spinoza, whose name they would doubtless at that period have pronounced as in English "spine").

18. Geoffrey Wheatcroft, "The Jewish Answer?" *Spectator* (London), Christmas issue, December 14–21, 2002, p. 48.

19. Dennis Sewell, "A kosher conspiracy?," *New Statesman*, Jan. 14, 2002, p. 16.

20. Dennis Sewell, "A kosher conspiracy?," *New Statesman*, Jan. 14, 2002, p. 16.

3

JEWS AGAINST ISRAEL

A SENSE OF THE RIGHTS OF THE OTHER

In a certain sense one can sympathize with the difficulties faced by those inclined to toy with the vocabulary and iconography of anti-Semitism in dealing with the phenomenon of Jewish disagreement over Israel. The divisions among Jews over their national state fly in the face of experience and seem, at times, even, *contra naturam*. An excessive concern for national identity—of the sort of which Jews themselves have so often been accused—is commonly attended among non-Jews, after all, by some degree—usually marked—of one-sided partiality, verging in extreme cases on xenophobia, on the part of virtually all patriotic members of the nation concerned. One does not hear many strident attacks on Arab anti-Semitism or sturdy defenses of the right of Israel to exist emanating from the Muslim lands. Serbs rarely express warm feelings toward Albanians or Bosnian Muslims. English admiration for Germany and its culture has since 1914 been decidedly, and, it is possible to think, regrettably, thin on the ground, as has, immemorially, anglophilia in Ireland or Scotland. Yet there can surely be no more unreserved expression, not merely of sympathy with the Palestinian people, but of support for their claim to the whole of the land presently occupied by Israel than that to be found on the web site of *Neturei Carta*,[1] an organization of Orthodox rabbis who believe, like many pious European Jews from the 1880s onward, that the attempt by Zionist Jews to end the Exile is impious and contrary to the will of God. Nor is this the limit of Jewish sympathy for people who do not, to put it mildly, take overmuch care to present themselves as friends of the Jews.

There is presently in Britain, as in Europe at large, a good deal of popular anti-Muslim feeling, which it is to be hoped will prove temporary, but which possesses, for the moment, thanks to such things as the murder in an Amsterdam street of the filmmaker Theo van Gogh and the London suicide bombings of 2005, a good deal more in the way of factual basis than any form of anti-Semitism has ever possessed. Those of my acquaintance who denounce this—it is to be hoped passing—Islamophobia most violently, who insist most vehemently on the reality of the credentials of Islam as a religion of peace and brotherhood, are, surprisingly enough, very often Jews. Nor are they kidding, or indulging in the common British pastime of staking out more or less hypocritical but politically correct *prises de position* (and they are not "trying to assimilate themselves" either, more about that in a moment). Stare as deeply into their eyes as one will, waiting for a flicker in the gaze or some other betrayal in body language of quite contrary thoughts proceeding deep within, and one will be disappointed. They really mean it. And one falls silent, feeling in one direction the acute pathos of the situation, in another, perhaps, impatience at a certain willed disregard for uncomfortable facts displayed in the political stance of one's interlocutor; but feeling also, if one has any sense of the realities of the Holocaust—the sort of sense to be gained, for instance, from the excellent recent English translation of *Nine Suitcases*, a Holocaust memoir by the Hungarian liberal writer Bela Zsolt[2]—abashed in the presence of a moral strength, a hardness in the service of forgiveness and fair-mindedness, which one might be very hard put to emulate.

DIVERSITY DENIAL

All Jews support Israel is thus a proposition rather remote from reality. It is also one which displays—or rather one such that the naive conviction of its unarguable truth displays—one of the most striking and depressing features, not only of anti-Semitism, but of racism in general. I have in mind the universal tendency of racists to lump together whole nations as bearers of whatever characteristic it may be that excites their dislike and contempt. The term *stereotyping* is sometimes used to gesture toward this feature of racism, but it is an unhappy term because it suggests that what is going wrong—all that is going wrong—is merely the giving of credence to a "stereotype" in the sense of a false, even absurdly false, *image* of the people concerned: the Frenchman as conceived by the English with his beret and string of onions, the Englishman as conceived by the French with his *chapeau melon* and *pantalon rayé*, and so forth. What I have in mind is something different and rather more sinister in its effects—something, incidentally, which is pretty standard in the discourse of a great many academic cultural relativists of all political stripes—namely, the refusal to grant or recognize the existence in the alien group of that most human of cultural characteristics, *diversity*. Since "stereotyping" won't quite fill the bill, and since one needs a suitable pejorative term for this aspect of racism, I propose to introduce one: *diversity denial*. That done, it is at once evident that the contempt for human reality involved in diversity denial need not, and may not, be uniquely linked to "racism" in the familiar sense of dislike or hatred of an alien people or race. It can display itself just as markedly in contexts of romantic admiration for the Other.

If someone, say around 1900, carried away by romantic enthusiasm of a generally right-wing flavor for the cause of Ruritanian independence from the trammels of the Austro-Hungarian Empire, manages to persuade himself, in the face of the facts, that there are no Ruritanians, or at least—saving phrase—no *authentic* Ruritanians—who would vastly prefer the rule of *Unser lieber Kaiser Franz* to that of whatever gang of more or less unsavory nationalist politicians stand to gain by the collapse of the Empire, such a person is just as much guilty of diversity denial as the pillar of that part of the present-day British Left which thinks that all Jews support Israel, despite the fact that the feelings of the former toward Ruritania and Ruritanians are quite glowingly positive while those of the latter toward Jews are distinctly chilly. People hold increasingly, in this intellectually and morally disheveled age, that there are no sins against Truth but only sins against Charity, or to put it in a less high-flown way, that it doesn't matter what nonsense you permit yourself to think as long as your heart is in the right place. The sin committed by the diversity denier against the collective Other, however, is a sin not against Charity but against Truth, and hence is quite independent of whether his feelings toward that Other are bitterly contemptuous or warmly empathetic. His error consists in treating the collective Other, not as the intricately connected, but also awkwardly diverse, collection of individuals constituting that Other in real life, but as a theoretically convenient dummy Other; a mere counter, that is to say, constructed, by topping and tailing the facts, to serve the convenience of the diversity denier's own ideological commitments. The diversity denier's sin, whether he loves or hates, is that his love and hate relate not to anything instantiated in reality, but to fictions elaborated in the service of whatever story he tells himself about himself.

It is evident that diversity denial has always constituted a leading feature of political anti-Semitism. Having brought it into the light—we shall come back to it later—let us leave it on one side and look a little further into the curious fact of its entire absence from so much Jewish thought and feeling concerning the non-Jewish collective Other who, for so many centuries, has brought so much suffering into Jewish life.

THE ROOTS OF JEWISH XENOPHILIA

Individual Jews often find this Jewish sympathy for their professed enemies difficult to comprehend and still more difficult to distinguish from (non-Jewish) anti-Semitism. The (Jewish) journalist Jonathan Freedland, for instance, after condemning Sharon's victory as "a dark hour" for Israel in his *Guardian* column, recounts how he found himself accused of anti-Semitism by a reader.

> I explained to Mr. M that I am in fact a member of "we (the Jewish people)." I asked, given his branding me an antisemite, what language he would use for the real enemies of our people. He responded, minutes later, that I was "the real enemy"! And that, actually, compared to Israel's Arab adversaries and indeed to neo-Nazi groups around the world, I was "the biggest problem."[3]

Alan Dershowitz, in his recent book defending Israel, offers two explanations for the remarkable preponderance of Jewish sympathy for the Palestinians over Arab sympathy for the Jews. The first, which is surely correct, is that the political authoritarianism at present dominant in the Arab world stifles the expression of generous or magnanimous views.

> The reality is that complete freedom of information and freedom of speech among Israelis and Jews allows for the widest array of views to be presented, whereas virtually total control over information to most residents of Arab and Muslim states, coupled with extreme sanctions for expressing dissenting views, makes any realistic comparison impossible.

The second, though, is roughly in line with the stance of Jonathan Freedland's "Mr. M." It is that there are, and always have been, "self-hating Jews."

> There has always been a small element within the Jewish community that for largely inexplicable reasons has been hypercritical of everything associated with Judaism, Jews and the Jewish state. Karl Marx, Noam Chomsky, and Norman Finkelstein come easily to mind. . . . There are also some Jews for whom Israel's growing unpopularity among the rad-

ical left is something of an embarrassment. These Jews want to be liked by those whose policies they support on other issues. Accordingly they tend to distance themselves from Israel and often support the Palestinian side without much thought about the merits of the case. Opposing Israel and supporting the Palestinians is, for some Jews, a way of establishing their left-wing credentials and proving that their political correctness trumps any ethnic solidarity.[4]

So far as it is in the power of an outsider such as myself to determine, there is a real phenomenon hiding behind the notion of "Jewish self-hatred." But I think it may need subtler and less forensic dissection than it receives from Dershowitz in the above passage, or for that matter from Freedland's "Mr. M." Here, for contrast, are some remarks of Aharon Appelfeld's which, it seems to me, both render it more explicable and also, I want to suggest—though I'm not sure that even Appelfeld quite sees this—rob it of a good deal of its force as an accusation of moral weakness or betrayal.

> The place of the non-Jew in Jewish imagination is a complex affair growing out of generations of Jewish fear. Which of us dares to take up the burden of explanation? . . . I said fear, but the fear wasn't uniform, and it wasn't of all gentiles. In fact there was a sort of envy of the non-Jew hidden in the heart of the modern Jew. The non-Jew was frequently viewed in the Jewish imagination as a liberated creature without ancient beliefs or social obligations, who lived a natural life on his own soil. The Holocaust, of course, altered somewhat the course of the Jewish imagination. In the place of envy came suspicion. Those feelings which had walked in the open descended to the underground.
>
> Is there some stereotype of the non-Jew in the Jewish soul? It exists, and it is frequently embodied in the word goy, but that is an undeveloped stereotype. The Jews have had imposed on them too many moral and religious strictures to express such feelings utterly without restraint. Among the Jews there was never the confidence to express verbally the depths of hostility they may well have felt. What hostility they permitted themselves to feel was, paradoxically, directed at themselves.
>
> What has preoccupied me, and continues to perturb me, is this anti-Semitism directed at oneself, an ancient Jewish ailment which, in modern times, has taken on various guises. I grew up in an assimilated Jewish home where German was treasured. German was considered not only a language but also a culture, and the attitude towards German culture was virtually religious. All around us lived masses of Jews who spoke Yiddish, but in our house Yiddish was absolutely forbidden. I

grew up with the feeling that anything Jewish was blemished. From my
earliest childhood my gaze was directed at the beauty of non-Jews.
They were blond and tall and behaved naturally: they were cultured, and
when they didn't behave in a cultured fashion, at least they behaved naturally. . . .

From my earliest youth I was drawn to non-Jews. They fascinated me
with their strangeness, their height, their aloofness. . . . The change took
place when we were uprooted from our house and driven into the ghet-
tos. Then I noticed that the doors and windows of our non-Jewish
neighbours were suddenly shut, and we walked alone in the empty
streets.[5]

Three things resonate in this passage. One is love of, and admiration for, the
non-Jew, this large, blond, beautiful, and above all *natural* being. The second
is a profound sense of betrayal at the hands of these terrible, ambiguous objects of Jewish love. The third is the destructive inward-turning of the resulting sense of failure; the mutation of the original sense of the glories of
the non-Jew relative to one's own status as the bearer of a "blemished" culture, into the terrible fear that perhaps that rejection, that appalling betrayal,
may actually have been deserved! There is much that is poignant, even tragic
here, but surely, pace Dershowitz, nothing that is *inexplicable*. This is the familiar geometry of love bestowed on an essentially alien, and because alien,
partly unknowable object; the kind of love that Proust explores, for instance,
in the love of Swann for the courtesan Odette de Crécy, or of the young
Marquis de Saint Loup en Bray for the actress and cheap prostitute Rachel,
both of whom seem to their lovers seductively "natural" beings, and for
both of whom their lovers find it in themselves to make endless self-
deceiving and self-flagellating excuses.

Despite my general admiration for Dershowitz, therefore, I feel disinclined to accept his explanation of the stand of Chomsky, Finkelstein, and
other Jews on the Left in terms of "inexplicable" self-hatred and a contemptible desire to seek acceptance by groveling to the non-Jewish Left.
Indeed, such an explanation seems to me itself flavored with more than a
whiff of Jewish self-hatred. It is surely more complex than that. For one
thing it is difficult to see anything contemptible, anything to despise, in
many of these Jewish pillars of the pro-Palestinian Left, and certainly no element of groveling. There is, of course, on the Jewish Left, a tradition to
which Marx, Rosa Luxembourg, Trotsky, and others belonged, that of
denying any cultural or religious specificity to Jews considered as a people.

According to this line of thought there is, in effect, no such thing as a Jew. Jews are constituted as such purely by the hatred of non-Jews, and that hatred in turn is hatred toward, as Luxembourg put it, "the *spirit of huckster-ism and swindle*, which appears in *every* society where *exploitation reigns*"[6] and will disappear of its own accord when exploitation ends with the revolution. A late version of this—at one and the same time culturally illiterate and almost feeble-mindedly optimistic—story can be found faithfully parroted in Sartre's *Antisemite and Jew*,[7] but I have never met any Jew who believed it. Whereas I *am* acquainted in Britain with fiercely pro-Muslim Jews, "on the Left" but unconnected with any organized branch of the Left, whom it would seem absurd to accuse of anything but love and respect toward their Jewish heritage.

If I were asked, as an outsider, to propose an explanation for the remarkable tendency of individual Jews to take up positions critical of what others, and some of their fellows, construe as "their own side," I would myself be inclined to look for it in two rather central features of Jewishness. The first is religious: the ancient belief in Judaism that it is the task of Jews to redeem the world, and that this task imposes special requirements not binding upon non-Jews. A rather clear, though entirely secularized, expression of this ancient conviction can be found in Daniel Lindenberg's little pamphlet *Le rappel à l'ordre*—which caused a furor in France in 2002 by its accusation of a shift to the Maurrasian Right among French intellectuals, particularly Jewish ones. In the section titled (in English, inexplicably) "When Jews turn right." Lindenberg offers the following account (my translation) of the Franco-Judaic tradition to which he sees himself as belonging:

> The original kernel of French "judaicity". . . sought, within the elites of the first two or three emancipated generations, a new "civil religion." It is conventional nowadays to call this civil religion "franco-judaism." It produced developments such as the Alliance Israélite universelle (1860) supported by Saint-Simonian intellectuals and those inspired by the events of 1848, responsive to the message of Jewish prophecy. It also achieved considerable penetration of rabbinic circles, even that which, with Isidore Loeb, created in 1880 the Société des études juives, which published the Revue des études juives, which continues to appear to this day. The principal theme of franco-judaism is the substantial identity between the "mosaic" or "prophetic" message, once extracted from its matrix of ritual, and the spirit of 1789 and the Rights of Man. The great voices of franco-judaism (Joseph Salvador, James Darmeester) thought

that Judaism, which they preferred to call Hebraism, is called to *regenerate the civilized world* [my italics], permitting the democracies of the future, like the Christian churches, to drink from the common and convergent springs of the Sinaitic Revelation and the Declaration of the Rights of Man and of the citizen.[8]

It is entirely explicable, surely, why someone who views his activity as a Jew in this light should be inclined to minimize, as Lindenberg does, the seriousness of the present spate of Muslim attacks on Jews in Western Europe—attacks which have grown in seriousness in France over the past few years until the French government has been forced to take note of them—in the hope of preventing these attacks from producing the general migration of French Jewish opinion to the Right, which Lindenberg sees as already beginning to occur. On the one hand, pace Dershowitz, one can hardly see in this rather moving passage grounds for dismissing Lindenberg either as a self-hating Jew or as a lickspittle of the non-Jewish Left. On the other hand, as a non-Jew aware of the full horror of what Jews in general, and French Jews in particular, have suffered over the past century, one can do little but stand respectfully in silence in the face of this willingness to find excuses for a further wave of rabid anti-Semitism, in the hope of preserving the commitment of Jews to the essentially redemptive goals of the first generations of emancipated Jewry in France.

The second factor motivating Jews in general to take up left-wing positions, and in particular to sympathize with Muslims and resist what has begun to be called Islamophobia, is, it seems to me, the same as we found in Appelfeld's earlier quote: the tendency of Jews, far from wishing to hurt, let alone dominate or supplant, gentiles, actually to fall in love with gentiles taken collectively. In the context of relations between Israel and Palestine this Jewish tendency to xenophilia is well illustrated by Meron Benevisti's book *Sacred Landscape: The Buried History of the Holy Land Since 1948*.[9] The book, written by an Israeli whose father had been a geographer and mapmaker, is a prolonged and detailed lament for the destruction of the Arab rural landscape of Palestine after the Israeli victory in the 1948 war. Benevisti is under no illusions that the same would have happened to the Jewish landscape had the Arabs won, but finds in that no consolation. The last paragraph of Benevisti's anguished Introduction is worth quoting in full.

It wasn't my human landscape, nor was it the physical space that my people created: they were its destroyers. But the pain and the sorrow were deep and genuine, and with them arose a compelling need to commemorate the vanished landscape, both because it was a human creation and because it was my homeland, a land that never forgets any of her sons and daughters. I cannot envisage my homeland without Arabs, and perhaps my late father, who taught me to read maps and study history, was right in his naïve belief that there is enough space, physical and historical, for Jews and Arabs in their shared homeland.

The late Isaiah Berlin wrote well about this Jewish xenophilia in a well-known essay, connecting it with the redemptive task of Judaism I mentioned a moment ago. In that essay he offers a parable of the condition of the emancipated Jewry that arose in Europe from the Enlightenment onward, comparing them to travelers who by some accident find themselves among a strange tribe whose customs they do not, at first, understand. They set themselves to become like that tribe and in the process come to love it.

> The strangers become primary authorities on the natives: they codify their language and their customs, they compose the tribe's dictionaries and encyclopedias, they interpret the native society to the outside world. With every year their knowledge and love of it, their fascination with all that it is and does, become greater. If their enterprise is successful, they feel that they understand the natives so profoundly, so much better than they understand themselves, that they feel—not unjustifiably—that they are its best friends, its champions and its prophets. In the end they are prepared not merely to live but to die for it and, if need be, with it, no less bravely, and perhaps with greater passion, than the natives themselves. Nevertheless, the natives often fail to reciprocate these sentiments. They may wonder at, admire, sometimes be spellbound by the strangers, grow fond, even very fond, of them, but their feelings, however benevolent or respectful or fascinated, are, at best, those felt towards strangers—persons the very quality of whose excellence goes with their being in some sense different from, and outside, the tribal structure.[10]

This is another version of the Jewish dilemma, the same dilemma formulated by Appelfeld reflecting on his childhood in *Beyond Despair*. The depth of the commitment of the strangers to the tribe may be familiarly gauged by any gentile, cynically critical of Britain as so many of us are, who has observed, possibly with amusement, the sincere alacrity with which a Jewish compatriot leaps to the defense of our common native land; or who has watched over the decades the little cortège of Jewish ex-servicemen, growing ever smaller with the years, travel down Whitehall to the Cenotaph on Armistice Day. For Berlin, of course, as for Appelfeld, the culmination in the Holocaust of the post-Enlightenment Jewish drive toward assimilation has made that kind of patriotism seem both foolish and self-deceiving.

> But second nature is different from nature, and the desperate self-identification of the Jew does not ring wholly true. Walter Rathenau once wrote, "My people are the Germans, no one else. For me the Jews are a German tribe, like the Saxons, the Bavarians or the Wends." No sensitive person—particularly if he is German—can read this without embarrassment. And when he was killed by the kind of young German nationalist whom, in some moods, he seemed to admire most, his assassination was doubtless a great crime and a tragedy for his country, but it had a dreadful pathos about it too—since it was something which Rathenau himself was all his life too blind, or too self-blinded, to allow to be possible.[11]

Berlin's bitterness and embarrassment is understandable enough. We gentiles, though, might do well to curb any embarrassment on Rathenau's behalf, along with large and loose talk about "kosher conspiracies" and the like, and reflect instead on the crime and the tragedy.

Now for a postscript on the dangers of failing to take sufficient account of intracommunal diversity, as illustrated, this time, in my own case. When a Jewish friend who had been raised in Egypt read through the foregoing, in an earlier draft, he became steadily more irritated by the passages I had selected, particularly those from Appelfeld and Berlin. He insisted that, when he was growing up, neither he nor his friends had ever felt anything of the kind: neither the admiration for non-Jews nor the desire to imitate them, nor the fear. "In Egypt we just took non-Jews for granted, as they did us. Those feelings Appelfeld and Berlin express, they are not in fact *Jewish* feelings, they are *Ashkenazi* Jewish feelings!" How right Ludwig Wittgenstein was, it seems, to hold that salvation lies in detail, and that generalization about human affairs is usually a sure path to error and intellectual muddle.

NOTES

1. The web address of *Neturei Carta* is http://www.nkuza.org/.
2. Bela Zsolt, *Nine Suitcases*, trans. Ladislaus Löb (London: Jonathan Cape, 2004).
3. Jonathan Freedland, "Back to 1948: Sharon's Election and the Dilemma for the Diaspora," *Jewish Quarterly* 181 (Spring 2001): 13.
4. Alan Dershowitz, *The Case for Israel* (Hoboken N.J.: John Wiley, 2003), p. 218.

5. Aharon Appelfeld, *Beyond Despair: Three Lectures and a Conversation with Philip Roth* (New York: Fromm International, 1994), pp. 76–77.

6. Rosa Luxembourg, cited in Paul Johnson, *A History of the Jews* (London: George Weidenfeld and Nicholson, 1987), pp. 448–49.

7. Jean-Paul Sartre, *Antisemite and the Jew* (New York: Grove Press, 1962).

8. Daniel Lindenberg, *Le rappel à l'ordre: Enquète sur les nouveaux réactionnaires* (Paris: Seuil, collecion La république des idées, 2002), pp. 62–63 (my translation).

9. Meron Benevisti, *Sacred Landscape: The Buried History of the Holy Land Since 1948*, trans. Maxine Kaufman-Lacusta (Berkeley: University of California Press, 2002). I am grateful to Gabriel Josipovici for putting this book into my hands.

10. Isaiah Berlin, "Jewish Slavery and Emancipation," *Jewish Chronicle* (1951) cited here from the version reprinted in Isaiah Berlin, *The Power of Ideas*, ed. Henry Hardy (London: Pimlico, 2001), pp. 166–67.

11. Berlin, *The Power of Ideas,* pp. 170–71.

4

POLITICS AND THE
CONCEPT OF EVIL

THE LIMITS OF FAIR REPORTAGE

I return in this section and the next to the central claim motivating the new anti-Semitism, that from a humanitarian perspective, the perspective of "human rights" as people say nowadays, the State of Israel is evil, both in its constitution and its conduct, to a degree which so transcends the wickedness of any other state, in a world not, one would have said, poor at present in political depravity, as to justify demands, not merely for a change in its government, but for its dissolution as a state.

The concerns of those who fear the growing dissemination of such views frequently focus on the very things—selective reporting, omission of essential background facts, "creeping cultural and moral relativism"—which Sewell blithely admits to be leading features of the coverage of Israel offered by "the liberal press almost any day of the week" and which many consider to have become equally evident of late years, in the broadcast media, particularly the BBC. Douglas Davis, a distinguished South African journalist and London correspondent of the *Jerusalem Post*, asks:

> How does the BBC fill the interval during live broadcasts of the Proms? The problem did not stretch the imagination of the Radio 3 producer on the evenings of 13 August and 20 August 2002. The gap was filled by a recitation of poems that compared the acts of Israelis to those of the Nazis and asked Holocaust survivors why they had "not learnt their lesson."
>
> . . . I do not deny the BBC's right—the right of any news organisation—to be critical of Israel. Criticism of politicians and political institutions is an integral part of the democratic process and our political

discourse would be unthinkable without it. I have never shirked from criticizing a range of Israeli administrations, from Rabin and Peres to Netanyahu, Barak and Sharon, when I considered such criticism appropriate, Unlike the BBC, however, I have also been critical, when I considered it appropriate, of the Palestine Authority chairman, Yasser Arafat, whose despotic rule has brought tragedy to hundreds of Israelis and impoverished the Palestinian people.

But while I acknowledge the right of the BBC to be critical, its relentless, one-dimensional portrayal of Israel as a demonic, criminal state and Israelis as brutal oppressors responsible for all the ills of the region bears the hallmarks of a concerted campaign of vilification that, wittingly or not, has the effect of delegitimizing the Jewish state and pumping oxygen into a dark, old European hatred that dared not speak its name for the past half-century.[1]

At the same time there are plenty of journalists, and no doubt others, who fail to see why unfairness to *Israel* in the media, even gross unfairness, should be considered *anti-Semitic*.[2] Two arguments for this position suggest themselves. The first, brutal but realistic, and because of that seldom stated openly, is that, whether one likes it or not, vilification by means of selective reporting is a technique endemic to the press and broadcast media of all advanced countries. The Serbs suffered heavily from it in the late Balkan wars, in the sense that while Serb atrocities received blanket coverage, and were generally reported in a tone of moral outrage, Bosnian and Croatian atrocities, such as the "ethnic cleansing" of the Serbian population of the Krajina, and earlier, and again more recently, of Kosovo, received, at most, muted and neutral treatment. More prosaically, all news organizations have a political slant. None is fair to the political parties it opposes, or to their supporters. Why should the Jews suppose themselves to be uniquely entitled to scrupulously fair treatment in the media? Anti-Semitism, so the argument goes, involves bad treatment directed, *specifically and differentially*, at Jews; but in this respect Jews are being treated, if no better, at any rate no worse, than a lot of other groups.

The second counterargument Davis faces is one stated quite openly at the moment, in articles in the *soi-disant* responsible press, and around *soi-disant* respectable dinner tables. It is that, if "Israel" and "the Jewish people" are indeed separate entities, as so many Jews allege, then antagonism toward Israel, robustly partisan antagonism included, and even antagonism aimed at stigmatizing Israel as a wholly evil, criminal state, cannot be antagonism toward *Jews as such*, and hence cannot be *anti-Semitic*.

Both of these arguments seem to me profoundly, and also importantly, sophistical. To take the second first, it is not clear how, if Israel were a wholly evil, criminal state, its criminality could be prevented from attainting equally those, Jews or non-Jews, who support its right to continued existence, as a large number, possibly a majority, of Jews do, and, of course, as a vast number of non-Jews, beginning only slightly to the right of the promoters of the analogy, also do. There is general agreement, after all, that, if the Third Reich was, as most of us take it to have been, a criminal state, then those who actively supported it must be regarded as participating, if not necessarily, in particular cases, to a very high degree, in its criminality. It is thus simply disingenuous to suppose that one can demonize Israel, or "Zionism," as *evil* without thereby demonizing Jews as evil.

THE CONCEPTUAL CONTENT OF THE NOTION OF EVIL

There is more to be said, however. To get at it, we need to begin at some—only apparent—distance from the matter in hand, with the concept of evil itself. George W. Bush famously described a number of states as constituting an "Axis of Evil." No doubt because of this, it is rather commonplace at the moment to hear, from many people, in academia and elsewhere, those who would describe themselves in America as liberals, or in Britain, quaintly, as "wishy-washy liberals," that the very word "evil" has, or should have, no place in political discourse. Quite recently, for instance, someone at a dinner table told me that he "could attach no meaning" to the term "evil." One grasps, of course, the place occupied by these moves in the current left-liberal worldview. The thought is that, if one regards people as "evil," one can no longer negotiate with them, because one can no longer think of them as fellow human beings, as people with whom a negotiated settlement is, even in theory, possible. And it is a central plank of one current left-liberal belief system, with what relationship to reality, or for that matter to the internal coherence of that system, remains to be seen, that all human conflict without exception can be resolved by negotiation; with the further proviso that where negotiation fails it is invariably because one has not gone far enough in viewing matters from the standpoint of those with whom one is negotiating.

Nevertheless, setting this standpoint on one side for the moment, "evil" is a familiar English word, and I doubt whether those who object, for the above sort of reasons, to its use, have really any difficulty in understanding its meaning. Indeed, they show by their choice of contexts in which to object to its use that they understand its meaning very well. But for their benefit let us attempt a little conceptual analysis. It is surely conceptually written into the notion of evil, part of the meaning of the term, that for what is evil there is nothing positive, nothing even mitigating, to be said. There are no shades of gray, no silver linings, where evil is concerned. Evil is, as Thomistic moral theology would have it, simply the privation of good, meaning by that that an evil thing is one from whose constitution all goodness, and with it the last shred of possible justification, has been expelled or exhausted. One cannot—and this also is a conceptual point—compromise with evil. One can only fight it and attempt to eradicate it.

One might well agree with current left-liberal thinking to this extent, that there are indeed very few things, and certainly no peoples or religions, which are evil in the conceptually required sense that there is nothing whatsoever to be said in their favor. Human affairs are seldom safely to be depicted in black and white. Nevertheless, there is one twentieth-century political movement which many, perhaps most, people would consider evil in that sense, namely Nazism. So deeply rooted is this judgment, indeed, that Nazism, and its symbol the swastika, have become universally recognizable stereotypes of evil. Hence, to assert of any group or movement that it is indistinguishable from the Nazis or from Nazism is precisely to stigmatize it *as evil*, with the conceptually licensed implication that there is, literally, *nothing* to be said in its favor; that it is so irredeemably bad that compromise with it is out of the question; that the only desirable thing, so far as it is concerned, is that it should be brought to an end, expunged from the face of the world. That, of course, is precisely what the Nazis thought about the Jews, and by extension about every expression of Jewish life, religion, thought, and feeling. That the Jews are an inherently, irredeemably evil race is, after all, the central proposition of political anti-Semitism. To attach the label "Nazi" to Israel, or to couple the Star of David with the swastika is thus not just to express opposition, even "robust" opposition, to the policies of one or another Israeli government. It is to defame Israel by association with the most powerful symbol of evil, of that which, because it contains not the least scintilla of goodness, must be utterly rejected and uprooted from the face of the earth, available at present to Western and world culture. Moreover, as we have already noted, the use of the Star of David in this context, a Jewish rather than a specifically Israeli symbol, makes it easy to extend the identification with absolute evil from Israel to the Jewish people in general. No doubt there are some people prepared to defend the identification of Israel as a uniquely evil state who would resist, particularly in public and before the media, its extension to "the Jews" in general. But there are others who would not, and in any case demons, once let out of bottles, are prone to ignore caveats and qualifications on the part of those who released them.

Davis thus gains his point. The material broadcast by the BBC in the evenings of 13 and 20 August 2002 was not merely anti-Israel but, in the strongest political sense, anti-Semitic. The same goes for the banner carried in a pro-Palestinian march in the photograph on the back cover of Kosmin and Iganski's book, which consists of a mock Israeli flag, bearing between the blue lines a Star of David followed by a swastika, the two connected by the mathematical greater-than symbol (>), signifying, presumably, that the crimes of Israel are greater than those of the Nazis. But the matter does not end there. If Davis is on firm ground on that issue, it follows that he is also on perfectly solid ground in characterizing as anti-Semitic the systematic suppression of any countervailing fact, any piece of background information, which could soften the overwhelmingly hostile impression of Israel presented by certain British newspapers and television news services, with the BBC, the *Guardian*, and the *Independent* leading the way. That which is inherently evil, that which should not be compromised with, but expelled, if possible, from the world, is, comes to the same thing, conceptually speaking, as that for which there is nothing whatsoever to be said. To constantly reinforce the impression that the news and current affairs editors of *soi-disant* "responsible" news-gathering organizations can find *nothing whatsoever positive to say in favor of Israel* can convey no other message than that Israel is, as the Nazis were, an evil state, and that those who support it and endeavor to set the record straight are, therefore, supporters of evil. There is no escape to be had from this conclusion by pointing out that other groups suffer the same distortions, that the Tories, the Serbs, and more recently, in connection with the second Iraq war, the British Labour government, have been equally the butts of distorted and selective reporting by the BBC and other news organizations. In the case of Israel and the Jews, however, one has to take into account not only what the editor of the *New Statesman* (as we noted in Chapter 2) delicately terms "historical resonance," that is to say, the past horrors wrought by political anti-Semitism, but also the widespread persistence of political anti-Semitism today, not only in the press and television of the Muslim world, but, as we have argued, in sections of the Western media. Political hyperbole coupled with selective reporting and the suppression of relevant facts are evidently bad, destructive things in themselves, and sometimes, in the influence they exert upon policy, potentially lethal things. In the case of Israel and the Jews they fall squarely into the latter category. Where these

matters are concerned they give a new twist to the Manicheanism, the belief that the battle against the Jews is a battle of good against evil, which
has always been at the heart of political anti-Semitism. Sartre saw this, at
least, clearly.

> Anti-Semitism is thus seen to be at bottom a form of Manichaeism. It
> explains the course of the world by the struggle of the principle of Good
> with the principle of Evil. Between these two principles no reconcilia-
> tion is conceivable; one of them must triumph and the other be annihi-
> lated. Look at Céline: his vision of the universe is catastrophic. The Jew
> is everywhere, the earth is lost, it is up to the Aryan not to compromise,
> never to make peace. . . . Others . . . are less discouraging. They envisage
> a long and often doubtful struggle, with the final triumph of Good. It is
> Ormazd and Ahriman. The reader understands that the anti-Semite does
> not have recourse to Manichaeism as a secondary principle of explana-
> tion. It is the original choice he makes of Manichaeism which explains
> and conditions anti-Semitism.[3]

RESERVATIONS REGARDING THE JEWS

There is, in short, something profoundly hypocritical about the stance of
those who denounce the use of the word "evil" in connection with, say, suicide bombers, while at the same time finding nothing to complain about in
the sort of press and media treatment of Israel that we have been considering. They hold, they say, that all intrusion of the notion of evil into political discourse is inadmissible. This is no doubt a fatuously overgeneralized
claim, since some acts, some regimes, even if not peoples or religions, surely
are evil. Within limits, nevertheless, it admits of defense on the entirely laudable grounds listed earlier. But to the extent that the covert, or implicit, intrusion of the notion of evil into much current debate about Israel remains
unrecognized, there remains in effect a tiny reservation at the heart of this
laudable reluctance to judge in black and white; a reservation inserted to en-
sure that it is, of course, not to be taken as applying to the Jews. In the same
way there is a tiny reservation, of the same purport, at the heart of Wilby's
"vigorous anti-racism": the one that excludes from "seriousness" racism
against "white people." Neither reservation can be rationally defended because neither is rationally defensible. They are maintained by the process
which Derrida calls marginalization: that is to say, by the relegation of contradictions essential, paradoxically enough, to the internal coherence of a

text, to the margins, the understory, the crypt, of a discourse which continues to flow above or beside them, in happy self-ignorance of its own founding incoherence.

ISRAEL AND THE JEWISH PEOPLE

One can now see what is both sophistical and anti-Semitic about the latter of the two counterarguments thrown up with a view to defeating Davis's and others' claims of anti-Semitism in the current treatment of Israel by sections of the media in Britain and Europe. The argument is that the vilification of Israel, however extreme, and even when conducted by means of selective reporting and suppression of relevant facts, cannot be construed as anti-Semitic because, as Jews themselves insist, Israel and the Jewish people are separate entities. The answer to this is, surely, that to represent Israel as a polity for whose continued existence there is nothing whatsoever to be said is conceptually equivalent to representing it as evil to a degree justifying its removal from the face of the earth; and thus, by extension, to represent the vast majority of Jews who, however critical they might be of individual acts of particular Israeli governments, would not support the dissolution of the State of Israel as supporters of evil. In other words, if we were dealing with measured and balanced criticism of Israel, the counterargument would be sound enough. Merely to criticize, say, the Sharon government for being insufficiently ready to trade settlements for peace in the Occupied Territories is plainly not to bring any charge against Jews as such, either diaspora Jews or Jewish citizens of Israel, many of whom in either group would uphold the same or similar criticisms. But we are dealing, in large sections of the European media, not with limited and reasoned criticism of that sort, but rather with a sustained campaign of vilification amounting to demonization, and in those circumstances the argument becomes entirely specious, since to condemn Israel as an embodiment of evil more or less unique in the world since the overthrow of the Third Reich is to adopt a stance which in logic must compel anyone who holds it to stigmatizing as evil, in line with the central claims of political anti-Semitism, all those Jews, possibly the majority, who support Israel's right to exist. Coupling the Star of David with the swastika, and Israel with the Nazis, while sedulously promoting by underhanded means the impression that there is as little to be said for the former as for the latter, is not to engage in "criticism of Israel"; it is rather, as Jews have been entirely correct to point out, to engage in the dissemination of political anti-Semitism in its most traditional form.

AN ALLEGED DILEMMA

The point can be stated from yet another angle. The second counterargument can with minimal adjustment be reconstrued as an ad hominem argument in the form of a dilemma. So reconstrued it says: Opposed to Israel though we are, we are not opposed to Jews or to the Jewish people per se, to the extent that Jews, or the Jewish people, are prepared to dissociate themselves altogether from Israel. The aim is to present the Jew, any Jew, with a dilemma. He can either admit that the opprobrium visited upon Jews in virtue of the crimes of Israel is in his case justified opprobrium, fueled not by anti-Semitism but by moral concern, or he can dissociate himself entirely from Israel by granting that it has no right to continued existence. At this point, of course, the importance, for those who wish to deny Israel the right to exist as a state, of establishing a parallel between Israel and Nazi Germany becomes clear. It was widely accepted at the time, and is widely accepted now, that those Germans, like, say, Werner Heisenberg or Heidegger or Leni Reifenstahl, who either supported the Nazis, or simply failed to flee Germany after 1933 and remained there throughout the War, had in some sense a case to answer. The aim of those who pursue a parallel between Israel and the Nazis is to promote the idea that Jewish, and for that matter non-Jewish, supporters of Israel are in, or ought to be regarded as in, a similar position.

It is a tribute to the patience and moral earnestness common among Jews that some Jews on the "liberal Left" seem prepared to accept this sort of thing at face value, as fair dealing. Thus, for instance, Jonathan Freedland, the liberal columnist for the *Guardian* and the *Jewish Chronicle* whom I mentioned earlier, writing in early 2001 after the victory of Ariel Sharon, about the resulting "dilemmas for the Diaspora," locates the central dilemma in terms not too remote from the one we have been examining. He goes to the length of chiding the "peacenik" Israeli Left for not turning their backs on their country and leaving it "for ever," despite the satisfaction of a condition—the election of Sharon as prime minister—which they had always sworn would make them do so, and notes wryly that they, the Israeli Left, will be shielded from being forced to realize the enormity of their sins by not being "out there" in the diaspora, like himself:

For those inside the Jewish state will be shielded from the full force of the international backlash, already under way, against Ariel Sharon. They will not read the op-ed articles, like the one that appeared in the Guardian days after the election, branding the new PM "a man of blood" who should rank alongside Augusto Pinochet and Slobodan Milosevic as an internationally wanted man—a war criminal.[4]

By the end of the article Freedland has wisely refused to accept as exhaustive the pair of choices proposed by this style of political rhetoric: of denying the right of Israel to exist, or supporting "war criminals." But should he have worried in the first place? Can one really frame in these terms a "dilemma" worth two minutes' attention from diaspora Jews or anyone else? Freedland's quotation from the *Guardian* goes to the heart of the underlying sophistry. The Middle East presents a vast rogues' gallery of "men of blood," but only Ariel Sharon, of all people, counts as such for the *Guardian*. The Israel/Arab conflict is an immense and shifting web of shades of gray, but for the body of left-wing opinion represented by the *Guardian*, and for much of the time in recent years by the BBC, it often appears to be a matter of black and white. The Palestinian leadership can do no wrong and the Israelis can do no right. The anti-Semitism resides precisely in the absurdly one-sided moral hyperbole of these claims. So far as Sharon was concerned, such hyperbole, as seen so often in journalism, was swiftly overtaken by events, as the great architect of settlement in the Occupied Territories transformed himself into the architect of the unilateral withdrawal from Gaza. Rational, reflective journalism, and there is plenty of that about also, foresaw this as one political possibility. To the peddlers of the Zionism/Nazism analogy, on the other hand, the development necessarily came as a surprise: necessarily, because the analogy itself ruled it *conceptually* out of court. What is evil has no power, *conceptually* speaking, to change its nature; since that which is evil can, given the meaning of the term "evil," contain no trace of good from which such a change could spring. Of course, real politics is not like that: anything can happen in real politics. But then, real politics is a department of the empirical world, the world of change and accident; not, except when people so motivated briefly gain absolute power, the domain of totalitarian metaphysics.

THE NAZI ANALOGY

Now for a brief postscript. One thoughtful, incensed, and anonymous reader of an earlier draft of this book had two critical points to make against the argument as it has developed so far. The first is that, while wishing to oppose the characterization of Zionists or supporters of Israel as Nazis, I seem quite happy to smear journalists and others opposed to Israel in that way.

> It is surprising to see [Harrison] agree that the cover of the New States-
> man he discusses is akin to the Nazi propaganda sheet Der Sturmer, or
> that those who oppose Jewish settlements in the territories are advocat-
> ing "judenrein" areas. Why it's okay to compare journalists who ques-
> tion Israeli government policy or opponents of Israeli settlements in the
> territories with Nazis but it's forbidden to use any Nazi analogies to crit-
> icize Israel's policies is not at all clear.

The second is that to accept the illegitimacy of such analogies, and by way of doing so, to insist on balance and fairness in criticism of Israel, would be to draw the teeth of criticism, to "defang" those protesting against man-ifest injustice to the Palestinians. Again quoting my anonymous reader:

> Not surprisingly, the only acceptable criticism of Israel [to Harrison] is
> that which simultaneously describes other countries or the other side as
> worse on a particular issue. Of course there are examples in the press
> when a moral double standard has been applied to Israel compared to
> other countries, but the real goal of the author's approach is to defang
> any serious criticism by Israel and human rights groups or others. It
> would be tantamount to saying that any criticism of anti-black racism in
> the U.S. must be balanced by a discussion of how much better life in the
> U.S. is for blacks than [those] living in various African countries.

I hope it will be by now evident to the reader that the first of these criticisms is misplaced and why. It is no part of my purpose to character-ize, absurdly, Wilby or any other contributor to the January 14, 2002, issue of the *New Statesman*, or other journalists on the Left, let alone "the Left" in toto, as *Nazis*. My view, as already explained, is that the vast majority of the people in these categories, who invite the criticisms I have been de-veloping, are sincere humanitarians, led by the force of their emotional commitment to the Palestinian case, into propagating a new version of anti-Semitism which, although largely inadvertent, is dangerous, for reasons I have already set out, and which in any case disfigures their cause. In the case of the *New Statesman's* cover, it is not, absurdly, a putative *neo-Nazism* on the part of its originators that I and others object to, but the rash deployment, by professed antiracists, and supposedly in the service of humanitarian ends, of an iconography, of expressly anti-Semitic content, pioneered by the Nazis. The objection to it, and to my critic's suggestion that such proceedings might be "okay," is that to use "Nazi analogies to criticise Israeli policies" is to disseminate the suggestion that Israeli policies are morally indistinguishable from Nazi policies, and hence that the State of Israel is therefore in no way morally distinguishable from the Third Reich, from which, if true, it surely follows that the existence of the State of Israel has as little to be said for it as the existence of the Third Reich; which is to say, nothing; and from that that the Jews, since so many of them support the existence of Israel, are, collectively, enemies of mankind. To disseminate such suggestions, for whatever reason, and with whatever color of moral commitment or humanitarian concern, is, I submit, to disseminate anti-Semitic views of a rather traditional kind.

Criticism of the administration by Israel of the Occupied Territories, a disastrous policy both in political and in humanitarian terms, a policy moreover, which at the time of writing Israel has in part unilaterally abandoned and seems likely to abandon in its entirety, need, in itself, be in no way anti-Semitic. Hence, it is no part of my purpose to blacken those, Jews and others, who have long opposed Jewish settlement in the Occupied Territories, by associating their positions with Nazi demands for a *judenrein* Europe. Perhaps the most vehement recent defender of Israel, Alan Dershowitz, in this case in company with a host of Jews on the Left, is on record as an opponent of settlements in the Occupied Territories. My own view is that the demand that Palestinian cities, Hebron, for instance, be *judenrein* is not, and never has been, absent as a political demand on the part of those sections of Palestinian and Arab opinion which have made the political running since the collapse of the Ottoman Empire; that this fact has done much to hinder prospects of peace and economic progress in the area, by exacerbating Jewish fears, and by giving the Israeli Right a not unreasonable basis for demands that the settlements be retained; and that the establishment and successful policing of the right of Jews to reside peacefully in self-governing Arab areas, paralleling the existing right of Muslim and Christian Arabs to leave peacefully within the self-governing Jewish polity of Israel, would do more than anything else to reduce tensions in the area.

The second objection is at least an objection to an actual thesis advanced in this book, namely, that as the writer grants, much press and media criticism of Israel applies a "moral double standard." And it has the merit of clearly stating and defending what I and many others take to be the reason for that, namely, the feeling that for critics of Israel to adopt a more balanced standpoint would be, or at least would be felt by them to be, tantamount to weakening, to "defanging," their criticism.

To address that criticism, one needs to ask what "balanced" criticism, *criticism* as distinct from anti-Semitic defamation, would involve. For a start, there is a distinction to be drawn between balance, on the one hand, and moral non sequitur on the other. What my critic offers as an instance of the absurdity of attempting *balance* in the discussion of what is inherently morally scandalous is in fact an instance of moral non sequitur. It cannot, plainly, mitigate *racism* against blacks in the United States, that African Americans enjoy, on the whole, a *better standard of living* than people of the same race living in Africa. The reason is that racial prejudice and economic welfare are not morally comparable, because they are not morally relevant to one another. You might as well say that if an English resident, because he is English, is hit on the head with a bottle in a pub in Glasgow, it diminishes his right to police concern that he has done very well economically since moving to Scotland. A journalist who reported the incident in those terms would not be displaying "balance," but, on the contrary, aligning himself with the very racism which led to the attack in the first place. It follows that *if* the avoidance of "moral double standards" in criticism of Israel could only be achieved at the expense of absurd moral non sequiturs of this sort, it would indeed be difficult to demand their abandonment. But my critic has so far shown no reason whatsoever why that need be the case.

To take the case of the Occupied Territories, indeed, it is rather easy to see the lines along which a vein of criticism of Israel wholly devoid of anti-Semitic overtones might be, and, indeed, long has been, opened up. Israel's occupation and administration of the Occupied Territories is one instance among many of a type of situation which frequently repeats itself in world affairs, and which since the start of the nineteenth century and the rise of Romantic conceptions of national identity, has become a fruitful source of war, namely, the attempt by one nation to administer territories whose majority population belongs to another. Examples are very numerous, and include, for example, the Austro-Hungarian control of Serbia, which led to World War I; the British presence in Ireland; German control of Alsace-Lorraine after the Franco-Prussian war; the Chinese presence in Tibet; the control by Thailand of a substantial Muslim minority locally dominant in its southern provinces; the control by the Arab population of the north of Sudan of the Christian and Animist south; the occupation of Lebanon by Syria; the rule by the Sunni minority over the Shi'a majority in Iraq, and the reverse situation in parts of southern Iran; the occupancy of

Kurdish lands by, variously, Turkey, Iraq, and Iran; the rule of the Tamil Hindu majority in the north of Sri Lanka by the Buddhist Sinhalese majority in the island as a whole, and so on. Any situation of this type offers, by its nature, rich possibilities for the rise of terrorist groups. With terrorism come counterinsurgency measures by the occupying power, and with them equally rich possibilities for the occurrence of human rights abuses, which duly occur. It is entirely reasonable, and not in the least anti–Semitic, to criticize Israel for having allowed the occupation and administration of the West Bank, with all its evident potential for conflict and human–rights abuse, to get under way after the victory of 1967. However, there are considerations which are by no means moral non sequiturs, and which therefore might reasonably be advanced, in any balanced discussion, and seen as mitigating, if not necessarily exculpatory, considerations. First among these is, of course, that Israel is not alone among the nations of the world in being involved in such situations, and therefore is not *uniquely* open to such criticisms (is not "the last colonial regime," or any such nonsense; there are plenty of others). Second, it might be argued that the circumstances in which the policy was adopted are such as somewhat to mitigate the culpable folly of its adoption. At the time Israel had survived a second war of aggression designed to wipe it and its Jewish population from the map. It felt a need, for reasons of military security, to push back its effective frontiers precisely in the very narrow central zone between the Judean mountains and the sea; ceding the Occupied Territories would once again give the Arabs control of the aquifers, and so on.

Stating these circumstances might indeed weaken, in some eyes, though not in others, the force of objections to the occupation on humanitarian grounds. But I am afraid that just is the nature of fair, balanced, rational debate, and it just has to be endured. What is neither fair, nor balanced, nor rational is to "use Nazi analogies." For what is the force of the "Nazi analogy"? Had the Germans won World War II, the situation of Germany in the bulk of Western Europe outside its frontiers would have mirrored that of Israel in the Occupied Territories. Germany, that is, would have found itself holding down a number of subject, non-German populations, a situation with exactly the same potential for insurgency, counterinsurgency, and human–rights abuse. It is not for that reason, however, that Nazism has become an object of universal horror and moral condemnation. A German Empire arising on the ashes of World War II would have been, no doubt, a very bad thing, but its badness would have been of a type wholly familiar in Europe, a continent, after all, for centuries racked by imperial ambition, war, and the invasion by one nation of the territory of another. What has made so many people regard Nazism as *evil*,

what has made its name stink in the nostrils of the civilized world, was its pros-
ecution of an ideology of racial superiority by means of mass murder, on an
industrial scale, aimed at the total extermination of the racially impure, mainly
Jews, but also including gypsies, the disabled, and others. If one is to promote
an "analogy" between Zionism and Nazism, then, let alone to claim, as has
been claimed, that the crimes of Zionism *exceed* those of the Nazis, it is *that*
aspect of Nazism that one must be assumed to have in mind because that is
the one aspect of Nazism indelibly imprinted in the mind of anyone who
hears the word Nazi. But where are the grounds for its application to Israel?
Where is the ideology of racial superiority, the *Rassentheorie*? Where are the
pogroms? Where is *kristallnacht*? Where are the armed police rounding up
members of the inferior race and the trains carrying them to destruction?
Where are the extermination camps, the gas chambers, and the crematoria?

In fact, the "Nazi analogy" contributes nothing whatsoever, either in
terms of force or in terms of content, to "serious" criticism of Israel. Its effects,
on the contrary, can only be deeply harmful to the process of securing peace
and a long-term settlement in the region. On the one hand, by exacerbating
Jewish fears of a revival of anti-Semitism, it tends to harden Israeli opinion; on
the other hand, by giving the appearance of providing anti-Semitism with a respectable, "humanitarian" basis, it gives aid and comfort, not only of the per-
sisting anti-Semitism of the European Right, but to the new wave of rancorous
and entirely traditional anti-Semitism emanating from the media and popular
opinion in the Middle East.

NOTES

1. Douglas Davis, "Hatred in the Air: The BBC, Israel and Anti-Semitism," in
Paul Iganski and Barry Kosmin, eds., *A New Anti-Semitism? Debating Judeophobia in
the 21st Century* (London: Profile Books, 2003), pp. 130–31.

2. This line is urbanely pursued, for instance, by Geoffrey Wheatcroft in "The Jewish Answer? Why Many Jews Were Hostile to Zionism," *Spectator* December 14 and
21, 2002, pp. 45–48. A good deal of Wheatcroft's case rests on the non sequitur that
since Jewish opposition to Zionism of the type that survives in *Neturei Carta* cannot
be construed as anti-Semitic, current non-Jewish opposition to Zionism, "however
stringent, however vehement, however unfair even," cannot be construed as anti-
Semitic either. That the second claim is in no way entailed by the first (even if the first
is taken to be true, which, of course, it need not be) is, I take it, evident to inspection.

3. Sartre, *Antisemite and Jew* (New York: Grove Press, 1962), pp. 41–42.

4. Jonathan Freedland, "Back to 1948: Sharon's Election and the Dilemmas for
the Diaspora," *Jewish Quarterly* 181 (Spring 2001): 13–16.

5

AGAINST DEMONIZING ISRAEL

PERSECUTION AND THE ORIGINS OF ISRAEL

> Besides, there is nothing so plain boring as the constant repetition of assertions that are not true, and sometimes not even faintly sensible; if we can reduce this a bit, it will be all to the good.

> —J. L. Austin, Sense and Sensibilia[1]

Thomas Friedman of the *New York Times* makes the same point against the combination of moral hyperbole and deliberate disinformation—disinformation, moreover, trading upon a spurious humanitarian justification—characteristic of much current talk and writing on the topic of Israel:

> Criticising Israel is not anti-Semitic, and saying so is vile. But singling out Israel for opprobrium and international sanction—out of all proportion to any other party in the Middle East—is anti-Semitic, and not saying so is dishonest.[2]

We have begun to see why this point is sound. When criticism of Israel modulates into the suggestion that only one side of the argument is worth hearing, that there is, in effect, *nothing to be said* for Israel, and when that impression in turn is reinforced by the effective denial of a hearing to contrary voices, with the general object of stigmatizing Israel as a "criminal state" and "the mirror image of Nazism,"[3] then criticism of Israel becomes little more than a convenient fig leaf for a revived version of the central, and as Sartre

79

pointed out, essentially Manichean, thesis of political anti-Semitism: that the supposed World Jewish Polity (or "conspiracy"), and by extension individual Jews, are inherently evil, a suggestion, that, as we have seen, carries trivially with it all the consequences that flow merely from the conceptual content of the notion of evil: most notably, that only good could come from the extirpation of Israel from the face of the earth, and the silencing of all those who support the right of Israel to exist. The problem remains of why such a stance should be attractive to so many people of generally "liberal" sentiment in the media, and, more generally, to so many members of the academic and intellectual elites of Western countries. I shall try, perhaps less than wholly successfully, to address this genuinely puzzling question in Chapter 9. In part, though, I think that this is, as I shall argue there, only a symptom of a deeper malaise; it is a matter of a widespread longing among intellectuals at present for simple answers, for moral and political schemata which appear to condense a vast amount of complex and morally ambiguous detail into a phrase, a sound bite, which will carry, or appear to carry, instant moral conviction when intoned before a camera, inserted into a piece of copy written at speed, or flung across a table to silence an opponent.

A case in point: Some years ago, a university colleague of mine, a highly intelligent and decent man with strong Christian beliefs, remarked to me that the foundation of the Yad Vashem memorial to the victims of the Holocaust in Jerusalem left a "bad taste in the mouth" because, to him, it represented an attempt on the part of "the Zionists" to establish an illegitimate claim to a Jewish state in Palestine on the basis of the sufferings inflicted by the Nazis on European Jewry. This line of talk, variants of which are by no means uncommonly heard in non-Jewish intellectual circles when Jews are absent and occasionally voiced out loud—that is, in public—by university academics with the air of indomitable freethinkers bravely attacking a disreputable shibboleth, has three defects which should be obvious to immediate inspection. First, it implies that, among Jews, the expression of grief is always secondary to the sort of scheming ulterior motive "one" expects from Jews (though the person who utters it, or some cognate, will almost always cheerfully add: "Of course, I'm not saying that in any anti-Semitic spirit").[4]

Second, it suggests, without exactly saying so, that no justification of the right of Israel to exist as a state can be offered except by way of a grotesque moral non sequitur, and that this same moral non sequitur is actually advanced, in that capacity, by "Zionists" whose pockets may therefore safely be assumed to be empty of other justification. Third, it smuggles out of sight the actual legal and moral basis for the existence of the State of Israel.

The sufferings visited upon European Jews, not just in the period from 1933 to 1945, but in the rather longer period from 1880 to 1945, evidently do not in themselves establish the "right of Israel to exist." That would be as absurd as to suggest that the religious persecution suffered by Mayflower Pilgrims before their departure, first for Leiden and then for the New World, established the "right" of the State of Massachusetts to exist. But they do have a causal, if not a juridical, bearing on the existence of Israel as a state. And they have, further, a bearing on the most common criticism to be heard of Israel from some voices on the Left, namely, that it is the "last colonial state," or words to that effect.

The function of the term "colonial" in such contexts is primarily emotive or polemical. By that I do not mean that it falls on the wrong side of the distinction, beloved of academic moral philosophers, between "descriptive" and "emotive" discourse. The term possesses, after all, a perfectly clear descriptive content. The trouble is that it is a content which, in the present context, drifts loosely, airily above the state of affairs singled out to receive the moral and political condemnation it serves to mediate. Its function is less to inform than to call up in the mind of the hearer a certain picture, which will in turn, it is hoped, evoke moral condemnation; the passage from picture to condemnation being accomplished within the hearer's mind in one easy stride, without, as it were, his feet ever touching the ground.

According to the picture commonly associated with the term colonialism, a colony is set up when the armies of one people march into the territory of another, take control, establish a permanent presence founded on substantial immigration drawn from the population of the occupying power, and in due course, as a result of this inward immigration, reduce the former proprietors of the land to the status of second-class citizens in their own country. That picture, quite properly, evokes a moral response of disapproval. But there remains a further question, frequently suppressed or disregarded in discussions of these issues, both in the media and in academia: namely, how accurately and exhaustively does such a picture, or rather thumbnail sketch, capture the historical and social realities of actual political relationships?

Once this question is seriously addressed, the moral waters soon become muddied, at least to the extent that it ceases to be clear either that colonialism is always necessarily a bad thing or that bad forms of colonialism are necessarily the preserve of "white" nations or of the nationalist Right. On the one hand, the picture fits rather well a range of present-day occupations, such as the Chinese annexation of Tibet, the Indonesian occupation, only recently ended, of East Timor, or the war fought for the past quarter century by the radical Islamic government of the Sudan against the Christian and animist tribes of the South; abuses which have been and are to a greater or lesser extent passed over in silence by Western "left-liberal" opinion, perhaps, by a sort of extension of Wilby's principle, because they have been conducted by Marxist or non-"white" states. On the other hand, it fails to fit many instances of nineteenth- and early twentieth-century "white" colonialism, such as the British presence in India or in many West African countries. Here there is an initial military incursion, but no subsequent introduction, as, say, in French Algeria or British East Africa, of large numbers of settlers drawn from the population of the occupying power. Moreover, in both India and West Africa it is arguable that the British presence, far from permanently disenfranchising the native population, functioned to ease the transition from medieval or Iron Age societies to a society capable of surviving and developing independently in the modern world. Indeed it is arguable—weakly, perhaps, in the case of India but powerfully in the case of many West African states, Sierra Leone being an obvious example—that British colonialism in these countries ended prematurely, with tragic consequences for the native population which endure to this day.

The moral of these reflections is, of course, that anyone who proposes to reason morally by analogy has a duty also to attend to disanalogies. It is a duty seldom recognized by those who hasten to characterize Israel as a colonial state. And yet when one lays the above thumbnail sketch of the nature of a morally reprehensible colonialism, or even less tendentious characterizations of colonialism, against either the historical or the present-day realities of Israel, it seems evident that the disanalogies outnumber the analogies to such an extent as to make it scarcely possible to class Israel as a "colonial" state at all.

To begin with, there was no initial military incursion by Jews against a preexisting Arab population. Nor were Jews, as such, strangers to the land. Prior to the nineteenth century, a Jewish population had been immemorially present in Palestine, augmented over the centuries by a steady trickle of Jews immigrating either for religious reasons or to escape European persecutions. The nineteenth-century immigration, the so-called First Aliya, which in time became associated with nascent Zionism, began as a reaction to the widespread pogroms of 1880–82 throughout the pale of western Russia and Poland (with the exception of Lithuania, where there were no pogroms until 1941) and peaked once again as a result of the Russian pogroms of 1903–6. The tens of thousands of Eastern European Jews who participated in the first and second Aliyahs, respectively 1882–1903 and

1904–14 (a far smaller group than the million who emigrated to America), were in many cases socialists or members of other radical groups. They were, in short, not colonists but refugees who neither could have nor would have wished to carry the flag for the countries from which they came, which they perceived as their persecutors. They were thus in no sense acting in furtherance of the national enterprises of the European nations, Russia, Poland, or Lithuania, from which they came. They were emigrating, moreover, to a part of the territory of a major player in the European power politics of the time: the Ottoman Empire. Even if they had wished to overthrow Ottoman rule, it is very hard to see how they could conceivably have hoped to do so. They constituted, in effect, a late peak in the general pattern of emigration of persecuted European Jews to Ottoman lands which had been proceeding at intervals at least since the end of the Spanish *reconquista* in 1492, with its consequent mass expulsion of Jews and Moors from Spain and Portugal.

The Palestine to which they emigrated was, in the 1880s, very thinly populated, but had never, unlike the lands for the most part colonized by Europeans, been without a significant Jewish presence. These included some Jews who had simply remained in the main cities, despite the fall of the last independent Jewish kingdom suppressed by the Romans, the suppression of Jewish revolts in 70 C.E. and 135 C.E., and repeated efforts by the Romans, the Crusaders, and some Muslims to empty Palestine of Jews. The Jewish population had been augmented over time not only by Jews fleeing persecution in Europe, but by Jews displaced from elsewhere in the nascent Muslim world, such as surviving members of two tribes of Arabian Jews, who, having survived extensive massacres at the hands of followers of Muhammad, were expelled from the Arabian peninsula. At the time of the first Ottoman Turkish occupation of Palestine in 1516 "approximately 10,000 Jews lived in the Safed region alone,"[5] while "Jerusalem . . . has had a Jewish majority since the first population figures were gathered in the nineteenth century, and, according to the British consul in Jerusalem, the Muslims of Jerusalem 'scarcely exceeded one-quarter of the whole population.' Jerusalem, was a predominantly Jewish city well before the First Aliyah. By the middle of the nineteenth century—thirty years before the First Aliyah—Jews also constituted a significant presence, often a plurality or majority, in Safad, Tiberias, and several other cities and towns."[6]

The Jews of the First Aliya, in short, were not, unlike the British in Australia or New Zealand or the French in Algeria, an alien implantation, imposed by the military power of an alien state, in a land where their presence had been previously unknown. They entered the territory of the Ottoman

Empire as individual immigrants, to settle in a part of the empire where many of their coreligionists had preceded them and where there had already existed immemorially a substantial population, and in some places a majority or plurality, of Jews.

When they arrived, many of them bought land, often at inflated prices, from "absentee landlords and real estate speculators."[7] What is now called by the name, of Roman derivation, Palestine was at that time divided between an Ottoman *vilayet*, ruled from Damascus by a *pasha* in the north and in the south by the independent *sanjak* of Jerusalem. The whole area was, to judge by the accounts of contemporary travelers, very sparsely populated. It was certainly not in the phrase dear to early Zionism "a land without people for a people without a land." But the population of the area covered by contemporary Israel, the West Bank, and the Gaza Strip, today more than ten million, was at that time probably "in the neighbourhood of half a million,"[8] including Jews, Muslims, and Christians. Much of the land was owned by absentee landlords, many living in Beirut or Damascus, and there was very little commercial demand for it. "Even . . . when Jewish land purchases were increasing, it was found that the quantity of Arab land offered for sale was far in excess of the Jewish ability to purchase."[9] Relatively few Arab families were displaced by these purchases. Dershowitz notes that according to Benny Morris, the Israeli "new historian" who has been attacked from the Jewish side for hostility to Israel and praised by Chomsky, the late Edward Said, and others for his "nuanced" treatment of the Arab/Israeli conflict, "Historians have estimated that only 'several thousand' families were displaced as a result of Jewish land purchases between the 1880s and the late 1930s,"[10] which as Dershowitz observes, "is a fraction of the number of people displaced by the Egyptian construction of the Aswan Dam, the Iraqi displacement of the Marsh Arabs, and other forced movements by Arab governments of fellow Arabs."[11]

The result of this immigration was that by World War I the racial and religious patchwork of the Ottoman Empire had been enriched by a Jewish majority in parts of what is today Israel. The collapse of the Ottoman Empire left the Great Powers with the problem of what to do with its predominantly non-Turkish areas formerly part of the empire. The situation in Palestine was complicated by the fact that there had never been a Palestinian state. Palestine was simply an area of forty-five thousand square miles, captured from the Ottoman Empire and occupied by Muslim Arabs, Christian Arabs, Jews, and others. The choices lay between giving all the land to the Arabs, giving all of it to the Jews, turning the whole area over to the new State of Syria, or dividing the land between the Arabs and the Jews so that each could develop there a self-governing homeland. The latter choice gained additional support from the fact that a political movement advocating a self-governing Jewish state had existed since 1897, when Theodore Hertzl organized, in Basel, Switzerland, the first Zionist Congress. Zionism gained the support of Winston Churchill, who saw the establishment of a Jewish state as "a notable step towards harmonizing the disposition of the world among its people."[12]

COLONIALISM OR SELF-DETERMINATION?

The establishment of distinct Jewish and Arab states in the wake of Ottoman rule in Palestine was not, in short, an attempt to install or reimpose Jewish colonial hegemony over the entire Arab population of the area. It was an exercise in applying the Wilsonian principle of national self-determination. The not unreasonable ground for including the Jews in the roll call of nationalities eligible for self-determination in Palestine was that, over the preceding two or three generations under Ottoman rule, there had built up, not by military means or conquest, but by normal processes of immigration, including purchase and reclamation of often very marginal land, a substantial Jewish population which had the same right to consideration as any other national or religious group. The declaration to that effect in 1917 by the British foreign minister Lord Arthur Balfour was by no means an isolated one: Balfour's statement had been submitted to, and approved by, President Woodrow Wilson before being released; the French foreign ministry had issued a similar statement some months earlier; and its principles were shortly to be reaffirmed by the League of Nations mandate, with the result that the establishment, in principle, of a small Jewish national state within the boundaries of the large territory then known as Palestine became a matter of binding international law.

The Balfour Declaration by no means "gave Palestine to the Jews." One of its clauses was, indeed, that the establishment of a self-governing Jewish enclave within the territory of Palestine must not "prejudice the civil and religious rights of existing non-Jewish communities in Palestine."[13] Nor is there any reason in principle why it should have done so. An arrangement similar to the division of Switzerland into cantons, each with a different linguistic or religious complexion, but all cooperating fruitfully within a single federal constitution is entirely conceivable, and the material benefits to Arab cantons in association with an economically progressive Israel within such a structure would doubtless be considerable. In any case the National Home proposed by the Great Powers for Palestinian Jews at the end of the Great War was, as Israel indeed still is, in comparison to the full territorial extent of "Palestine" as then understood, a very modest affair indeed. Despite the fact that the Jewish Legion had fought on the side of the Allies, while the bulk of Palestinian Arabs supported the Ottoman power, the first act of the victorious Allies was to set aside the eastern 80 percent of Palestine, renamed Transjordan, as a wholly Arab emirate under the rule of Abdullah, the brother of the new ruler of Iraq. Many Jews formerly resident in that eastern 80 percent of Palestine, some for generations, were forced to leave by episodic pogroms, and the few remaining were forced to relocate, since, by law, Jews were forbidden to live in Transjordan. This left the western 20 percent of Palestine to be divided between its Jewish and Arab residents.

One might ask why it should be divided: why there should not be a single, pluralist or, in terms of modern jargon, multicultural state embracing both Jews and Arabs, Muslims and Christians. The reason lies in the reluctance of many, though not all, Arab leaders to countenance any Jewish presence whatsoever in the former Ottoman lands and in the resulting frequency of massacres and acts of terror directed against the Jewish population. To use an expression later coined by the Nazis, the goal for some influential Arabs was a *judenrein* Palestine, as empty of Jews as Transjordan. Thus, Aref Amin Pasha, a Jerusalem notable of the period, states:

> It is impossible for us to make an understanding with [the Jews] or even to live with them. . . . In all the countries where they are at present they are not wanted . . . because they always . . . suck the blood of everybody. If the League of Nations will not listen to the appeal of the Arabs, this country will become a river of blood.[14]

The tone of this kind of Arab bigotry, immensely magnified in recent years by the Western media, has become very familiar to us. Are we to regard it as the "authentic voice" of Islam, or for that matter "the Arab world" or "the Palestinian people"? There are, and always have been, other, equally Arab, equally Islamic, voices to be heard. Emir Feisal, the son of the Sherif of Mecca, in 1919 signed an agreement with Chaim Weitzmann, representing the Zionist organization. It called for the taking of all measures necessary to

> Encourage and stimulate immigration of Jews into Palestine on a large scale [in order to achieve] closer settlement and intensive cultivation of

the land, [so long as] Arab peasant and tenant farmers shall be protected in their rights, and shall be assisted in forwarding their economic development.[15]

In a later letter to Felix Frankfurter, Feisal elaborates on this stance:

> We feel that the Arabs and Jews are cousins in race, having suffered similar oppressions at the hands of powers stronger than ourselves, and by a happy coincidence have been able to take the first step towards the attainment of their national ideals together. . . .
>
> We Arabs, especially the educated among us, look with the deepest sympathy on the Zionist movement. Our deputation here in Paris is fully acquainted with the proposals submitted yesterday by the Zionist Organization to the Peace conference, and we regard them as moderate and proper. We will do our best, insofar as we are concerned, to help them through: we will wish the Jews a most hearty welcome home. . . . We are working together for a reformed and revised Near East, and our two movements complete one another. The Jewish movement is national and not imperialist, and there is room in Syria for us both. Indeed I think that neither can be a real success without the other.[16]

The existence at this period of the body of liberal and progressive Arab opinion to which Feisal appeals is surely enough to reveal the absurdity of the dismissal of Arabs, or of Islam, as *intrinsically* bigoted and reactionary, so frequently heard nowadays, in the aftermath of the attacks of September 11, 2001. Resistance to anti-Semitic, anti-Israel posturing on the Left should, in other words, have as its natural accompaniment resistance to Islamo- or Arabophobic posturing on the Right. Certainly had the body of opinion represented by Emir Feisal proved capable of extending itself in the Arab world and of directing subsequent events, there can be little question that a "one-state" settlement, of the sort currently promoted by Chomsky and others on the Left, might have proved workable, perhaps on the Swiss federal model of semi-independent cantons, no doubt to the enormous economic advantages of all the cooperating communities, Muslim, Christian, and Jewish alike.

The reason why a "one-state" solution was not considered in the interwar period was that the body of opinion represented by Emir Feisal proved incapable of stemming the contrary tide of opinion, governed by nationalist or religious bigotry of the type represented by Aref Amin Pasha. Pursuing its goal of a *judenrein* Middle East, a succession of political movements on that wing of Arab politics continued to foment terrorist attacks on Jews.[17] After a very long series of attacks on, and massacres of, Jews by predominantly Muslim Arabs, the Peel commission in 1937 recommended in the following terms a partition of the remaining 20 percent of Palestine between areas of majority Jewish and majority Arab population:

> Manifestly the problem cannot be solved by giving either the Arabs or the Jews what they want. The answer to the question "Which of them in the end will govern Palestine?" must surely be "Neither." We do not think that any fair-minded statesman would suppose, now that the hope of harmony between the races has proved untenable, that Britain ought either to hand over to Arab rule 400,000 Jews . . . or that if the Jews should become a majority, a million or so Arabs should be handed over to their rule. But, while neither race can justly rule all Palestine, we see no reason why, if it were practicable, each race should not rule part of it. . . . There are many who would have felt an instinctive dislike to cutting up the Holy Land. The severance of Transjordan, they would have thought, from historic Palestine, was bad enough. On that point we would suggest that there is little moral value in maintaining the political unity of Palestine at the cost of perpetual hatred, strife and bloodshed. . . . Partition seems to offer at least a chance of ultimate peace. We can see none in any other plan.[18]

Partition, for the same reasons, was the option adopted by the United Nations in 1947. The area of majority Jewish settlement proposed by the (British) Woodhead Commission in 1938 was very small and in two sections. The area proposed by the United Nations in 1947 was not much larger. The Jews accepted the United Nations proposals; the Arabs did not.

The issue of whether Israel is correctly to be described as a "colonialist" state comes to a head precisely at this point. Left-wing Jewish defenders of the Palestinian cause—as I noted earlier this is a numerous category—like many on the non-Jewish Left, defend the Arab refusal in 1947 as a reasonable stand against an attempt to impose colonialism under the color of international mediation. Thus Ilan Pappe, a member of the political science department at Bar-Ilan University states:

> But we don't even have the right to say they were wrong to refuse the partition. They viewed Zionism as a colonialist movement. And there are very little reasons [sic] not to understand that point of view. Just imagine the Algerian national movement agreeing in the fifties to divide Algeria into two states, between them and the white settlers ("les pieds-noirs"). Who would have said to the Algerian leadership "Don't miss the historic chance?"![19]

Certainly one could very well argue that such a division in Algeria would have saved a great deal of bloodshed, as well as serving the economic interests of both sides. The root-and-branch opposition to colonialism Pappe needs if his argument is to go through is not, in other words, the only relevant value worth mentioning in the traditional moral lexicon of the Left: the interests of peace, conciliation, and economic progress surely also make moral demands on us which deserve consideration. And even if one were to grant, for the sake of argument, the implausible proposition that overriding moral value attaches to the extirpation of every trace of a colonial history, Pappe still needs the balance of analogies over disanalogies between the historical position of the *pieds-noirs* in Algeria and the Jews in Palestine to be overwhelming. And as we have already seen, the reverse is true. The *pieds-noirs* in Algeria were there, historically speaking, as a direct result of a transfer of population from France in the wake of a French conquest of the country. The Jewish population in Palestine was either autochthonous or had resulted from processes of immigration in no sense organized by, or in the interests of, any European colonial power. Neither the United Nations nor the various British Royal commissions who considered the problem were wrong, therefore, to exclude considerations of colonialism or imperialism from their purview, since the two latter notions simply find no foothold in the situation. What those bodies considered, rightly, to lie *morally* at the heart of the situation were, on the one hand, Wilsonian principles of self-determination, and on the other hand, the avoidance of conflict. What we find on the Arab side, then and since is an unwillingness to contemplate the existence of any Jewish presence whatsoever, self-governing or otherwise, on any part of the historic territory of Palestine, however small. No doubt a poll of the white population of Bradford would reveal, if not a majority, at least a sizable body of opinion opposed to any Muslim presence on British soil. There seems no reason, however, given the traditionally antiracist stance of the Left, why either sentiment should be felt as morally compelling by anyone on the Left, and every reason why neither should. To that extent, therefore, the attempt to demonize Israel by playing the currently fashionable card of anticolonialism falls to the ground. There seems every reason to agree with Dershowitz's summary of the matter:

> The decision to partition Palestine—at least that portion not already allocated to an exclusively Arab emirate, renamed Transjordan and then Jordan—into Jewish and Arab states was not a reflection of the discredited colonialism or imperialism of the past. Rather, it was among the first examples of the new self-determination that President Woodrow Wilson

and many other progressives had championed. . . . The establishment of Jordan and the selection of its Hashemite ruler by the British government in 1923 was an act of imperialism and colonialism. Its formal exclusion of all Jews was an act of blatant racism. . . . The Jewish claim to govern the Jewish area of Palestine allocated to it by the United Nations is certainly more consistent with self-determination than the Hashemite claims to rule over the majority of the Palestinian population of Jordan. Yet the selective name-callers and sloganizers aim their misguided rhetoric only at the Jewish state. The burden falls on them to explain why.[20]

One might object to Dershowitz's comment that, even if there was a substantial Jewish population immemorially in Palestine, the arrival of substantial numbers of refugees in the First Aliya and subsequently created conditions for a partition which could not but displace many Arabs from the land. Here one needs to remember that

> From the very moment when it [Jewish Statehood] became "a concrete political prospect"—that is, the League mandate, Zionist settlement policy was "based on the idea of avoiding any conflict with existing demographic realities. The idea was to settle Jews where Arabs were not in firm possession." Since Arab settlements followed ancient Israelite ones, the modern Jews went to the old coastal plain of the Philistines and the valley of Jezreel, which the Arabs had avoided because of malaria. . . . Hence, in the UN negotiations [in 1947] we relied on the general premise of a historical connection, but made no claims whatever for the inclusion of particular areas on our side of the Partition boundary on the grounds of ancient connections. Since Hebron was full of Arabs, we did not ask for it. Since Beersheba was virtually empty, we put in a successful claim. The central Zionist thesis was that there existed sufficient room within Eretz Israel for a densely populated Jewish society to be established without displacing Arab populations, and even without intruding upon their deep-rooted social cohesion.[21]

Following similar principles the Peel Commission in 1937 had offered the Jews "only Galilee from Metulla to Afula, and the coastal strip from a point 20 miles north of Gaza to Acre, the latter being broken by a corridor to a British-held enclave around Jerusalem."[22] The 1947 partition reflected continuing settlement, in the interval, of unattractive or semidesert land. "It did not give the Jews Acre or Western Galilee, which were then mainly Arab, but it added to the Jewish portion almost the whole of the Negev and part of the Dead Sea area. It was not the Promised Land by any definition, because it excluded Judaea and Samaria, the whole of the West Bank, and, above all, Jerusalem itself. But the Jews, however reluctantly, accepted it."[23] Had the Arab leaders not rejected this partition, as they had done the partition proposed by the Peel Commission and as they would subsequently reject the Camp David–Taba proposals, there would have come into existence a Palestinian state covering half of Cisjordanian Palestine, in combination with a Jewish state which would have been "extremely awkward to run and defend."[24] But they did reject it. The result was that the United Nations voted in favor of the creation of the State of Israel. On November 29, 1947, a partition plan involving Arab and Jewish states, together with an international zone in Jerusalem, was endorsed by the General Assembly, thirty-three votes to thirteen, with ten abstentions. As Paul Johnson points out, this decision can hardly be regarded, as it still is in some left-wing quarters, as a capitalist conspiracy. It was hotly opposed both by the British War Office and Foreign Office, and by the U.S. Defense and State Departments. The Left in both countries, however, were in favor of the creation of Israel, as was the Soviet Union in the immediate aftermath of the war. Stalin not only recognized the new state de jure, whereas President Harry Truman recognized it only de facto, but gave instructions to the Czech government to sell arms to the new state.[25]

UN ANIMAL MÉCHANT

Cet animal est très méchant. Quand on l'attaque, il se défend.

—Voltaire[26]

Once the UN vote was taken, Arab forces began to attack Jewish settlements with the object of destroying the new state. Azzam Pasha, secretary general of the Arab League, said in a broadcast, "This will be a war of extermination and a momentous massacre."[27] Jewish resources were limited, amounting to just over sixty thousand men in various stages of training, a large quantity of small arms, but virtually no armor, aircraft, or heavy guns. The Arabs disposed of "a Liberation Army of considerable size but with a divided leadership,"[28] plus the regular forces of Egypt, Syria, Iraq, and Lebanon, plus the 4,500-strong British-officered army of Transjordan. The results are well known: by the time armistices were successively agreed upon in 1949, with four of the Arab belligerents (Iraq excluded) Israel controlled by far the bulk of Cisjordanian Palestine, excluding the Old City of

Jerusalem, taken by the Arab legion on May 28, 1948. No permanent peace plan had been agreed upon with the Arab states, however, and none has to this day, other than with Egypt and Jordan.

The 1947–48 War of Independence created both the well–documented Palestinian refugee problem and the less well-documented but numerically greater expulsion of Jews from Arab countries. According to UN figures, 650,000 Arab inhabitants of mandatory Palestine fled Israeli–held territory to destinations including the West Bank of the Jordan, Transjordan, Lebanon, Iraq, Syria, Egypt, and the Gaza Strip (Israel puts the total figure lower, at 550,000 to 600,000). Correspondingly, in the wake of the establishment of Israel, between 1948 and 1967, an estimated 750,000 Jews living in Arab countries were encouraged or forced to flee the Arab world, for the most part suffering massive losses of property. The Arabs who left Israel did so for several reasons: to escape the fighting, because they were advised or ordered to do so by Arab broadcasts and also because of the publicity attending a massacre of Arab villagers at the village of Deir Yassin by two Jewish terrorist groups—the Irgun and the Stern Gang. The vast majority of Jewish refugees were resettled, the majority, a substantial number, in other Western countries. The Arab governments, on the other hand, with the assistance of the UN, refused to resettle Arab refugees from Israel, preferring to keep them in camps, which exist to this day, pending an Arab reconquest of Israel which has never come.

That, however, has hardly been for want of trying. Between the War of Independence and 1978, no Arab state proved willing to conclude a peace treaty with Israel. On May 15, 1967, the military dictator of Egypt, Gamal Abdel Nasser, having reorganized and reequipped his forces, moved 100,000 men into Sinai and expelled the UN force there. On May 22 he blockaded the port of Aquaba, and eight days later Jordan signed a military agreement with Egypt. On the same day Iraqi forces entered Jordan and took up positions there. On June 5 Israel carried out a preemptive strike which destroyed almost the whole of the Egyptian air force on the ground. Jordan and Syria immediately entered the war on Egypt's side and proceeded to suffer heavy defeats on all fronts. On June 7 Israel took the Old City of Jerusalem, and by the end of the following day she had occupied the entire Left Bank. During the next two days Israeli forces stormed the Golan Heights, establishing forward positions a bare thirty miles from Damascus, and reoccupied the whole of Sinai, finally obtaining reasonably defensible frontiers as a result.[29] Six years later, on Yom Kippur 1973, Egypt and Syria attacked Israel without warning. Achieving complete surprise, they broke through the Israeli lines and inflicted significant losses on Israeli planes and armor. On October 9 the Syrian advance had been stemmed, and the following day America began an airlift of advanced weapons to Israel. Two days later the Israelis counterattacked in Egypt, crossing to the West Bank of the canal and encircling the Egyptian forces in Sinai. By the time a cease-fire came into effect on October 24 the victory of Israel was as decisive as those of 1948 and 1967.

LAND FOR PEACE

In 1977 the Labour coalition which had governed Israel since independence lost power to the main party of the Right, Likud, under Menachem Begin. It is one of the standing illusions of the Left, that right-wing politicians are without exception warmongers and that only the Left is the party of peace. Begin and the Likud in fact proved willing to trade conquered land for peace and found a willing partner in the Egyptian leader Anwar Sadat. After a difficult and extended peace process presided over by the United States under the Jimmy Carter administration, a treaty was signed in September 1978. Egypt recognized Israel's right to exist and guaranteed her southern borders. Israel in return handed over the Sinai peninsula, with all its oilfields, air bases, and settlements. Later Israel concluded a similar treaty with Jordan, handing over land captured from the Hashemite kingdom. At the same time the Begin government expressed its willingness "to negotiate away much of the West Bank, and even to make concessions over Jerusalem, in return for a complementary treaty with the Palestinians and the other Arab states."[30] The occasion was propitious for the Palestinian side, not least because of the increased economic and political power conferred upon the Arab states at the time by the rising demand for oil in the West. A successful negotiation at this point might well have left the Palestinians with a state whose territorial extent would have been at least comparable with the area assigned to them by the rejected United Nations partition of 1947. The Palestinian leadership, however, made no attempt to negotiate, with the result that Judea and Samaria were left in the hands of Israel, without international recognition, as "occupied territories."

For all practical purposes, therefore, relations between Israel and all the Arab states except Egypt and Jordan remained after 1977, and have remained ever since, on a war footing. The wars of 1947, 1967, and 1973, without exception wars of aggression initiated by the Arab side, have failed to produce a peace treaty with any Arab state except Egypt and Jordan. Nor has any Arab state except Egypt and Jordan recognized the right of Israel to exist. One very commonly hears it asserted on the Left that Israel has consistently refused to negotiate with the Palestinians, and that Israel has, equally consistently, refused to obey United Nations resolutions. The reality is very different. The basis for the repeated claim that Israel has no "legal" right to the territories it conquered as a result of successfully resisting Arab aggression in 1948, 1967, and 1973 is UN Security Council Resolution 242. This resolution announces the hitherto unheard-of claim that war, whether aggressive or defensive, cannot be allowed to change the preexisting boundaries of the belligerent states. It goes without saying that if this proposal were to be applied retroactively, the boundaries of many, if not most, states would undergo surprising changes. It has in the past been taken for granted that territory lost as a result of an aggressive war is lost for good. The redrawing of European frontiers at the end of World War II represents only the latest application of this principle. Nevertheless, Resolution 242 requires Israel to withdraw from "territories"—not, it should be noted, from "all territories"—gained in 1967. However, that is not all it requires. The text of the resolution runs as follows:

> [The Security Council] (1) Affirms that the fulfilment of Charter principles requires the establishment of a just and lasting peace in the Middle East which should include the application of both of the following principles: (i) Withdrawal of Israel armed forces from territories occupied in the recent conflict; (ii) termination of all claims or states of belligerency and respect for and acknowledgement of the sovereignty, territorial integrity and political independence of every state in the area and their right to live in peace within secure and recognised boundaries free from threats or acts of force.[31]

It is evident that clauses (i) and (ii) state equally necessary, and complementary, conditions for a lasting settlement. No state in Israel's position, facing bitter hostility from neighboring states determined to bring about its obliteration, could realistically be expected to accede to (i) without believable guarantees from her neighbors on the issues specified in (ii). In both cases in which the required guarantees were provided, namely by Egypt and Jordan, Israel has implemented Resolution 242 by returning the relevant tracts of land. The other Arab states and the Palestinian leadership under Yasser Arafat, however, have repeatedly and categorically rejected the principles of Resolution 242. Examples of Arab rejectionism include the famous "three no's" resolution: "No peace with Israel, no negotiations with Israel, no recognition of Israel," and the adoption, in response to Israel's acceptance of Resolution 242, of the Palestinian National Charter. This document expressly denied Israel's right to exist and pledged to continue "armed struggle" as the only way to liberate all of Palestine. It defined Palestine to include all of Israel (as well, apparently, as all of Jordan): "Palestine, with the boundaries it had during the British mandate, is an indivisible territorial unit." In defiance of the United Nations, the Palestinian Charter declared the U.N. "partition of Palestine in 1947 and the establishment of the State of Israel [to be] entirely illegal," because they "were contrary to the will of the Palestinian people." And it rejected "all solutions which are substitutes for the total liberation of Palestine" through armed struggle, declaring Zionism and Israel to be racist, colonial and fascist.[32]

The Palestinian leadership has since said, under pressure and with some backsliding, that they accept the existence of Israel, provided it returns to boundaries previously rejected with violence. But other Palestinian and Arab groups (Hamas, Hezbullah, Islamic Jihad) and states (Syria, Iran, Libya) continue to reject a two-state solution. And it must be said that the actual conduct of the Palestinian leadership hardly suggests that verbal declarations of support for such a solution reflect any very deep political commitment. Most recently, in 2001–02 Palestinian rejectionism expressed itself once again in the rejection by Yasser Arafat of the Barak–Clinton offer of a Palestinian state in the West Bank and Gaza, including the removal of Jewish settlements, so often cited as a barrier to peace. Negotiations ended when Arafat, rejecting the advice of other Arab leaders, including the Egyptians and the Saudis, flew home without making any counterproposals.[33] Shortly afterward Palestinian terrorism rose to new levels of murderousness with the opening of the Second Intifada. The "Armed Struggle" had resumed.

It seems evident to inspection that the policy of rejectionism and armed struggle espoused by the Palestinian leadership and the rejectionist Arab states has seriously, not to say devastatingly, harmed the interests of the Arabs and above all the Palestinian people, on any reasonably utilitarian account of the notion of harm. An Israeli colleague of mine remarked to me once that there was really no reason why Palestine should not be organized into Jewish, Muslim, and perhaps Arab Christian states within a federal structure, with cross-communal residence and employment rights. Had the Palestinian leadership and the Arab states accepted the United Nations partition of 1947, or had they exploited Israeli readiness to negotiate in 1978 or 2001–02, it might have been possible for such an arrangement to evolve, with consequent economic and social advantages to all sides. The debacle of 2001–02 contrived by Arafat was particularly effective in demolishing any immediate prospect of such a solution, in that it more or less totally undermined the position of the Israeli Left, not the only, but a major, force behind a two-state solution, by making it clear to the mass of the Israeli public that Israel could hope, for the moment at any rate, for no reasonable or even plausible negotiating partner on the Palestinian side. As Benny Morris, the "revisionist" Israeli historian frequently quoted with approval by Chomsky and others on the Left, stated:

> One of the characteristics of the Palestinian national movement has been the Palestinians' view of themselves as perpetual victims of others—Ottoman Turks, British officials, Zionists, Americans—and never to appreciate that they are, at least in large part, victims of their own mistakes and iniquities. In the Palestinian Weltanschauung, they never set a foot wrong; their misfortunes are always the fault of others. The inevitable corollary of this refusal to recognise their own historical agency has been a perpetual Palestinian whining—that, I fear, is the apt term—to the outside world to save them from what is usually their own fault.[34]

NOTES

1. J. L. Austin, *Sense and Sensibilia*, reconstructed from the manuscript notes by G. J. Warnock, (Oxford: Clarendon Press, 1962), p. 5.

2. Thomas Friedman, "Campus Hypocrisy," *New York Times*, October 16, 2002.

3. Alan Dershowitz, *The Case for Israel* (Hoboken, N.J.: John Wiley, 2003), p. 1.

4. In fact, the idea that when Jews complain of injuries they are after something, most probably money, is a hallowed traditional motif of anti-Semitism. A nineteenth-century French version of it is deployed, for instance, in Alphonse Daudet's Algerian sketch "A Milianah," *Lettres de mon Moulin* (Paris: Livre de Poche Classique, n.d.), pp. 148–59.

5. Dershowitz, *The Case for Israel*, p. 17.

6. Dershowitz, *The Case for Israel*. Dershowitz gives abundant references to sources for these historical claims

7. Ibid., p. 23.

8. Ibid., p. 24.

9. Benny Morris, *Righteous Victims* (New York: Vintage Books, 2001), p. 111.

10. Ibid., p. 123.

11. Dershowitz, *The Case for Israel*, p. 25.

12. Cited in Morris, *Righteous Victims*, p. 72.

13. Ibid., p. 75.

14. Ibid., p. 91.

15. Walter Laqueur and Barry Rubin, *The Israel-Arab Reader*, 6th ed. (New York: Penguin, 2001), p. 19, as cited in Dershowitz, *The Case for Israel*, p. 38.

16. Laqueur and Rubin, *The Israel-Arab Reader*, as cited in Dershowitz, *The Case for Israel*.

17. Dershowitz, *The Case for Israel*, pp. 40–44.

18. Peel Report, p. 59, cited in Dershowitz, *The Case for Israel*, pp. 47–48.

19. "An interview with Ilan Pappe," *Le Soir* (Belgium), November 29, 1999, cited in Dershowitz, *The Case for Israel*, pp. 63–64.

20. Dershowitz, *The Case for Israel*, pp. 65–66.

21. Abba Eban, Israeli foreign minister and chief negotiator of the new state, cited in Paul Johnson, *A History of the Jews* (London: Weidenfeld and Nicholson, 1987), pp. 531–32.

22. Ibid., p. 531.

23. Ibid.

24. Ibid., p. 532.

25. Ibid., pp. 525–26.

26. "This is a very dangerous animal: when it is attacked, it defends itself." Couplet frequently ascribed to Voltaire (François Marie Arouet, 1694–1778), but by other sources to a comic song of 1828, *la Ménagerie*, by one Theodore P. K. (unknown), music by Edmond L'huillier.

27. W. D. Davies, *The Territorial Dimension in Judaism* (Berkeley: University of California Press, 1982), pp. 114–15.

28. Johnson, *A History of the Jews*, p. 527.

29. Ibid., p. 534.

30. Ibid., p. 536.

31. Cited in Dershowitz, *A Case for Israel*, p. 96.

32. Ibid., p. 97.

33. Ibid., pp. 117–22.

34. Benny Morris, "Rejection," *New Republic*, April 21–28, 2003, p. 37.

FASCISM AND THE IDEA
OF TOTAL WAR

THE PALESTINIANS AND THEIR LEADERSHIP

Why should the Palestinians have continued to act in such a way as to undercut repeatedly their own interests for fifty years on end? The answer requires us to confront a certain ambiguity surrounding our use, in political debate, of such phrases as "the Palestinians," "the Arabs," "the Muslims," "the French," "the Scots," and so forth. In line with the besetting tendency I mentioned earlier, to deny, or simply to fail to notice, the diversity of alien groups, we tend naturally to fall into the delusion that these terms group "peoples" essentially united in their opinions, aims, *Weltanschauung*, and loyalties. The delusion is sufficiently deep rooted, even, to survive total and rapid transformations in the apparent political complexion of free nations. Twenty years ago, for instance, Britain was, to a legion of journalists and commentators, *Mrs. Thatcher's Britain*, a country overwhelmingly populated by enthusiastic free-enterprise Conservatives, with a capital "C," thirsting to roll back the frontiers of the state. In 1997, however, this extraordinary concentration of Friedmanite John Bulls metamorphosed abruptly, indeed overnight, into *Tony Blair's Britain*, a nation of early middle-aged, vaguely swinging, guitar-playing, flared-trousered political vacillators with a liking for rocket salad and vacations in Tuscany. In reality, of course, these abrupt changes of political style are an artifact of Britain's electoral system, which magnifies slight shifts of political allegiance into large, and occasionally massive, parliamentary majorities. The Labour Party under Tony Blair rules at present (2006), partly because of electoral anomalies involving constituency boundaries and other forms of over- or underrepresentation, with the support of approximately 21 percent of those entitled to vote; Mrs.

Thatcher ruled with somewhat more support, but never anywhere near an absolute majority. The demographic reality is that, while Britons exhibit many widely shared characteristics, few of those characteristics are political. Politically, the country is as divided now as it was in the seventeenth-century civil war, which led to the establishment of its modern political constitution; divided, moreover, along lines which reach back both emotionally and intellectually, even though remotely, to many of the issues which divided it then.

What is true of the British is true of other nations. The idea of a nation, defined as a body of people united by a common language and certain fundamental features of character, history, and traditions, has its feet firmly on the ground of empirical reality. The idea of a "people," envisaged as united by common political goals and by wholehearted and universal assent to a particular ideology, is a political illusion, though an extremely important one. It is part and parcel of the ideas which gave rise to the French Revolution and have formed an essential element in the intellectual basis of every subsequent form of revolutionary messianism, that the overwhelming majority of a nation, "the people," possess common interests which are being denied satisfaction by a tiny minority. These interests may not, of course, be recognized as such by those whose interests they "objectively" are, which is why they need to be articulated and proclaimed by a "vanguard" political movement which, by virtue of the superior political insight thus demonstrated, has a right to regard itself as the authentic representative of "the people" thus defined, to presume their loyalty on that basis, and to regard anyone not prepared to accept its right to govern as an "enemy of the people." This essentially absurd and fantastic set of claims has for the past two centuries been common ground between the extremes of Left and Right, providing the main moral basis for the claims of both fascist and communist regimes. That is no longer the case in European politics. The collapse, one after another, of the messianic totalitarian regimes of Left and Right which dominated the twentieth century, a historic process which began with the forcible extirpation of German National Socialism and Italian fascism and continued with the successive internal collapse first of Franco's Spain, Salazar's Portugal, and finally of the Soviet Union and all the other socialist despotisms of Eastern Europe, has carried down with it in common ruin the entire rhetoric of the People and the Vanguard Party. These notions are still, however, freely, and for the most part uncritically, applied by Western journalists and commentators to third-world nations and peoples.

FASCISM IN EUROPE AND THE THIRD WORLD

It is a habit we need to throw off if we are ever to think clearly about the Middle East. There is no Ideal Political Entity called the Palestinian People, to be distinguished from the collection of politically diverse individuals composing the real-life Palestinian people by the curious fact that its (the Ideal Political Entity's) interests are indistinguishable from those of Fateh, Hamas, or whatever other political clique happens to hold power, and thus the stage of the world political theater, at any given moment. For that matter there is no (Ideal) Syrian People whose interests are indistinguishable from those of the ruling Ba'ath Party, any more than there was ever a (Ideal) deutsches Volk whose interests were represented and served by Hitler and his clique. If the twentieth century has taught us anything it is that the rhetoric and political practice of the People and Vanguard Party leads nowhere but, at best, to stagnation and needless suffering on the part of the mass of the people, and at worst to war and utter catastrophe. The main reason why the twentieth century, despite the collapse of the Ottoman Empire, proved to be a century of losses and reverses for the Palestinians, and for the Arabs in general, is that for large tracts of that period a majority of states in the Arab world, and the Palestinians in particular, have been governed, or rather misgoverned, by essentially fascist cliques of one overt political complexion or another. The term fascist so deployed may need, in what Wittgenstein called "the darkness of this time,"[1] some explication. Since the 1960s, the terms *fascism* and *fascist* have come to be used by many on the Left as generalized terms of abuse directed at anyone not on what one or another left-wing faction chooses to recognize as "the Left," the object being to suggest that nothing of substance differentiated, or differentiates, Margaret Thatcher, or George W. Bush, or Tony Blair, from Adolf Hitler or Benito Mussolini.

Let us attempt a more careful definition. Fascism was, in its origin in the political chaos in Europe following World War I origin, a form of messianic nationalism which saw itself as called upon to rescue the world from a combination of evils seen as inextricably intertwined with one another, and including, as fascists saw things, free-enterprise capitalism, parliamentary democracy, any form of individualism crediting the individual with a sphere of "negative freedom" deserving legal and constitutional protection against the demands of the state, as well as any kind of cultural activity, art, or literature considered as "degenerate" in the sense of departing from the canons of a truly "national" culture. "The Jews" were seen, of course, less so by Italian fascists, but with pathological intensity by German, Austrian, and Hungarian ones, as among the most active, if not the main, agents of such degeneracy. Fascist parties saw themselves essentially as vanguard parties ruling over people whom it was their duty to render worthy of membership of the ideal, spiritual entity, the *People* (the *Volk*) whom they saw themselves as representing, and to which, rather than to the mere human fellow citizens confronting them, they understood themselves as owing fidelity. The political and moral corruption represented by the gutter-Romantic exaltation of People and Vanguard Party as representing supraindividual political-moral ideals reached its apogee in Europe in the first half of the twentieth century. Morally justified, as they saw it, by the urgent national necessity to extirpate the political Hydra of individualist degeneracy and establish a "pure" culture and society, fascist parties considered themselves under no obligation to observe traditional forms of restraint in the treatment of those they considered enemies of the people. The results are well enough known.

On the above definition, fascism is by no means confined to the political Right. The term *vanguard party*, if not the idea, was coined by Lenin, and the Soviet Union, for most of its history, in its despotism, its rejection of any form of negative freedom, its willingness to murder, as enemies of the people, millions of its own citizens through the Gulag system, and, last but not least, its endemic anti-Semitism, was as much a fascist state as the Third Reich, differing from it solely in its commitment to economic collectivism and a largely empty socialist rhetoric. The philosopher Julius Kovesi, in a penetrating, posthumously published collection of essays which deserves to be more widely known, explores the manner in which a powerful syndrome of political ideas and emotions can to a degree emancipate itself from the concrete circumstances which gave it birth and become a presiding structure, a quasi-platonic form. Such a schema can serve to articulate and give shape to specific political concerns which might appear not only to have otherwise little to do with one another, but to occupy opposite poles of what we ordinarily think of as the political spectrum.[2] I have been suggesting that something like this is true of the fundamental ideas of European fascism: that those moves compose a quasi-platonic form, an empty structure constituted by hatred of liberal economics and political and cultural individualism, coupled with messianic fidelity to some supposedly salvatory ideal, originally the Nation, the whole given political focus and direction by the idea of a Vanguard Party representing the interests of an initially, perhaps largely Ideal, but in some deep and mystical way transcendently real and morally pure community, a community opposed by evil forces—including "the Jews"—and commanding fidelity of a sort whose demands overrule in principle, deprive of moral force in the circumstances of the struggle against those forces, all traditional forms of moral restraint. This semiabstract structure, I want to say, following Kovesi, can be filled in by almost any detailed content you please. One can, for instance, replace the nation with the proletariat, the Jews as one's evil opponent with international capitalism, and one's messianic ideal with the revolution. Equally, in the style of many "Islamist" movements at the moment, you can replace the Proletariat with "the Muslims," considered as an ideal community sadly ill-represented by actual Muslims, many of whom, one will consider, deserve death as apostates; international capitalism with the demonic triad of the Jews, Israel, and America; and the equally ideal society of the communist millennium with the perfect purity of the restored caliphate.

Whatever new wine you pour into the schematic structure of fascism, however—this is the point—fascism it remains. That, of course, raises the interesting question of the relationship of "Islamism" as represented by a host of movements of the type of Hamas or Al Qu'aida, to Islam. What is not in doubt is that as with any religion, different sects and authorities take different views, all equally founded in the sacred writings, and there are many courageous Muslims to whom the activities of "Islamic" fascists are anathema, both a source of profound shame and regret.[3] Emir Feisal, the son of the Sherif of Mecca, the pan-Semite and friend of the Jews I mentioned earlier, was a great Muslim leader. Many Palestinians, for that matter, have sought friendship and reconciliation with the Jews, and many have paid for it with their lives, as "collaborators" at the hands of "Islamic" fascism.[4] The idea that the world faces a "clash of cultures" with its correlative suggestion that entire Muslim populations (the Turks? the Moroccans?) share a uniform sympathy with essentially fascist groups is simply another version of diversity denial: the tendency to deny the internal diversity of alien groups and societies which, as I argued earlier, functions equally as an essential component of anti-Semitic conspiracy theory. Nor is Muslim, or for that matter non-Muslim, opposition to fascism in the Islamic world in any way foolish, "merely" altruistic, or contrary to the interests of the Islamic world. The experience of Europe in the twentieth century has shown that no nation which embraces fascism, whether of the Left or the Right, profits by the choice. The reasons for this are complex. One is that the *Weltanschauung* of fascism is so remote from reality as to make a rather large proportion of the decisions taken under its influence counterproductive in the short or long term. Another is that the outlook of fascism is, to put it bluntly, intrinsically pro-war (one of the saddest events of the late twentieth century was what amounted to the refighting of World War I over the Shatt al-Arab, the river whose southernmost course divides southern Iraq from Iran, with all the accompaniment of immense slaughter achieving practically no territorial gain, between secular-fascist Iraq and theocratic-fascist Iran). A third is that it rather rapidly declines into forms of gangsterism whose main object is no longer the liberation of "the People" so much as the enrichment of the leadership. Hence, the point made by Dershowitz that

> Despite the enormous personal wealth accumulated by Palestinian leaders through personal corruption—Arafat's personal wealth according to Forbes magazine is in excess of $300 million—very little money has been allocated to upgrading the Palestinian Authority's primitive emergency medicine system.[5]

These are by no means the worst aspects of fascist messianism, however. Far worse is the tendency, fundamental to all forms of fascism, to treat whatever basic aims may happen to be central to a given fascist project as possessing a moral authority overriding, trumping, as it were, all traditional forms of moral restraint. Antinomianism of this type is of course in principle deeply hostile to all the monotheistic religions which descend from Judaism, including Islam, whose aim is precisely to bring about the ordering of life in terms of systems of rules—of *nomos*—considered as divinely ordained. Fascism derives its antinomianism, by routes which it would be tedious to trace here, from certain deep, and entirely secular, tendencies in the European Enlightenment: tendencies of which the work of Sade is another expression. Fascism, in short, even fascism with a non-European face, is a European export; part of the passage of radical ideas from the West to the rest of the world traced by Ian Buruma and Avishai Margalit in a recent book. Fear and hatred of the West, Occidentalism, as they call it, is, they argue, itself a Western product.

> Occidentalism cannot be reduced to a Middle Eastern sickness any more than it could to a specifically Japanese disease more than fifty years ago. Even to use such medical terminology is to fall into a noxious rhetorical habit of the Occidentalists themselves. It is indeed one of our contentions that Occidentalism, like capitalism, Marxism and many other modern isms, was born in Europe, before it was transferred to other parts of the world. The West was the source of the Enlightenment, but also of its frequently poisonous antidotes. In a way, Occidentalism can be compared to those frequently colourful textiles exported by France to Tahiti, where they were adopted as native dress,

only to be depicted by Gauguin and others as typical examples of tropical exoticism.[6]

The idea central to fascism, whatever its political color, of a suffering people both redeemed and restored to its own ideal nature by a fearless vanguard party capable of embracing death with joy, has after all, nothing specifically to do with Islam. It is an entirely secular, and entirely European, product, one of those "poisonous antidotes" to the Enlightenment of which Buruma and Margalit speak, and doubtless, as such, capable of evoking a response among certain sections of European and American opinion, not because of its alienness, but precisely because of its familiarity.

POLITICAL MESSIANISM AND THE IDEA OF TOTAL WAR

One consequence of the antinomianism central to fascism has been the denial that there is any valid moral distinction to be drawn in war between combatants and noncombatants as objects of offensive action. The consequences of that denial showed themselves for the first time in the twentieth century in the terror bombing of the Basque village of Guernica in April 1937 by German aircraft acting in support of General Francisco Franco, which killed or wounded more than sixteen hundred civilians. The savagery of this act rightly outraged the European Left of the period; there was, for instance, a march of more than a million protesters in Paris on May Day in 1937. But the principle that in war the only legitimate targets are combatants is not, any more than most moral principles are, a mere product of speculative reflection on the part of the middle-class liberal thinkers so despised by fascists from either end of the political spectrum. On the contrary, it is the fruit of bitter experience: a self-denying ordinance solidly rooted in self-interest. It can be safely rejected only on the presumption that one's adversaries will continue to abide by it. As we all know, that presumption, if it was ever entertained by the Nazi rulers of Germany, proved false. Terror bombing of British cities led to the terror bombing of German cities, the most famous instance being Dresden, where the resulting fire storm consumed more than a hundred thousand civilians. The war ended, eight years after the destruction of Guernica, with the destruction of the civilian population of Hiroshima and Nagasaki by the first atomic bombs.

In short, though the Nazis were first, both sides in World War II abandoned the principle that in war only combatants are legitimate targets. It is, therefore, remarkable that for over more than half a century Israel has maintained that principle in the face of an adversary that has long abandoned it. The principle that every Israeli, including women and children, is a legitimate target has been repeatedly and expressly proclaimed and acted upon by the Palestinians and the rejectionist Arab states both before and after the founding of Israel as a state. To kill civilians has been the whole point of innumerable actions both by al-Fateh and by such "Islamist" fascist groups as Hamas, Hizbolla, or Islamic Jihad. On the other hand, while actions undertaken by the Israeli armed forces have resulted in the deaths of Arab civilians, the object of these actions has not been to bring about those deaths. Further, although some civilian deaths are inevitable in a war conducted at such close quarters over heavily populated land, Israel has done, on the whole, everything in its power to keep such deaths to a minimum. Israel can with some justice be accused of two massacres of Arabs and is unjustly accused of a third. In the first group there is the massacre at the Arab village Deir Yassin, carried out by members of the Irgun and the Stern Gang during the War of Independence. A large number of civilians died in this action, and according to some accounts twenty-three Arab men were taken to a quarry and shot.[7] On the side of Israel, it can be urged that this was an isolated incident, that the forces involved were a political group acting independently, and that it occurred during a war in which the civilian Jewish population of Palestine was facing extermination. As the then secretary general of the Arab league Abd al-Alman Azzah Pasha stated, "This will be a war of extermination and momentous massacre, which will be spoken of like the Mongolian massacres and the Crusades."[8] The second is the massacre carried out in Hebron by a Jewish doctor, Baruch Goldstein, who machine-gunned twenty-nine Muslims at prayer. Goldstein, who was himself killed in the attack, had according to his family been reduced to despair by a long series of terrorist attacks on Jews. This attack was strongly condemned by Israel and by the majority of Israelis and Jews around the world. The third, the massacre of Palestinians at the refugee camps of Sabra and Chatila in Lebanon on September 18, 1982, was carried out by Lebanese Christian Phalangists in revenge for an earlier massacre carried out by Palestinians at the Christian village of Damour in northern Lebanon. An Israeli parliamentary commission (the Kahan Commission) subsequently censured Ariel Sharon for allowing the Phalangists into the camps.

There is a minor publishing industry, uniting the extremes of Left and Right, devoted to establishing that Israel is guilty of planning or—preferably—executing a "holocaust" against the Palestinians.[9] The above-mentioned three episodes are the major exhibit, along with a variety of claims to the effect that civilian deaths in Israeli antiterror operations constituted deliberate massacre of civilians. The most recent and celebrated example of these is the so-called Jenin massacre of April 2002. This was an operation against a center for bomb making and terror planning in the Jenin refugee camp. The operation was conducted by methods of street fighting which were costly to the Israelis, and resulted in the deaths of twenty-three Israeli soldiers and fifty-two Palestinians, many of whom were combatants. The episode is in fact a textbook example of the difficulties faced by those, whether on the Left or the Right, who wish, as part of the project of demonizing Israel, to set up a parallel between Israel and the Nazis. The Israelis could perfectly well have dealt with terrorist operations in the Jenin camp by bombing it comprehensively from the air, as the German air force did at Guernica, and as the United States has since done in Afghanistan and Iraq, and the Russians, to appalling effect, in Chechnya. Such a policy would in all probability have resulted in no Israeli losses whatsoever. Nevertheless, the Israelis chose the costly and difficult option of using ground forces to storm the camp, precisely because that option was likely to prove less costly in terms of civilian casualties. Nor was this accidental, or a mere device adopted in the hope of securing (*per impossibile*) favorable, or even fair, reporting abroad. The Israel defense forces operate under an exacting ethical code drafted by a team including Moshe Halbertal, a well-known peace activist who, like many Israelis and Diaspora Jews on the Left, supports, no doubt with a grasp of the possible consequences for Israel more extensive than can, on the evidence, be credited to many on the non-Jewish Left, withdrawal from the Occupied Territories.

That is half the story where Jenin is concerned. The other half is that the Jenin operation followed hundreds of successful and attempted suicide bombings, culminating in the Passover seder massacre of twenty-nine Jewish men, women, and children at prayer. And there one has both wings of the difficulty confronting left-wing would-be demonizers of Israel. However the difficulty is disguised, in Europe and in certain quarters in America, by selective reporting and disinformation, it remains the case that while Israel chooses freely to conduct a defensive war—a war not of its choosing, a war which it has repeatedly offered to end, and with two former combatants ended, by implementing a two-state solution with exchanges of land—in a manner designed to minimize civilian losses on the Palestinian side, and to do so in a manner which increases its own risk of losses, its adversaries reject the distinction between combatants and noncombatants and make no secret of the fact that their object is to kill as many Israeli civilians as possible. Where the civilian deaths inflicted by fascism on innocent Basques at Guernica in 1937 brought a million members of the Left onto the streets of

Paris, a certain section of the present-day Left, and its academic and intellectual fellow-travelers, in articles, books, and around polite dinner tables,
finds nothing to complain of, but rather to celebrate, in the deaths of innocent Israeli civilians not merely inflicted, but exulted in, by contemporary
Arab fascism.

DEFENDING TOTAL WAR: "YOU'RE GUILTY IF I SAY SO."

Some line of talk, some fig leaf, is necessary to cover this glaring contradiction at the heart of the current left-liberal climate of opinion of which I
spoke earlier. In fact there are two responses in current service. The first is
to brazen it out by, in effect, grasping the nettle and denying that there *is*
any valid moral distinction to be drawn between combatants and noncombatants when it is a matter of dealing with Israelis (or Jews, or Americans,
depending on the interests of the given polemicist) on the grounds that in
such circumstances the notions of "innocent civilian" or "noncombatant"
are empty. On this view no Israelis (or Jews, or Americans) are either innocent or noncombatant. All are, whether they like it or not, combatants in
the war against "progressive" causes, and all are guilty, sufficiently guilty, indeed, to deserve death, and they are both of these things simply in virtue of
being Israelis (or Jews, or Americans) and thus complicit in the guilt—from
the point of view of certain minds on the left—of Israel (or the World Jewish Community, or America). A recent example of this line of rationaliza-
tion was provided by the infamous edition of the program *Any Questions*
broadcast by the BBC immediately after September 11, 2001, in which both
contributors and speakers from the audience asserted that the murder of
close to 3,000 civilians was a legitimate punishment for the crimes of
"American Foreign Policy." Another contributor to the genre is Tom
Paulin, the Oxford poet and academic, who said in an interview with the
Egyptian paper *Al-Ahram Weekly* that "Brooklyn-born Jewish settlers" deserved to be murdered. "They should be shot dead. I think they are Nazis,
racists, I feel nothing but hatred for them. I never believed that Israel had
the right to exist at all."[10]

All that needs to be said, it seems to me, about the attitudes expressed
by Paulin and the *Any Questions* audience is that they are, in principle and
in effect, indistinguishable from those of the fascist politicians and military
commanders who engineered the bombing of Guernica. Indeed, that Paulin
should imagine himself to have the right to deploy the terms "Nazi" and

"racist" as if they applied only to others, and not to himself, argues either monumental stupidity, as Howard Jacobson has suggested,[11] or monumental brass neck. It also says something about the climate of some current British institutions which like to present themselves as "progressive," as well as about the current ambiguities of that much-abused term, that Paulin, who would, I fancy, have found grave difficulty in maintaining his standing as a pillar of the Left, fifty or sixty years ago, in the face of outbursts which would then have been considered to express parlor fascism of the deepest dye, should have no trouble at all in continuing to enjoy not only an Oxford fellowship but a regular contract as a broadcaster with the BBC.

But at the same time Paulin and others who imagine that they can deal by simple nettle grasping with the disparity between an Israel which sustains, at some cost to itself, the combatant/noncombatant distinction, and a range of various Palestinian and Arab groups and states who reject it, do us a service. The very political naïveté, the artlessness with which they rush to confer "radical," "progressive" legitimacy on an essentially fascist style of warfare, forces them to thrust to the center of the moral stage precisely those consequences of eroding the combatant/noncombatant distinction which shrewder political operators might wish to see confined to the shadows, or as Derrideans would say, to the margins of discourse.

For Paulin, plainly, the notion of guilt, as deployed by a given speaker, is answerable only to that speaker's feelings or political beliefs. If you are a "Brooklyn Jew" who has moved to, or is even living in Israel, you deserve to be ("should be") "shot dead." Why do you "deserve" this? Because Paulin's heart, and his sectarian political worldview, say you do. Suppose you are not a "Brooklyn Jew," as many Israelis, and even many "settlers" in the Occupied Territories are not, but some other sort of Jew? Paulin has given us few grounds to suppose that his heart would be any warmer, or the verdict of his politics any less tremendous (or, to speak plainly, grandly fatuous).

A concept of desert, thus made the toy of sectarian political polemic, is vacuous: no concept at all, but a mere *flatus vocis*. "Guilt" and "desert" become not words but angry mouthings flung into the wind. We are in Carroll's Wonderland listening to the prophetic words of the Queen of Hearts. "Off with their heads!" ("All their heads," say her modern imitators, "and do not spare the children"). With those words, one might say, Carroll inadvertently caught the first whisper of the prevailing winds of the century to follow his.

But the words themselves, insofar as they seek to erode the conceptual distinction between murder and punishment by assimilating the former to the latter, are nonsense: mere empty ranting. Even if one were to assent to the idea of capital punishment, there can be no intelligible notion of punishment without some way of giving sense to the notion of desert, no non-vacuous concept of desert without the prior existence of a practicable *and practiced* system of law, no law without general acquiescence in its operations, no general acquiescence without reconciliation, no reconciliation without both the admission of one's own crimes and errors and the right of the adversary (at the very least) to exist. Paulin's words, "I think they should be shot. . . . I never believed that Israel had the right to exist at all," do not point in the direction of progress along that long and difficult road. They point in the opposite direction: into a darkness filled with the stench of blood. But they resonate nonetheless at present among people who regard themselves as possessors of delicate consciences: produce echoes heard far beyond the High Table which Paulin graces with his presence.

In Chapter 4 I mentioned Jonathan Freedland's toying, in an article in the *Jewish Quarterly*, with the idea that members of the Israeli "peacenik left" might, perhaps ought to, have considered themselves morally obliged to leave the country "for ever" after the election of Ariel Sharon as premier. One can only make sense of the suggestion on the assumption that to stay in the country after Sharon's election is precisely to have failed in a duty: to be guilty. Then are *all* Israelis to be considered "guilty," either because they voted for Sharon or because they failed to leave when others did? And is the penalty for this "guilt" to be Paulin's? This is crazy talk. It is crazy talk for the same (ultimately Wittgensteinian) reason that Paulin's similarly structured talk is crazy talk: because it uses, and uses with a fine flourish, grand terms like guilt, obligation, and morality, in a manner which divorces them from all of the ordinary contexts from which they take their meaning, and provides them with no other source of intelligibility. Crazy talk; vast, hollow gesticulations of sound from empty heads. But it is a line of talk, it seems, very easy to fall into at present if you read too many *Guardian* op-ed articles.

DEFENDING TOTAL WAR:
"UNDERSTANDING" THE MURDERERS

Normally, however, liberal-left defenders of the political murder of randomly targeted civilians do not grasp the nettle with quite Paulin's robust enthusiasm. The more usual move is to grant that such tactics are, or might be considered, very wrong, but to plead mitigating circumstances. Although suicide bombing, for example, might be considered wicked by apolitical moralists (so this argument goes), from a more intelligent political standpoint, it can be understood, nevertheless, as a "natural" reaction of concerned individuals to the very much worse atrocities of "state terrorism" committed by the Israelis, the Americans, the British, the Russians, the Hindus, Westerners in general, or any non-Muslim group with whom any Islamo-fascist group may regard itself as at war. A recent instance of this kind of stance was provided by a British Liberal Democrat member of Parliament, Jenny (now Baroness) Tonge, who was reported early in 2004 as saying publicly that she herself would consider becoming a suicide bomber if forced to live like Palestinians, and chose, rather bravely, to stand by these remarks. At a pro-Palestinian rally in Parliament she said, among other things, "I think if I had to live in that situation—and I say that advisedly—I might just consider becoming one [a suicide bomber] myself."[12]

It may to some extent reassure those whose only contact with British politics comes via the media that she was sharply censured for these remarks within her own party, whose leader, Charles Kennedy, was at some pains to divorce the party from remarks which, as he said, "are not compatible with Liberal Democrat party policies and principles."[13] Tonge was duly dropped from her post of Liberal Democrat spokesperson for children.

It is perhaps not obvious, however—patently it is not obvious to Tonge, who is a medical doctor and no doubt a highly intelligent woman—why her remarks are neither morally nor politically sound. If one is being made to suffer daily humiliation and poverty, is it not at least understandable that the frustration and resentment of individuals should rise to the point at which they feel impelled to strike back by any means, be those means never so reprehensible in themselves, at those they perceive as responsible for their sufferings? This is the entire sense, after all, of Tonge's remarks. She does not claim that suicide bombing is morally defensible: she says only that *if* she had to live like the Palestinians she herself would be tempted to become a suicide bomber. The London *Daily Telegraph*, a newspaper generally sympathetic to Israel, coupled its report of Tonge's dismissal as a Liberal Democrat spokesman with a report on an Israeli woman whose mother and five-year-old daughter were killed and her three-year-old son injured by a suicide bomber at a bus stop in Jerusalem. The circumstances recorded are, as usual, harrowing in the extreme. But on the one hand, could not Tonge point out that equally harrowing deaths of Palestinian children have occurred as a result of Israeli antiterrorist actions? And on the other hand could she not reasonably retort, to the implied suggestion that she is defending the murder of children, that her view is not that the murder of children by suicide bombers is justified, but only that it is the sort of thing to which individuals can be driven by prolonged oppression?

Were one to wish to give Tonge a serious answer, an answer which avoids the ineffectual moral non sequitur implicit in the *Telegraph's* juxtaposition of reports, and one which cuts off at the root the possibilities of plausibly moral-sounding retort which non sequiturs of that type leave open to her and those who think like her, one would have, no doubt, to draw attention to two features of suicide bombing which are evident enough but are seldom noted or discussed. The first is that, while becoming a suicide bomber is certainly something which an individual can decide to do, it is not something which an individual *unconnected with a political group* can decide to do. The second is that suicide bombing, in addition to the deaths of Jewish children which result from it, very frequently involves first the mental and moral subversion, and then the death, by sedulously encouraged suicide, of Palestinian children. It is a very dreadful feature of current controversy over Israel that not only many of those who aspire to the leadership, either of the Palestinians or of the Muslim world, but certain Western journalists,[14] daily show themselves capable of exulting in the discovery that political power may spring, not just "out of the barrel of a gun"—for we have come a long way indeed from the relative innocence of the terrorism of forty years ago, or that of the Camus of *Les Justes Assassins*—but from engineering the deaths of children.

To take the first point first, an individual cannot decide, *of him- or herself, and without reference to questions of political engagement,* to become a suicide bomber, for one thing, because the manufacture of the right sort of bomb would be far beyond the technical expertise of the vast majority of individuals. Political groups committed to terrorism maintain people with the right sort of expertise to get around this difficulty. But to avail oneself of that expertise it is necessary to join the group and subject oneself to its internal discipline. Becoming a suicide bomber cannot, for that reason alone, be the response of a politically isolated individual to frustrations which have "caused him to snap." Suicide bombing is an essentially political enterprise, a form of warfare organized by political groups and covertly financed by certain states. Hence, to say that suicide bombing is "understandable given certain circumstances," meaning by that that one would *oneself,* under those circumstances, consider becoming a suicide bomber, is not merely to confess to an emotional sympathy with those who do, but to assert that, in those circumstances, one would consider the *political* enterprise of organizing suicide bombings as, politically speaking, *worthy of support.* Hence, if one says, like Tonge, that one can imagine circumstances in which that enterprise would seem *emotionally* compelling, and if one affirms also, as she does, that those circumstances presently obtain, one would appear to have left oneself, in logic, with no means of avoiding embracing the conclusion that the enterprise of organizing suicide bombings is (not merely hypothetically but categorically) worthy of *political* support.

Of course this is not what Tonge, and those who think like her, think they are saying. They think they are saying merely that someone enduring the conditions endured by Palestinians, who "snapped" and blew up some Jews, would be acting understandably under the circumstances. It is worth noting in passing that, if one *is* clear about what one is saying, and says *that*, one is obliged, again in logic, to say the same thing about Baruch Goldstein, who machine-gunned twenty-nine Muslims at prayer in Hebron, whose family claimed, no doubt with reason, that he had "snapped" under the pressure of repeated terrorist attacks, and who really was acting on a purely individual basis. But, leaving that on one side, this whole line of empathetic mitigation is inappropriate to the Palestinian case, because we are dealing there not with individuals who snap but with a well-organized political campaign.

Tonge is, in short, grossly politically naive about how one actually sets about organizing a terror campaign. She reminds me of the story in the journalist Claude Cockburn's autobiography about an elderly gentleman at an antifascist meeting in the 1930s who rises to his feet, overcome with emotion, and shouts "Arm the workers!," then sinking back into his seat, turns to his neighbor and in worried tones mutters, "By the way, how does one actually set about arming the workers?" But her naiveté has a darker tone to it. It might partially save her remarks from moral absurdity if Hamas, Islamic Jihad, and the rest did, as a matter of fact, rely for their supply of willing suicide bombers on public-spirited persons of mature years, much like Tonge—persons who have no doubt "snapped," but not in any way harmful to their capacity for forthright moral decision—walking into their offices and asking to be used as human bombs. One imagines that this is how the parliamentary representative for Richmond Park would herself set about it. I don't know what would happen if one were actually to try to do that. I imagine that there could be few better ways of marking oneself out as a potential infiltrator or *agent provocateur*—or simply as a romantic fool. Terrorist groups need to be sure, above all things, of the unquestioning, unflinching loyalty of those they employ in such roles. I doubt whether an independent-minded sixty-two-year-old Liberal Democrat member of Parliament for a wealthy borough by the Thames would quite fulfill that requirement. Those who can most easily, and best, be persuaded to fulfill it are, in common experience, children or very young adults. Anyone who has taught philosophy in a university knows very well how easily very young people can be persuaded to give serious intellectual credence to the most insecure propositions on the basis of weak but plausible arguments. The business of the tutorial very often consists first of presenting such arguments, then getting the student to see by further, often difficult, passages of reasoning, how feeble they in fact are. The object of the exercise is to train young minds in critical rationality, a faculty of the highest use both to society and to those individuals who possess it. But a proportion of students, usually the weaker ones, resent the process. They were charmed by the first position they were induced to take up. They imagine they thought of it for themselves. They do not wish to have its weaknesses pointed out to them. They see the process as one in which a delightful landscape of seductively colored absurdities is being wantonly reduced to a wasteland of aridly logical tergiversation, to no profit save that of linguistic or logical pedantry. In fact, though they do not know it, these attitudes prepare them to be the prey of any stronger and more ruthless mind which cares to make use of them. They are, and wish to remain, manipulable. One could, no doubt, if one wished, persuade young people like this of more or less anything, with the virtual certainty of their being devoid, certainly for the time needed to employ them as political tools, of the ability to think their way out of whatever sectarian worldview they had been induced to accept as sound. Terrorist organizations, as well as tutors, are well aware of these facts and know how to employ them for their own ends. That is why most suicide bombers are either children or very young, impressionable people. The following cases, among others, are quoted by Alan Dershowitz:

> On July 6, 2002, two eleven-year-olds were caught trying to plant a bomb near an Israeli outpost, and one of them said he hoped to become a martyr. . . . A fifteen-year-old girl was arrested after confessing that her uncle, a senior Tanzim operative in Bethlehem, had recruited her to become a suicide bomber and she had agreed to recruit additional girls from her school. . . . terrorist operatives deliberately seduced Andalib Suleiman, a twenty-one-year-old woman from Bethlehem. When she became pregnant, she was told that the only way to avoid shame was to die a martyr's death. She then agreed to blow herself up in a Jerusalem shopping market, killing six civilians, including two workers from China.

A similar example is Ayat al-Aryas, an eighteen-year-old woman from Dehaisi, who blew herself up in a supermarket, killing two civilians, after having been seduced and made pregnant.[15]

The exact nature of the processes by which young people are induced to sacrifice themselves in this way, though entirely understood in Israel, is seldom, if ever, raised in Western media reports on Israel. Many Western journalists accept without question the absurd claim, made by Islamo-fascist groups and their fellow-travelers, that Muslims simply "love death" and are content to transmit it without further inquiry, often accompanying it with a delicious frisson of radical awe, embroidering it in the process, ironically enough, with various "orientalizing" fantasies of precisely the sort which the late Edward Said was at such pains to expose.[16]

Nor do Western media reports on Israel inquire overmuch into the feelings of Palestinian families who lose children or young people in this way. Journalists not uncommonly show themselves ready to accept the bona fides of families paraded in front of them by Hamas minders to express their satisfaction at having produced a martyr. It does not seem to occur to them to inquire what would happen to these, usually working-class, Palestinians if they chose to protest their loss, thus identifying themselves as collaborators with the Israelis and enemies of "the Struggle." It was, in the days of the Soviet Union, and still is, very difficult to impress upon a certain type of politically engaged Western mind that when it is very unsafe indeed to tell the truth, people tell lies. Nevertheless, grief commonly transcends political "commitment." An Israeli friend tells me that when one unfortunate Palestinian family lost a promising daughter who had been induced to blow herself up in a supermarket, members of the family required hospitalization for psychological trauma over the loss. And it is possible that things may be changing. Samirah Abdullah, the mother of the sixteen-year-old suicide bomber who blew himself up in the middle of the Carmel market in Tel Aviv on November 1, 2004, is reported as saying, "It's immoral to send someone so young . . . they should have sent an adult who knows the meaning of his deeds."[17]

Middle-class Palestinians, to whom relative affluence affords more options, do what they can to keep their children of vulnerable ages out of the reach of Hamas and the other "radical" groups by sending them abroad. This again is a well-known feature of the situation which I had never seen mentioned in the Western media until a recent article by

Inigo Gilmore, describing an exodus of middle-class Palestinian youths from Hebron:

> As Tareq sat in the spacious living room of his family's three-bedroom house, where a portrait of his late father, a lawyer, hangs alongside elaborate Palestinian tapestries, he acknowledged that Hamas had had extraordinary success in secretly recruiting and persuading young men to die for the cause.
>
> One of them was his friend Bassem Takhouri, a 19-year-old student and the son of a well-off shop owner, who blew up himself and 16 other people on a Jerusalem bus a year ago.
>
> "Basem was a quiet person," said Tareq, "it was unexpected. Of course there is plenty of anger towards Israel over the killings, the checkpoints and so on. But Hamas has been able to brainwash these young men."
>
> The response of dozens of young men from Hebron's middle-class families has been to flee the spreading influence of Hamas—which is now reaching beyond its usual recruiting ground in the ranks of poor and dispossessed Palestinians from the refugee camps.
>
> Tariq's older brother, Sami, 21, also plans to move to the US—following another brother, Ramzi, 26. Yet another brother, Basel, 27, is already in France. Sami said that those who cannot escape resent those who do, but added: "It is hard, but we have no choice. We have to make a future for ourselves, and the best way for us to do that now is to go somewhere else."
>
> Some now face parental pressure to leave. Omar Jaber, 19, who lives in a spacious home a few minutes drive from al-Jama, said his father had grown so concerned about his welfare that he had imposed an 8 p.m. curfew. "We are so tired of the violence that maybe it is better to get out now," Omar said.[18]

I shall leave it to a Muslim voice, that of Abdel Rahman al-Rashed, general manager of the Al-Arabiya news channel to sum up this part of my argument:

> We cannot clear our names unless we own up to the shameful fact that terrorism has become an Islamic enterprise, an almost exclusive monopoly, implemented by Muslim men and women. We cannot redeem our extremist youths, who commit all these heinous crimes, without confronting the Sheikhs who thought it ennobling to reinvent themselves as revolutionary ideologues, sending other people's sons and daughters to certain death, while sending their own children to European and American schools and colleges.[19]

THE "HOLOCAUST DAY" CONTROVERSY IN BRITAIN: A POSTSCRIPT

In January 2006, as I was finishing the final draft of this book, a familiar annual controversy erupted once again in the press and broadcast media in Britain, when the Muslim Council of Great Britain, an organization generally regarded as moderate, headed by Sir Iqbal Sacranie, announced that once again this year, as in previous years, it would boycott the Holocaust Day commemoration. As is previous years, a good deal of outrage was voiced in the popular press, and the cause of Islamophobia in Britain no doubt received a small but significant fillip in consequence.

Both BBC radio and independent television, however, produced programs in which a wide variety of opinions concerning the affair, Muslim and non-Muslim, were aired and argued over in a not unenlightening way. BBC radio (Radio 4) contributed an edition of the long-running program _The Moral Maze_, which gave an airing to arguments from all sides of the controversy. Independent Television screened, on January 20, a one-off program in the Channel 4 series _30 Minutes_, under the title "Why do we need Holocaust Day?" In this, the Scottish Sikh television producer Hardeep Singh Kohli interviewed a number of people, both controversialists and bystanders, on the issue. They included Inayat Bunglawala, a spokesman for the Muslim Council; the Jamaican poet and novelist Benjamin Zephaniah; the Jewish academic and novelist Howard Jacobson; the journalist, author, and regular _Guardian_ columnist George Monbiot; the amiable Leslie Bunder, one of those "Brooklyn Jews" who so excite the ire of Tom Paulin, who has lived in Britain since 1977 and edits the website Something Jewish;[20] and Sir Greville Janner, now Lord Janner of Braunstone, the Labour politician and member of Parliament successively for Leicester NW and Leicester West, who has also been president of the Board of Deputies of British Jews (1978–84), and has been internationally active in efforts to secure restitution for victims of the Holocaust.

The observance of a special day to commemorate the Holocaust is not a long-standing tradition in Britain. It was first instituted by the Labour government under Tony Blair in 2001. Some of Kohli's Jewish respondents express doubts about it. Howard Jacobson records that he was initially unconvinced, seeing it as an example of the sort of rather meretricious "care/Blair" politics that expresses itself in "saying-sorry days." Leslie Bunder worries about whether it is not in the end unhelpful for Jews to dwell too much on the Shoah, on the grounds that it helps to embed in the consciousness, both of Jews and others, an image of Jews as victims.

The objections brought by the Muslim Council of Great Britain, in this program represented by Inayat Bunglawala, in justification of the council's repeated decision to boycott observances of the day, run along different lines. Bunglawala proposes that Holocaust Day should be abolished, and replaced by a Genocide Day, on two main grounds. The first, as Bunglawala put it, is that the concentration on the Jewish Holocaust, the Shoah, deflects attention from other more recent acts of genocide, in particular those, in Srebrenica, Kosovo, and Chechnya, in which large numbers of Muslims have suffered death at the hands of non-Muslims, but also the massacre in Rwanda, in which huge numbers of Tutsi tribesmen, women, and children, were slaughtered by their ancestral tribal enemies, the Hutu. The second ground advanced by Bunglawala for abolishing Holocaust Day as such is that observing it carries the suggestion that Jewish lives "matter more" or "are worth more" than those of people of other racial or religious groups who have suffered similar fates.

Hardeep Singh Kohli has no difficulty in finding non-Muslim contributors to second both these arguments. The poet Benjamin Zephaniah, while making it clear that he is not a Holocaust denier, and that he recognizes the terrible nature of the sufferings inflicted on European Jews, still wants to say that talk and preaching about the Holocaust still take an unjust precedence over the sufferings inflicted by slavery on black people. White people, he says, go on and on about the Jews and the Holocaust, but when we, blacks and West Indians, want to talk about slavery, they say we have a chip on our shoulder. He draws the conclusion that the lives and sufferings of black people are held less valuable than the lives and sufferings of Jews. George Monbiot further amplifies both of Bunglawala's grounds of objection. He suggests that the official commemoration by the British of a foreign holocaust, for which they share no guilt, serves to "let the country off the hook" by deflecting attention from the numerous holocausts for which the British Empire, or British colonists, *were* directly responsible. He instances the destruction to the last man of the Tasmanian aboriginals, and a famine in India in the 1870s which killed large numbers of poor farmers and their families, and which, according to him, although it was caused primarily by a drought in the Deccan, was greatly augmented in gravity by the economic policies pursued by the Viceroy of the day, Lord Lytton.[21] And he suggests that the only reason *these* holocausts are not given equal prominence with *the* Holocaust is that *some people* are better organized and more adept at putting forward their case for sympathy than others.

What are we to make of these arguments? On the one hand, Hardeep Singh Kohli has clearly done us all a favor by showing that support for the suggestion that Holocaust Day be replaced with something along the lines of a Genocide Day extends sufficiently far outside the limits of the British Muslim community to find supporters both in other ethnic communities and in parts of the native British Left.

On the other hand, there hangs about the arguments he marshals for this proposal, and about the program itself, a curious air of what I feel inclined to call moral strangeness, of something approaching paradox, though the nature and source of the paradox, if it exists, is not all that obvious, or easy to put one's hand on. Howard Jacobson, in what is evidently a further extract from what must have been a longer filmed interview, confesses himself baffled by the suggestion that observing Holocaust Day could be seen as "divisive," and compares it to sibling rivalry: it's as if, he says, the critics were saying, "Why can't we have a holocaust ourselves?"

In the same statement he goes back on his earlier suggestion that introducing the special day was a bad idea in the first place, and says that the Muslim boycott has convinced him, despite his initial doubts about the wisdom of introducing it, that Holocaust Day, now that it exists, should be retained at all costs. Just what one would expect a Jew to say, of course, though it doesn't fit that stereotype that he didn't say it to start with.

But, even more curiously, at the end of the program, the British Sikh presenter, Hardeep Singh Kohli, joins Jacobson in affirming almost exactly the same position. Kohli is filmed making a visit to Auschwitz and inspecting the machinery of destruction. He comes across in the film as fairly shattered by this experience. In his concluding remarks he says two, not entirely mutually consistent, things. The first, apparently motivated by his experience at Auschwitz, is that Holocaust Day should not be abolished, or replaced by a Genocide Day. Now that it exists, and is observed, it should go on being observed. The second is that he still thinks Holocaust Day should not have been introduced in the first place, because it is, for all the reasons canvassed in the earlier part of the program, "divisive."

Once more, what is one to make of this controversy? Can anything more concrete, perhaps, be made of my suggestion that an air of paradox lurks about some of the arguments deployed in it? Maybe it can. The massacre of around 8,000 Bosnian Muslim men and boys at Srebrenica in the concluding stages of the civil war following the breakup of the former Yugoslavia produced a wave of entirely justified outrage in Britain. If British Muslims had pressed for the institution of an official annual commemoration of this outrage, it seems quite likely, especially in the early days of the Blair administration, that they might have succeeded. Suppose such a day were to be instituted. And suppose various groups on the Right, supported, let's say, by a tabloid newspaper or two, were to decide to boycott it, not, according to them, on grounds of Islamophobia, but on the grounds that, since it did not commemorate, equally, deaths caused by Muslim suicide bombers, it was inherently divisive and likely to set one community against another? I think the reaction of most ordinary British people would be one of disgust and contempt. Why? Because, since the object of such an observance is to express, publicly, respect for the dead, regret at their deaths, and moral censure toward the injustice of their fate, the effect of a boycott is to *withhold* from the dead respect and regret, *and from their murderers censure.* It is easy to imagine, is it not, the editorials and commentaries which would be devoted to exposing the latent, if unconfessed, Islamophobia inherent in such a boycott, and deploring its tendency to divide society, alienate moderate Muslim opinion and set one community against another?

At this point, perhaps, the nature of the moral paradox implicit in the reasons offered for opposition to the observance of Holocaust Day becomes clear. To attempt to justify the boycott of a memorial observance for the unjustly murdered dead of one community on the grounds that *the observance* is divisive, is paradoxical—not to say incoherent, morally speaking, because *the boycott itself*, given what it says in terms of the deliberate refusal of both regret and condemnation, *is itself divisive*, and extremely so.

There are other problems. Why, for instance, pick on Holocaust Day? Hardeep Singh Kohli and every contributor to his program were careful to stress that they were not denying that the Holocaust took place or that its victims were innocent and unjustly murdered; only saying that "concentration on the Holocaust" was "unfair" and "divisive" because it deflected attention from "other holocausts." But in that case, why stop at Holocaust Day? Does not the honor and remembrance paid to the British dead of the two world wars on Armistice Day in Britain serve to deflect attention from the dead of other wars and other nations? Why is a memorial to the dead of the Glencoe Massacre, say, not an obstacle to the remembrance of other massacres? Once we grant the proposition that the remembrance of one injustice can serve to cloud or obscure our remembrance of others, is it not a very short step to the paradoxical conclusion that we should remember none of them?

Might there, though, be some feature unique to Holocaust Day, which exposes it to criticism, on grounds of "divisiveness," to which other public acts of remembrance are not, in the nature of things, exposed? The suggestion before us is that there is indeed such a feature, namely, that Holocaust Day singles out for remembrance one specific holocaust, one specific genocide, among many. This is the whole force, after all, of the suggestion that

Holocaust Day be abolished and replaced by Genocide Day. Jacobson, it seems, is wide of the mark. It is not that everyone "wants to have a holocaust of his own"; it is rather that everyone thinks that he already *has* a holocaust of his own.

This argument can get off the ground, it seems to me, only by a certain stretching of the meaning of the terms *holocaust* and *genocide*; with each step in the direction of greater generality accompanied by a corresponding shift in the speaker's sense of what is being, or ought to be, commemorated. Suppose, when asked for examples of holocausts-in-the-plural, we offer, say, the massacre of Srebrenica and the extermination, by nineteenth-century British settlers, of the Tasmanian aboriginals. If by genocide we mean the extermination of an entire people, the second certainly was genocide. But there are substantial differences between it and what happened in Europe between 1933 and 1945. In the latter case the murderers and the victims were fellow citizens, members of the same community. The latter were singled out for extermination by a political movement disposing of an elaborate theory of racial superiority, with the goal of "purifying" the superior race. That feature is lacking in the Tasmanian case, where the victims were simply a different people from the settlers who exterminated them. And while the settlers certainly regarded the aboriginal population as racially inferior, in fact as animals (I once heard a drunken young man in a bar in Perth, Western Australia, boast that his grandfather had organized "Abo hunts"), they did not exterminate the aboriginals with any notion of purifying the race, but simply with a view to protecting their livestock, as they exterminated the "Tasmanian Tiger," a wolflike marsupial predator. In the case of the Srebrenica Massacre also, the motive of racial purification is absent. The victims were not murdered because they were held to belong to an inferior and impure race. The *racial* composition of the vast majority of the population of the former Yugoslavia, so far as one can speak sensibly of such things, is uniform. Virtually everyone, whether Roman Catholic, Orthodox, or Muslim in religion, belongs to the same southern Slav population. The victims at Srebrenica were killed because they were Muslim males of fighting age. That there was no intention to commit *genocide*, in the sense of wiping out the entire Muslim population of the region, is shown by the fact that the systematic murder of women and children, which formed such an essential part of the Final Solution, was in this case absent.

Some readers might take me to be arguing that the Holocaust was worse *for the victims* than these other massacres, or that a Jewish life is for some reason to be regarded as of more value than an aboriginal or Bosnian Muslim life. Not at all. Death is death. A life, whomever's it is, is a life. My point is Bishop Butler's point; the one that G. E. Moore used as an epigraph for *Principia Ethica*: "Everything is what it is, and not another thing." Butler's thought has a bearing on a question unraised, for the most part, in the controversy over Holocaust Day in Britain: the question of what exactly we are commemorating, forcing ourselves to remember, in commemorating the Holocaust. We live in a culture very powerfully influenced by utilitarianism, the late-eighteenth and nineteenth-century philosophical doctrine whose central plank is that nothing is good save pleasure and nothing bad save pain. One effect of that influence is to make it difficult to grasp the actual variety, the diversity, of kinds of good and evil. In the essay *On Liberty*, for instance, that chronically uneasy utilitarian John Stuart Mill struggles manfully to persuade himself, and us, that the values of freedom and self-determination can be accommodated within the austere terms of the version of utilitarianism bequeathed him by his father and Jeremy Bentham, but fails.

Utilitarianism, however, survived to become the basis of most people's moral thinking even today. Guided by its light, we tend to think that what was chiefly bad about the Holocaust, indeed all that was bad about it, was that it caused intense suffering to vast numbers of people. At this point there occurs to us the natural thought there are historical events—slavery, great famines, Stalin's forced collectivization of agriculture, Pol Pot's revolution in Cambodia—which have caused yet more intense suffering to yet vaster numbers of people. Should we not then be commemorating *these*, rather than the Holocaust, whose Jewish toll, after all, ran only to a relatively modest six million? Isn't it, in fact, sectarian, even racist, to only give such attention to the latter? Doesn't the fact that we—evidently, since we appear to hold them for some reason more worth commemorating—take the deaths of six million Jews to be of more moral importance than the deaths of Monbiot's sixteen million to twenty-nine million Indian peasants in the Deccan in the 1870s show something rather discreditable about us: that we value the life of a Jew more than that of someone with dark skin? This is the seductive moral and intellectual garden path up which we find half of Kohli's interviewees, along with, I suspect, a very large number of decent, youngish middle-class Western people of respectably radical sympathies.

The answer is that what made the Holocaust bad was not, or not only, the suffering it caused. Suffering, though an evil, is not the only evil. There is also (among other things) irrational racial, and, more generally, intercommunal hatred, and the corruption which springs from it: corruption of the social order, corruption of relationships between individuals, corruption of the individual heart and mind. The commemoration of the Shoah which, since 1945, has taken its place as a part of the great cycle of the Jewish liturgical year is, indeed, a commemoration of *Jewish* suffering. The commemoration of Holocaust Day by society at large is not, for two reasons, exclusively a commemoration of the suffering endured *by Jews*. The first reason, of course, is that it commemorates also the suffering of other groups, gypsies, political enemies of the regime, mental patients, handicapped children, whom the Holocaust also consumed. The second, and more important reason, is that it commemorates, endeavors to keep alive in the collective memory, the true nature, and catastrophic consequences, for Europe and the world, of a certain sort of corruption: the corruption which sprang from accession to autocratic power under Hitler of a theory and ideology of racial superiority.

The problem with the idea that we should replace Holocaust Day with something, called perhaps, Genocide Day, designed to call to mind "other genocides" or "other holocausts," is that such a move would smuggle out of sight and out of mind precisely what is specific to the Nazi Holocaust: namely, the fabric of peculiarly and specifically European beliefs and feelings about "race" and racial inferiority which gave it both its justification and its power over the minds and actions of those many who either stood aside or actively enforced its decrees. If we take genocide to mean the actual or attempted extermination of an entire people or race, then very few massacres are genocidal, and only one genocide, that of the Holocaust, sprang from the specifically European combination of intellectual and moral developments commemorated, in shame, by Holocaust Day. If the phrase "the Holocaust" is used, as it has come to be used, as a name picking out precisely what is unique about, and specific to, the events of 1939–45, then there are no other holocausts, although there are other genocides, having different sources and consequences; and of course there are all the other landscapes of death and misery, the famines, the Gulag, slavery, all of which deserve to be remembered, but not at the cost of obliterating, of sweeping under the carpet, all recollection of what was both specifically evil and specifically European about the Nazi Holocaust.

The kind of outlook which gave Nazi racial doctrine, and ultimately the Final Solution, a populist political appeal is, after all, by no means dead in Europe, a Europe far more racially and communally complex than the Europe which emerged from the war of 1914–18. One would have thought that advocating the replacement, with a more anodyne, because more notionally "inclusive," version of a commemorative institution, whose main object is to keep in public recollection the past consequences of making a populist politics out of the idea of racial purity, would hardly be to the advantage of any minority community. In Kohli's program this is the point made by Lord Janner, who asks Kohli if it doesn't worry him that it might be the Sikhs next time.

Lord Janner's point can only be felt as powerfully convincing by those of us old enough to have been around, even as very young people, "last time." But it falls on very stony ground in the context of Kohli's program, in which "inclusiveness" is allowed to hold the floor as a determining moral consideration even after the presenter's chilling encounter with the gas chambers. I think there are several reasons for this, which I'll state in declining order of intellectual and moral respectability. The first is the prevalence of the idea of gutter-utilitarian provenance, that there is only one kind of evil, namely, experienced human suffering, with its corollary that there can be no morally compelling reason (indeed no *reason*, other than thinking one person's suffering worth more than another's) for commemorating a catastrophe in which a mere six million people died, when so many more people died in other catastrophes. The second is the natural tendency of political "activists" to fight for possession of a word, if that word possesses sufficient moral and political resonance. One of several impressive philosophers by whom I had the good fortune to be taught in the 1950s was the late C. L. Stevenson of the University of Michigan. In his book *Ethics and Language*, famous then, but nowadays perhaps less read than it should be, Charles has a chapter on "Persuasive Definition."[22] His thesis is that certain words, like "Democracy," are surrounded, as it were, by an aura of positive emotional connotation for a majority of hearers. This feature gives such words a certain value when it comes to securing agreement in political debate. The thought is, that if one can convince one's hearers that the policy one is proposing is the "democratic" one, while one's opponent's policies are "undemocratic," that in itself will give one an edge in debate. That gives one a motive for bringing the word democracy over to one's side in the argument, as it were, by subtly shifting its descriptive content and reference ("persuasively redefining" it) while leaving its emotional aura unchanged. Something like this is happening in the debates we have been investigating with the word holocaust. I argued earlier that Howard Jacobson fails to hit the nail on the head when he remarks in bewilderment, in Kohli's film, "It's as if they all wanted their own Holocaust!" But that isn't quite it either. It isn't, perhaps the *thing*, so much as the *word* they're after (how right Laurence Sterne was to set on the title-page of *Tristram Shandy* Epictetus's aphorism, "It is not the things themselves, but opinions concerning them, which disturb men").[23] The thought is: "Why should the Jews have sole use of this wonderful word, which draws so much sympathy, and money, to them. Why shouldn't we—my people, me and my political friends—have the use of it too?" It is this impulse which leads to the kind of attempt we have been witnessing to broaden the use of the term, to make the *term* more "inclusive," first by making it synonymous with "genocide," then by broadening its reference further to cover any massacre, then still further, in the manner of George Monbiot, to cover such phenomena as famines, or slavery. There is in all these attempts at persuasive redefinition, to return finally to the central topic of this book, a certain slight but perceptible edge of anti-Semitism, the sense that in having established, as it seems to the objectors, sole ownership over the word holocaust, those wretched conspirators "the Jews" have once again "gotten away with something," stolen other people's light, used their sufferings, real as those may be, to cast into the shade the sufferings of others.

In the Kohli program everybody is, almost obsessively, keen to make it clear that he is not a Holocaust denier, that the Holocaust really happened, that the sufferings of those Jews it affected have as much right to be commemorated as the anybody else's sufferings. The slight edge of anti-Semitism I'm talking about is at most, as literary critics say nowadays, a subtext, something haunting, as Derrida would put it, the margins of discourse. It makes itself most clearly felt in the recurrent charge that there is implicit in the observance of Holocaust Day, as it stands, a tacit assumption that the life of a Jew, the sufferings of a Jew, are "worth more" than the lives and sufferings of others. What is distressing about this contention is that the whole function of Holocaust Day, as it stands, is to recall to the collective consciousness the evil nature and worse consequences *of a populist politics which founded itself explicitly upon the very principle objected to*; that one race, one people, is of more value than another.

It is pleasant to be able to end this rather downbeat postscript with an upbeat one. There is now a Muslim, Fahmia Huda, on the board of the Holocaust Memorial Trust. Urging Muslim leaders to end their boycott, she is reported as pointing out "that Holocaust Memorial Day marks not only the deaths of six million Jews but also the killing of gypsies and other minority groups by the Nazis and more recent genocides including those in Bosnia and Rwanda"; and as saying, "I feel very confident that we are looking at genocide issues, that we are looking at racism, that we are looking at Islamophobia, that we are looking at anti-Semitism in the round."[24] This is fine. On the one hand, there are evident partial analogies to be drawn between what happened in Bosnia to Muslims, and in Rwanda to Tutsis, and what happened in Europe between 1939 and 1945 to the Jews and other victims of the Nazi genocide; and there is no harm and much good to be achieved by reflecting on those analogies. On the other hand, there is no good, and much harm, to be done by, in effect, *redefining* the term holocaust in such a way as to allow the concrete specificity of the Nazi genocide, and with it everything which links it to enduring aspects of European culture and politics, to fade from view. For that is what would happen if we were to allow ourselves to be led, through a persuasive reassignment of the descriptive content and reference of the term holocaust in the direction of greater generality, to imagine that every great evil done by human beings to one another, from slavery to intertribal massacre, from the hunting down like animals of aboriginal people, to the creation or exacerbation of famine by political malignity or ineptitude, is *a phenomenon of exactly the same kind as* the Nazi Holocaust. Everything is what it is, and not another thing. Evil is not a single recurrent feature of human life, eternally self-identical in its nature. There are many kinds of evil, springing from many different causes, some of them sui generis. If we are to think rationally about these matters, if our response to human evil is not to be reduced to futile and sentimental hand wringing, we need a vocabulary which allows us to keep track of the differences.

NOTES

1. L. Wittgenstein, *Philosophical Investigations*, 2nd ed. Trans. G. E. M. Anscombe (Oxford: Basil Blackwell, 1958), p. x.

2. Julius Kovesi, *Values and Evaluations: Essays on Ethics and Ideology*, ed. Alan Tapper (New York: Peter Lang, 1998/2001). See especially "Marxist Ecclesiology and Biblical Criticism," "Nature and Convention," and "Moses Hess, Marx and Money."

3. See, for example the article by Abdel Rahman al-Rashed, general manager of the Al-Arabiya news channel, in the pan-Arabic newspaper *Al Sharq Al Awsat*, September 4, 2004, English version, London *Sunday Telegraph*, September 5, 2004, p. 7 ("These hostage deaths shame the Muslim world"); and the article on the struggle of Ayaan Hirsi Ali, the Dutch member of Parliament of Somali descent, for the rights of women in Islam, in the Review section of the same issue of the *Sunday Telegraph*, p. 4 ("Why I Lifted the Veil on Islam").

4. Alan Dershowitz, *The Case for Israel* (Hoboken, N.J.: John Wiley, 2003), p. 124.

5. Ibid., p. 125.

6. Ian Buruma and Avishai Margalit, *Occidentalism: The West in the Eyes of Its Enemies* (New York: Penguin, 2004), p. 6.

7. Paul Johnson, *A History of Jews* (London: George Weidenfeld and Nicholson, 1987), p. 528.

8. Dershowitz, *The Case for Israel*, p. 81.

9. See, for instance, Michael A. Hoffman and Moshe Lieberman, *The Israeli Holocaust against the Palestinians* (New York: Independent History, 2002). The material on Hoffman's website places him, to put it mildly, on the far Right.

10. *Al Ahram Weekly Online*, April 4–10, 2002, available at http://weekly
.ahram.org.eg/2002/580/cu2htm.

11. "Let me be clear: I do not charge Paulin with antisemitism. I'm not sure I even
charge him with sensationalism, though I understand why a poet in our time must
grab a headline. What I charge him with is stupidity. He has a mind and in this instance he has refused to use it. He has chosen to be a fool." Howard Jacobson, "Word-
smiths and Atrocities against Language: The Incendiary Use of the Holocaust and
Nazism against Jews," in Paul Iganski and Barry Kosmin, eds., *A New Anti-Semitism?
Debating Judeophobia in the 21st Century* (London: Profile Books, 2003), p. 104.

12. See report in the *Daily Telegraph*, January 24, 2004, p. 4.

13. Cited in ibid.

14. Amir Taheri, in a biting, highly critical review (*Daily Telegraph* "Seven" Magazine, January 15–21, 2006, p. 43) of Robert Fisk's *The Great War for Civilization: The
Conquest of the Middle East* (London: Fourth Estate, 2006), makes the following observation: "Nevertheless, Fisk believes that, thanks to Islamist suicide-bombers, the
'Anglo-Saxons' and their Israeli appendage are doomed. He writes, 'The suicide-
bomber has become the nuclear weapon of the other.' And adds, 'In Lebanon, Palestine and Iraq the suicide-bombers have become the symbol of this new fearlessness.
Once an occupied people has lost its fear of death, the occupier is doomed.'"

15. Dershowitz, *The Case for Israel*, pp. 129–31.

16. Edward Said, *Orientalism* (New York: Random House, 1978).

17. London *Daily Telegraph*, November 2, 2004, p. 12.

18. Inigo Gilmore, "Hebron's Middle Classes Choose America Rather than
Martyrdom," *Sunday Telegraph*, September 5, 2004, p. 27.

19. Abdel Rahman al-Rashid, article in *Al Sharq al Awsat*, Sept. 4, 2004. An English version appeared in the London *Sunday Telegraph*, September 5, 2004, under the
title "These hostage deaths shame the Muslim World."

20. The URL is somethingjewish.co.uk.

21. A fuller version of this argument can be found in an article by George Monbiot, "How Britain Denies Its Holocausts," which appeared in the *Guardian* on December 27, 2005, and which can also be found on Monbiot's website at http://
www.monbiot.com/archives/2005/12/27/how-britain-denies-its-holocausts/.

22. C. L. Stevenson, *Ethics and Language* (New Haven: Yale University Press,
1944).

23. Laurence Sterne, *The Life and Opinions of Tristram Shandy, Gentleman*, ed. Gra-
ham Petrie (Harmondsworth: Penguin Books, 1967), p. 31.

24. Ben Leapman, "Holocaust Memorial Plea to Muslims," *Sunday Telegraph*, January 22, 2006, p. 4.

7

THE ACCUSATION OF RACISM

IS ISRAEL A "RACIST APARTHEID" STATE?

One of the main claims, if not the main claim, advanced by some sections of the Left in defense both of suicide bombers and of the further claim that "Israel ought not to exist," is that Israel is an "apartheid state," a state founded, to some unspecified extent, on "racism." The use of the term apartheid in this context serves much the same purpose in the polemics of certain sections of the European and American Left as the equation of the Star of David with the swastika, namely, to convey the impression that Israel no more "deserves" to exist as a state than the Third Reich or apartheid-era South Africa did. As it is usually stated, the accompanying implication is that no other country comes close to deserving, on these grounds, the hostility of all right-minded people. The claim therefore invites two questions: How far are the institutions of Israel analogous to those of apartheid-era South Africa? How far do other countries deserve censure on the same grounds?

Israel is in fact, for better or worse, almost a textbook example of a multicultural society. After the War of Independence Israel did not, as she might have done, expel all Arabs from the new state. Notice I say, "as she might have done." In Europe, the continent from which a majority of Israel's accusers are drawn, "ethnic cleansing" has provided one of the chief political leitmotifs of the past century. One has no need to confine oneself to Hitler's efforts to render Europe *judenrein*. After the war, very large German populations were expelled from Poland, the former East Prussia, and Czechoslovakia, and stand a vanishingly small chance of being readmitted on their prewar footing. A smaller, but significant Slav Muslim population fled Bulgaria in the 1980s to escape persecution by the Orthodox majority. Then there are the extraordinary mass deportations, of the Crimean Tartars, of the Volga Germans, carried out in the 1930s and 1940s by the Soviet Union, a state regarded at the time, by a majority of those on the Left, as unimpeachably "progressive." Again there are the mass exchanges of Greeks and Turks which took place after the failure of the Greek attempt at the end of World War I to reverse by force of arms the consequences of the historic collapse of Byzantium. Then there are the various "cleansings" of the Balkan wars that followed the breakup of the former Yugoslavia in 1992. Most people's media-influenced recollection of those wars is, I suspect, that the Serbs were the chief proponents of "ethnic cleansing," resisted by the "International Community," a somewhat nebulous and shifting collection of states, but one with which, I suppose, a significant proportion of "left-liberal" critics of Israel would identify. But this recollection is faulty. It leaves out the expulsion of the Serbian population of the Krajina by Croatian forces flying the Ustasha flag,[1] using American arms notionally supplied (in defiance of a UN embargo) to the Bosnian Muslims but landed in Zagreb and hijacked by Croatia; not to mention the steady elbowing of Serbs out of Kosovo by Albanian immigrants throughout the 1980s, a process finally completed under the auspices of the "International Community" as an in-direct but entirely predictable result of the bombing campaign which finally brought the Balkan situation, for the moment at least, under control. Mass deportations have also on occasion served as a technique of genocide. That is true, for instance, of the German deportation of the Hereros from south-west Africa, the deportation of the Cherokee nation from the southern Ap-palachians to Oklahoma in the early years of the nineteenth century, and the Navajo from their lands in the late 1860s, the deportations carried out against Armenians by the Ottoman Turks in 1914, Stalin's deportations of the Chechens and the Crimean Tatars, and others.

I cite these facts only to remind us that, if what we mean by "racism" is a preference for racial or cultural purity, Israel is hardly at the head of the list of racist states. Indeed, she is nowhere. Unlike the Croatians or the Czechs, victorious Israel did not expel en masse the aliens within her gates. Inevitably, many Arabs fled the country. There was a war going on, and when people are fighting for their lives and their families, bad things hap-pen. The residue of the defeated was not expelled. There was no "ethnic cleansing." Approximately 160,000 Arabs remained, and over the interven-ing half century the number has grown to approximately 1.5 million. Arab citizens of Israel include both Muslims and Christians. Although Orthodox Jews exercise a disproportionate influence in religious matters—an influence opposed within Israel by secularists, anti-Orthodox activists, and non-Orthodox religious Jews—there is no religious discrimination. Mosques and churches exist in Israel. They are not burned, as synagogues and mosques not infrequently are in Europe. Moreover, many immigrants to Israel are not Jewish. Israel has accepted half a million non-Jewish Russian spouses and children. Many Israelis are black, the Abyssinian Falasha, for example; very many are Arab Jews, from Yemen, Jordan, Iraq, the entire Middle East. Anyone, moreover, can convert to Judaism, and people of all races, colors, and religions do.

There is thus simply no basis in Israel for "apartheid" in the strict, South African sense, if one means by that the erection of legally enforceable barriers to keep two races from mingling socially or sexually, by setting up separate facilities for each—"whites-only" beaches, separate divisions of seats on buses, and so on. Nor is it true that there is *social* separation between Israeli Jews and Israeli Arabs on a de facto basis, something one might surely expect after fifty years of war. An instance: Sakhnin, an Israeli Arab village of twenty-four thousand in Galilee, with five mosques and three churches, has a football team, Bnei Sakhnin, which in May 2004 won the Israeli State Cup and so qualified to compete for the Uefa Cup. The team is a mixed one, containing both Arabs and Jews. I take it that, if Arab and Jew are supposed to stand as the Israeli equivalents of black and white in South Africa, this mingling of the "races" in a successful football team is not something which those charged with administering an "apartheid state" would, or could, allow to happen. The story, however, does offer a clue to how a serious, nonhyperbolic critique of Israel's treatment of its Arab citizens might run. Bnei Sakhnin has, at time of writing, no stadium. It plays on a grass plot. In May, when it won the cup, Ariel Sharon, the prime minister, pledged five million shekels (£600,000) to build a stadium, a promise recently raised to fifteen million, but no money has so far appeared, and only one Israeli company has so far come forward to sponsor the team. As one citizen of Sakhnin said to a reporter:

> The tragedy is that even though we obey the laws and pay our taxes, the Israeli government does not give a fair return. We have a third world status in a first world country. More and more, we feel we are being pushed into the corner.[2]

Arab Israelis, in short, find themselves treated, to a degree, as second-class citizens. Any visitor to Israel who bothers to talk to Israeli Arabs even on the most casual basis (to Arab tourist guides, for instance) can acquaint him- or herself with this piece of the jigsaw. Phyllis Chesler, the American feminist, in a recent, passionate book attacking, like this book, left-wing anti-Semitism and the demonization of Israel, puts the matter succinctly:

> Although Israeli Palestinian Arabs may privately admit that their lives as second-class citizens in Israel are far better than the lives of their counterparts all over the Arab world, they remain second-class Israeli citizens in Israel proper. . . . This means two very different things. First, those Palestinians who did not flee Israel in 1948, who chose to remain, were granted Israeli citizenship, which most value and will not give up. They vote in Israeli elections, have elected some of their own representatives to Parliament, travel on . . . Israeli passports, go to Israeli hospitals, receive the same medical care that Jewish Israelis do. However, Israeli Arabs were not granted equal citizenship. This is unforgivable, an understandable but huge mistake.
>
> Unequal citizenship for Israeli Palestinian Arabs means the following: the Israeli government has never allocated an equal amount of money for Arab community development, so many Arab village roads remain unpaved, and electricity and water supplies remain compromised. In addition, until recently, the government subsidised Jewish-only communities where Arabs did not live. The Israeli Supreme Court recently ruled that this is unjust and illegal. Communities who discriminate against home buyers or renters on the basis of religion or nationality are now violating the law of the land.
>
> At the same time the government has not allowed Arab farmers to grow certain crops that it has allocated to Israeli Kibbutzim (collective settlements), and it has not assisted Arab farmers in the distribution of their crops, on which their survival depends.
>
> Israeli Palestinian Arabs are not conscripted into the Israeli Defense Forces, but they may volunteer. Most do not, either because of antipathy towards the Israeli state or because they are afraid both of Israeli mistreatment and of Arab charges of disloyalty, which often carry a vigilante death penalty. Arabs have served in the Israeli army, but they have not risen to the level of major positions (members of the Druse religion have occupied high ranks and have tended to be loyal to the Jewish state). This means that the many benefits that flow from army service are not available to most Arabs. These benefits include access to a substantial array of educational, housing and civil service opportunities, as well as access to lifetime friendships and networks that begin with one's army experience.[3]

It is in no way anti-Semitic to criticize Israelis and the government of Israel for not doing more to correct these inequities. That the perpetuation of second-class status for any group of citizens, in any state, is a bad thing, inherently and irrespective of consequences, needs no argument. And, leaving aside the moral argument, it is plainly unwise, simply from a standpoint of political prudence, for Israel to allow a sense of exclusion and resentment to fester among its Arab citizens. But one should not imagine that foreign criticism is required to make such arguments heard in Israel. They are sustained politically within the country by the Israeli Left and by sections of the legal establishment in ways which are bringing about a steady erosion of disabilities affecting Israeli Arabs. Most recently, in 2002, the Israel Supreme Court struck down laws preventing Arabs from buying homes in certain areas formerly specified as Jewish. In delivering this decision, Chief Justice Aharon Barak wrote: "The principle of equality prohibits the state from distinguishing between its citizens on the basis of religion or nationality. . . . The principle also applies to the allocation of state land. . . . The Jewish character of the state does not allow Israel to discriminate between its citizens."[4]

No doubt much more needs to be done. But we are discussing, remember, the question of whether Israel is, or is not, an "apartheid state." It is not merely hard, but impossible, to imagine the South African Supreme Court, under the premiership of Hendrik Verwoerd, say, delivering an analogous decision, because to have done so would have struck at the root of the entire system of apartheid, which was nothing if not a system for separating the races by separating the areas they were permitted to occupy. Nor under apartheid were blacks allowed to attend white universities, to be treated in white hospitals, to enter white areas without a pass. None of the restrictions affect Arab, Druze, or other non-Jewish citizens of Israel. Moreover, and this is a point which needs to be repeated over and over again, so resolutely is it ignored in Western media, Israel stands virtually alone in the world, among nations facing an immediate military threat to their existence, in its willingness to countenance within her borders, neither interning nor expelling its members, a large population of people sharing the culture and religion of her declared enemies. Again the contrast with the "ethnic cleansing" carried out in the Balkan wars of the 1990s, and now sustained de facto by the various occupying powers because the expelled populations are by and large too terrified to risk returning to their homes, is glaring. But one is not confined to that example: one need only remember the treatment meted out to British residents or citizens of German culture or nationality at the outbreak of World War I, or to Japanese Americans at the outbreak of World War II, to see that Israel, far from having embraced apartheid or of the forms of racial intolerance so widely practiced outside her boundaries, is, admittedly within limits in part adumbrated above by Phyllis Chesler, not only a shining but a virtually unique instance of racial and religious tolerance and forgiveness.

It is not merely, however, that Israel is widely—and falsely—characterized on the Left as a "colonial," or "apartheid," or "Nazi" state. The journalists and public intellectuals who disseminate this line constantly speak as if Israel were the only state deserving to be discussed in such terms. The second of the two questions facing us in this section is, as we said earlier, whether this second claim is sustained by the facts. There is implicit in the claim a hidden agenda, which I shall get to in a moment, which renders it more explicable, if not more in tune with the facts, than it might otherwise seem to be. Taken at face value, however, it seems almost ludicrously unsustainable. Chinese colonialism in Tibet presents itself as an obvious, and massive, counterexample. Here we are dealing with colonialism in its purest and most straightforward form: an initial invasion leading to massive transfers of surplus population from the colonial power into the territory of the colonized nation. Other instances are provided by the efforts of the Islamist government of the Sudan to impose Islam on the Christian and Animist tribes of the south of the country, which led to a twenty-five-year civil war fought with almost inconceivable barbarity; the more recent support, by the same government, of Arab nomads against black African tribes in Darfur; the war against Russian colonial dominance in Chechnya; the genocide carried out, under French auspices, by the Hutu tribe against the Tsutsi people in Rwanda; the mass killings carried out by the Ba'ath Party under Saddam Hussein in Iraq, now being more fully documented as mass graves are uncovered and excavated, and, sadly, so on. All of these conflicts have resulted in suffering on a far greater scale than the conflict between Israel and its Arab adversaries. All of them are in part the outcome of actions of regimes which in varying degrees actually deserve the epithets "colonial," "apartheid," "Nazi." Yet the only one to which commentators and intellectuals associated with the Left have, over the years, devoted any serious attention, is the conflict in Chechnya, possibly because the others all involve non-European states, and thus fail to fit a worldview according to which all human suffering is the responsibility of the West. The allegedly exclusive and monocultural basis of Israeli society is sometimes claimed to follow merely from the existence of the "law of return" which allows any Jew to claim citizenship of Israel merely in virtue of being a Jew. It is alleged that this law is unique, and "racist." The first part of this claim is simply false.

Israel is far from the only country—and far from the only democracy—with comparable laws. Since the breakup of the Soviet Union, Russia has welcomed thousands of ethnic Russians from the former republics. Since 1945, millions of ethnic Germans have come to Germany from all over central and eastern Europe and the former Soviet Union. For almost fifty years, German immigration law even followed the official definition that "members of the German people are those who have committed themselves in their homelands to Germanness (Deutschtum), in as far as this commitment is confirmed by certain facts such as descent, language, upbringing or culture." Other states, too, have similar laws and similar connections with their diasporas.[5]

What about the second part of the claim? Are such laws, including Israel's, inherently "racist"? Only, one would suppose, if the law were designed to exclude from citizenship anyone not of the favored ethnic group, in order to produce a racially pure population. We have already discussed the issue of Israel's alleged, but fictional, racial purity. Here it is worth adding that in 1999 Israel offered citizenship and membership of Kibbutz Maagan Michael to more than a hundred Albanian refugees airlifted from Kosovo, having made similar offers to Muslim refugees from Bosnia, and to non-Jewish refugees from other conflicts, including a number of Vietnamese boat people. Given her readiness to offer asylum to non-Jewish refugees, in short, I do not see how Israel can be prevented from offering it, or for that matter morally accused for offering it, to Jewish ones. The double standard, and hence the anti–Semitism, implicit in such accusations is evident when we consider the law as it affects citizenship current in many Muslim countries. Jordan has a law of return which explicitly denies citizenship to Jews, including those who had formerly lived there for generations. Its laws specifically allow citizenship "to any person who is not Jewish" and who meets other criteria. Saudi Arabia explicitly bases eligibility for citizenship on religious affiliation. Iran under Islamist rule has persecuted non-Muslim minorities, most notably the Baha'i, the latter with a violence bearing comparison with the Holocaust. There is in all Muslim states from the beginning of Islamic rule a practice of reserving a special, second-class "Dhimmi" status for non-Muslim groups, including Christians and Jews, within the Muslim polity, and this treatment occurs widely today, although most of the states in question are now, of course, *judenrein*. Anti-Semitism is nothing if not the belief that "the Jews," that mythical polity whose agents are supposedly at work everywhere, are not only wicked per se, but wicked in ways unique to the Jews. Nothing could be more clearly demonstrative of the current penetration of the European, and to some extent the American left by anti-Semitism of the most childish kind, than the prodigies of self-deception necessary to sustain the belief in Israel, of all countries, not merely as a "racist" or "Nazi" state, which it is clearly not, but as *the uniquely glaring* instance of such a state, in a world which presents, as ours at present does, a largely unrelieved panorama of racism, genocide, religious bigotry, and political despotism of every shade and political hue.

It may be retorted that the characterization of Israel as an "apartheid" or "Nazi" state is founded, not on Israel's treatment of her non-Jewish citizens, but on her treatment of the Arab population of the Occupied Territories. These comprise the parts of Cisjordanian Palestine, together with the Gaza Strip, overrun by the Israel Defence Forces during the war of 1967. These territories were not annexed by Israel, but have been administered by Israel ever since. A very small minority in Israel would like to see the annexation of these lands and the expulsion or permanent occupation of their Arab population. Most Israelis have always wished to see these lands handed over to their Arab inhabitants in exchange for a permanent peace treaty, in the context of a two-state solution allowing self-determination to both the Jewish and the Arab populations. But, as we have seen, Israeli efforts in this direction have been consistently thwarted by the absence on the Palestinian side of any real will to negotiate seriously, an absence most recently demonstrated in the case of the Camp David–Taba peace negotiations of 2000–2001, which ended when Yasser Arafat, acting against strong urgings to the contrary from Prince Bandar of Saudi Arabia,[6] rejected the proposals put forward by the then Israeli prime minister Ehud Barak, and walked out of the peace negotiations without tabling any counterproposal, after which the Palestinian side returned to terrorism in the shape of the Second Intifada.

Since 1967 numbers of Jewish settlements have been set up on both the West Bank and the Gaza Strip, in defiance of opposition from the United Nations and the European Union, and intermittently from the United States; and the existence of these settlements is often cited by opponents of Israel as a major barrier to peace. Once again, as with the unequal treatment in certain respects of Israel's Christian and Muslim Arab citizens, we have in setting up these settlements a reasonable ground for criticism of Israel.

As one might expect, given the political and religious divisions in the Jewish community, vociferous criticism on this issue has not been slow in coming, from a multitude of Jewish voices, both inside and outside Israel.

There has been, and continues to be, a great deal of principled hostility on the part of the Israeli Left, still a force in Israeli politics despite the damage done to it, in terms both of influence and self-confidence, by the outcome of the Camp David–Taba negotiations, to the entire settlement program. Even Alan Dershowitz, of whom there can be no more vigorous and informed defender of Israel, confesses himself to be "personally opposed to the settlements."[7]

No doubt it can be powerfully argued that the existence of Jewish settlements in the Occupied Territories has exacerbated Arab hostility to Israel and done nothing to improve security within Israel proper. As with any other issue concerning the Middle East conflict, however, there is another side to the argument. On the one hand, there is the status of the territories as a bargaining counter. As recently as April 2003, Ariel Sharon repeated this offer, promising "painful concessions" with respect to the settlements in exchange for a peace treaty with the Palestinians. "I know that we will have to part with some of these places. As a Jew this agonizes me. But I have decided to make every effort to reach an accommodation."[8]

In the absence of such an accommodation for the past forty years, however, and for most of that time without the slightest prospect of one, the practical choice confronting Israel has been either to continue to conduct a military occupation of the West Bank and the Gaza, or to withdraw unilaterally from those territories. An argument for immediate withdrawal in 1968, as a pure *ex gratia* gesture of trust, could have been made at the time, and no doubt looks somewhat stronger in the light of subsequent history. But the military arguments against such an act are formidable. The West Bank cuts into the territory of Israel in such a way as to reduce the width of the country at its narrowest point to approximately eleven miles. The aquifers under the Judean Mountains are an important source of water both for the West Bank and Israel. Military control of the West Bank and the Gaza Strip is in all probability essential, both to control the flow of suicide bombers and to keep heavy military equipment at a reasonable distance from Israel's pre-1967 borders. No doubt also it can be argued from a military point of view that the existence of fortified settlements and the roads and other infrastructure serving them are a essential elements in the military control of the region by Israel, and thus, in the absence of a peace agreement, essential to Israel's security. At the time of writing, and despite those arguments, unilateral withdrawal, rather than any further exchange of "land for peace" seems the likeliest outcome, with the total withdrawal of Jewish settlements from the Gaza Strip being followed by the abandonment of a substantial number of settlements in the West Bank. Whether that will much improve the situation of the Palestinians, given the success of Hamas in the 2006 elections, remains to be seen.

The choices facing a nation in a continuing, unresolved state of war with very much more numerous and territorially extensive neighbors, who have demonstrated in the past, both in word and deed, their desire to wipe it off the map, are, in short, limited; and the punishment likely to be meted out by events, to those unwise and quixotic enough to make gestures of trust where there is no serious prospect of reciprocity, catastrophic and irrevocable. It is very easy for foreign observers living at peace to read moral lectures to such a nation, and easier still for international politico-legal organizations possessing neither the power nor the will to impose order on an increasingly chaotic world to pass paper motions condemning it. The seventeenth-century political philosopher Thomas Hobbes is famous for having held, for persuasive reasons, that it is the first duty of human beings to seek peace. But Hobbes also held, for essentially the same reasons, that in circumstances in which peace is unobtainable, because there is no power capable of both devising and enforcing a fair resolution of disputes between warring parties, it is the merest idleness and moral frivolity to imagine that one can accuse either party morally for doing what it can to protect itself. Law, Hobbes thought, rests on agreement, or "covenant." But for the benefits conferred by the rule of law to be more than air, agreements, once made, must be enforceable. "Covenants, without the Sword, are but Words, and of no strength to secure a man at all. Therefore, . . . if there be no Power erected, or not great enough for our security; every man will, and may lawfully rely on his own strength and art, for caution against all other men."[9]

If the United Nations, or the European Union, or for that matter the United States, were to take upon itself the duty of protecting in perpetuity Israel's frontiers, and with them the right of the historic Jewish community in Palestine to self-determination, and if the promise to do so were, improbably, accompanied with guarantees believable enough to make it worth more than the paper of the official document recording it, then indeed Israel might be asked with some color of moral plausibility to dismantle the settlements and withdraw from the territory it gained in 1967. But if that is a mere fantasy, as it is, then, it seems to me, following Hobbes, that Israel's leaders can only be guided, morally speaking, by the overriding duty of any democratically elected national government: to prevent harm to the people who elected them to power.

Over and beyond military necessity, there is a second ground for the existence of Jewish settlements in the Occupied Territories, namely, the desire, on the part of some Jews to establish and defend, in principle, the right of Jews to live in any part of the historic land of Israel. Before we dismiss this, in the spirit of the new anti-Semitism, as an atavistic Jewish *revanchisme* serving as a fig leaf for naked imperialism, let us look a little more closely at what we shall find ourselves supporting if we incautiously allow ourselves to be swayed by that particular line of political rhetoric. The entire dreadful situation in the Middle East has come about because, while some wise and far-sighted Arabs were at the turn of the past century prepared to welcome Jews as fellow Semites, and might well have been prepared to accept a self-governing Jewish political entity within some sort of federal or cantonal structure for Palestine conceived politically along the lines, say, of Switzerland, those Arab voices were at the time, and have ever since, been entirely drowned, deprived of political influence, by voices, European and fascist rather than Islamic in their inspiration, clamoring, in effect, not only for an altogether *judenrein* Palestine, but for a *judenrein* Islamic world. The latter aim, with the notable exception of Turkey, has been virtually achieved, at the expense of the three-quarters of a million Jews who have been forced, or found it prudent, to leave the area since World War II. The failure of a majority of nations in the Middle and Near East, since the fall of the Ottoman Empire, to free themselves from the political corruption and despotism, which have produced economic failure and social distress on a vast scale, has conveniently afforded a virtually free field of operation to numerous putatively "radical," but in fact profoundly reactionary, groups of a type increasingly marginalized in Europe since World War II. To condemn Israel, without qualification, in the familiar terms canvassed above, is in effect to accept, without the slightest pretense of critical scrutiny, the entirely specious claims of such groups to represent a respectable radical tradition and a serious hope for the future.

Alan Dershowitz, having expressed his willingness to see the tiny Jewish settlement in Hebron abandoned if that would help the peace process, observes that there is really no reason why Jews should not live in Hebron. And it is indeed hard to see how there could be, any more than reasons why they should not live in Finsbury Park, or Crown Heights, or any town in England. If, as seems at present almost inconceivable, some sort of federal or cantonal political arrangement were to be cobbled together west of the Jordan, then, just as it is at present contrary to Israeli law that Israeli Arabs should be excluded from Jewish neighborhoods, so the exclusion of Jews from Arab neighborhoods would have to be contrary to the laws of a future peaceful Israeli-Arab federation.

Jews in the West Bank and Gaza Strip settlements may or may not constitute, just by their presence, an obstacle to peace. Their argument is that, given the overwhelming climate of explicit, Nazi-flavored anti-Semitism which at present dominates in the Arab world, the abandonment of Jewish settlement in the Occupied Territories would be merely the prelude to further armed attempts to bring to an end Jewish settlement in Israel proper. They represent, rightly or wrongly, a strand of Jewish opinion which feels that a time has come in Israel for Jews to cease being pushed here and there around the world as the bloodthirsty whims of their enemies dictate. I do not think, given the history of the past century, including the history of the Muslim world—for it simply is not true that the Israeli-Arab conflict has roots only in the attitudes of Europeans toward Jews and none in the attitudes of people in the Middle East—that that strand of opinion either can be, or deserves to be, simply shouted down, especially by a moralizing "liberal-left" itself too deeply morally compromised to sit in judgment upon it.

In researching for this book I forced myself to read a great many published letters to the editors of a great many newspapers and magazines. The letter to the editor is a literary genre which deserves more attention from philosophers, critics, and textual analysts than it receives. It can at times offer a snapshot of a whole, structured attitude of mind, which, in its brevity and miniature dimensions, it illuminates more clearly and places under a sharper and more searching light than a more extended discourse could do. One letter that I came across, though I failed to make a note of its location at the time, was from a writer identifying himself as a young Jew on the Left. He wished to distance himself from the idea, which one felt might have been too much obtruded upon him by elders whom he took to be stick-in-the-mud reactionaries, that he should stick up for Israel because he was a Jew. The point he wished to make was that he himself felt no obligation to stick up for Israel on the grounds that it is a "Jewish state" because, so far as he could see, it is no such thing. The grounds he wished to adduce in favor of this conclusion were that very large numbers of the population of Israel are not "Jewish" in a religious sense, but secular people of Jewish ancestry, and that a smaller but still large number were not even Jewish, by ancestry in any other sense.

As an ad hominem argument aimed at an opponent for whom, in the face of rabbinic tradition, a Jewish state which allowed, as Israel does, a place to the non-Jew, could not be a *Jewish* state, or at an opponent for whom secular Jews do not count as Jews, the argument has force. As a general argument for not sticking up for the right of Israel to continue to exist, it has none, since it precisely undercuts the idea that Israel is a Jewish monoculture and, *therefore,* "racist," which provides the main motivation for the contrary view. I have no particular objection, myself, to monocultures, and I find the idea that any monoculture is inherently and de facto "racist" absurd. But the fact that Israel is by no means a Jewish monoculture, but a vibrant multicultural society committed to Western ideals of freedom and democracy under law, living under appalling circumstances of permanent armed attack from forces committed precisely to the extirpation of those ideals and their replacement by either a fascist or a theocratic monoculture, does give anyone who values those ideals, Jewish or non-Jewish, an excellent reason for supporting Israel's right to exist.

"DISMANTLING" ISRAEL

> A destroyer in function, a sadist with a pure heart, the anti-Semite is, in the very depths of his heart, a criminal. What he wishes, what he prepares, is the death of the Jew.
>
> —Sartre, Antisemite and Jew[10]

For many years the right of Israel to exist—a right, after all, arising from decisions concerning the partition of Palestine supported by United Nations resolutions—was scarcely contested in the West. Over the past few decades, however, a growing number of politicians and public intellectuals on the European and American Left have lined up to make statements denying Israel that right. Nor, to take the example of Britain, is the list confined to minor literary or media figures such as Tom Paulin, or to minor political ones such as the mayor of London, Ken Livingstone, or others of purely local influence, mainly backbenchers on the far left of the Labour Party, who provide regular political support to the pro-Palestinian lobby in Britain. Peter Hain, a very senior member of the Labour government under Tony Blair, a former Privy Councillor and foreign office minister, and presently Leader of the House of Commons, is quoted by Douglas Davis as follows:

> The present Zionist state . . . is by definition racist and will have to be dismantled. [The dismantling] . . . can be brought about in an orderly way by negotiation or it will be brought about by force. The choice lies with the Israelis. They can recognize now that the tide of history is against their brand of greedy oppression, or they can dig in and invite a bloodbath.[11]

What interests me about these remarks is, as usual, not so much the light they throw on Hain's opinions, as the light they throw on a state of mind shared by many, about which I shall have more to say in the final chapter of this book.

The reasons Hain gives for believing that "Israel will have to be dismantled" are both moral in character. Israel is (1) "by definition racist" and (2) guilty of "greedy oppression." Political invective can, of course, and usually does, proceed without the support of accurate reasoning; but the language in which these charges are put is quite unusually cloudy. It is unclear, for a start, what "definition" of the term "racist" Hain has in mind. Israel is in fact a racially mixed, multicultural representative democracy. I think the only thing that Hain can have in mind is that Israel is a "Jewish state": a state with a Jewish majority population, and *therefore* "racist." But if any state with a religious complexion shared by a majority of its citizens is "racist," there would be no nonracist states to be found in the world. Israel grants citizenship, as we have seen, to persons of any race or religious persuasion. Neighboring Jordan has a constitution which precisely denies citizenship to Jews. Unless one is missing something, that makes Jordan a racist state, Israel a non-racist one.

"Greedy oppression," likewise, is so vague a phrase that it is not easy to see what exactly Hain has in mind. Several possibilities suggest themselves. The charge might, on the one hand, suggest an account of the history of Israel according to which a ferocious Jewish army—rather than a ragged straggle of potential kibbutzniks purchasing marginal land from Arab landlords in a country with a large existing Jewish presence—marched, not into a desolate and barren wilderness but into a land not merely green and pleasant, but effectively *judenrein*, and took it by force from the inhabitants, whereupon the Jewish invaders proceeded to build themselves mansions on the proceeds of the sweated labor of the colonized peasantry. Who knows what putatively educated people believe, nowadays, about Israel, or about anything else; but I cannot think that, even in 2004, a leader of the British House of Commons believes an unhistorical farrago of nonsense as absurd as this. Let us try another tack. Maybe "greedy oppression" refers to the treatment of the population of the Occupied Territories. If so it surely cannot be irrelevant that Israel came into possession of those territories in the course of defending itself against a war of aggression, and that the task of dealing equitably with the Arab population has been rendered impossible by the refusal of the aggressors in that war to conclude a peace treaty, and by continued use of the territories to wage a war which has cost the lives of thousands of Israeli citizens. A third possibility: "greedy oppression"—inserting as a minor premise the common left-wing assumption that all differences in standard of living result from "greed" and are therefore a fortiori morally culpable—refers simply to the fact that Jewish Israelis enjoy a higher standard of living than most of the population of the Occupied Territories. To this—apart from the inherent absurdity of the inserted premise—it can be retorted that the standard of living of Arab Israelis is considerably higher than that of Arabs in the Occupied Territories, simply as a consequence of living in an advanced society. A fourth attempt: maybe Israel is guilty of "greedy oppression" in virtue simply of forming part of the advanced world, that world which Chomsky and others of the like persuasion love to paint as responsible, through its "corporate greed," "corporate racism," and the like, for all the ills of the world. I think, in fact, that the latter is probably the dominant chord which Hain is attempting to strike with his choice of words, with the other three possibilities we have just canvassed forming, as it were, the harmonizing chords of the diapason. But, then, if that is the drift of the remark, one would want to know why *Israel* in particular, deserves to be "dismantled," and not, say, France, or Germany, or even that great nation in whose government Hain himself has come to occupy such remarkable eminence?

The stated moral basis of Hain's demand for the "dismantling" of a country posing no threat to his adopted nation appears, in short, to be paper-thin, and the "moral high ground" on which, like so many others, he imagines himself to be standing, to be crumbling under his feet into an abyss of ideological nonsense, bad history, and special pleading. What about the demand itself? What could be meant, what could Hain understand, by the term "dismantling"? And if Israel "will have to be dismantled," who is envisaged as doing the "dismantling"? Hain says that the process can be "brought about in an orderly way, by negotiation" but that if the Israelis fail to recognize that "the tide of history is against their brand of greedy oppression" and "dig in," they will "invite a bloodbath." The implications, or presuppositions, of these remarks are interesting. It is implied, rather than asserted, that Israel, as a state, has proved in the past chronically unready to resolve conflicts with its neighbors by negotiation. As we have seen, this, whether asserted or merely implied, is false. It is further implied that Israel was more likely than not, at the time these remarks were uttered (1999), to "dig in its heels" against negotiations with the Palestinians. As is well known, a year later, at the time of the Camp David Accords, the Israeli government of Ehud Barak offered withdrawal from most of the West Bank and Gaza Strip, and the creation of a Palestinian State: the negotiations failed because Yasser Arafat walked away from them.

I think it is entirely possible that Hain, along with much of the Left, would reply that the Camp David negotiations were a sham, and that they were a sham because what the required "negotiations" have to address is not, or no longer, the desire of the Palestinians for a state of their own, but, precisely, the "dismantling" of Israel. On that reading of Hain's remarks, and for that matter a great deal of recent anti-Israel polemic originating on the left, what has to be dismantled is Israel *as a Jewish state.* What should be demanded by "progressive" opinion, on this view, is the so-called one-state solution advanced, among others by Noam Chomsky and the late Edward Said: that is to say, the replacement of Israel west of the Jordan by a single political entity, which would inevitably possess a Muslim and Arab majority population. It was perhaps this, then, that Hain had in mind when he said that Israel would have to be "dismantled," and indeed, that that must be the ultimate drift of his admittedly cloudy remarks is evident from the fact that any solution which left a self-governing majority-Jewish state in existence west of the Jordan could hardly be said to have "dismantled Israel." It is, then, after all, *the right of the Jews, considered as one people among others, to national autonomy,* the right defended by the Peel Commission and sanctioned in 1947 by the United Nations, that is presently at issue for sections of the liberal Left.

Hain's claim then, must, on that not unreasonable interpretation, be that it is the final ceding of Jewish political autonomy to the Arabs which can be "brought about in an orderly way by negotiation." A "bloodbath" is likely only if Israel "digs in its heels" and wickedly compounds its "racism," its "brand of greedy oppression," by attempting, in the face of the moral disapproval of Hain and his friends, to maintain the right to self-government of its mainly Jewish population. The implication of Hain's remarks is, further, that if Israel chooses the second course, the resulting "bloodbath" will be entirely her own fault: Hain, his political friends, and all those who participate in forming progressive opinion will find themselves, in other words, should those regrettable circumstances arise, with perfectly clean hands and a perfect right to say "we told you so."

Leaving aside the moral one-sidedness of this, in the shape of its blank failure to attach any moral weight whatsoever to considerations of national autonomy per se, is it true? Is it remotely likely, that is, that the "dismantling" of Israel as a Jewish state could be brought about "in an orderly way by negotiation"? It really does demand extraordinary reserves of credulity to believe, as Chomsky and others claim to do, that the ending of the right of the Jewish population of Israel to self-government and self-defense, as a distinct people with its own state, however it was brought about, would not lead immediately to attacks on the Jewish civilian population west of the Jordan conducted with a degree of ferocity amounting to a second Holocaust.

Consider the remarks in 1947 of Azzam Pasha, secretary general of the Arab League, quoted in Chapter 6, "This will be a war of extermination and a momentous massacre." Consider the extensive history of massacres of Jews by Arabs in the area, long antedating the foundation of Israel; the flood of anti-Semitic calumny presently inundating the entire Muslim world; the numbers of "radical" Sheikhs teaching their followers that it is a religious duty to kill all Jews, and the depressing increase of anti-Semitic attacks in Europe over the past decade which has occurred as a result. Lastly, consider the multitude of small and great persecutions which have led over the past half century to the vast majority of oriental Jews fleeing to Israel, Europe, or America.

One cannot reflect long, it seems to me, upon these depressing facts, without being forced to conclude that the idea of a "one-state" solution leading to justice, peace, and prosperity for all is a potentially murderous ideological fantasy.

Unlike the politician Peter Hain, the journalist and novelist Linda Grant, in a remarkably honest and poignant account of a journey to Israel published in the London *Guardian* earlier this year, is clear-sighted enough to grasp, to her own expressed dismay, the full ghastliness of the situation and in the process to prick this particular *bien-pensant* political bubble. She concludes:

> After four months in Israel, and hundreds of hours of conversations, I found not a scrap of evidence that Jewish Israelis will ever agree to a peace deal that will result in them becoming, within a generation or two, a minority dependent on the good-will of a Palestinian majority in a re- gion without democracy or any real human rights. As the novelist David Grossman told me, "There is not enough reassurance in the galaxy for Israelis." In an interview with Ha'aretz in August 2000, Edward Said was asked what would happen to the Jews if they became a minority in a sin- gle state: "It worries me a great deal," he said, "The question of what is to be the fate of the Jews is very difficult for me. I really don't know. It worries me."[12]

Clearly, given the history of the twentieth century, East and West, it should have worried Said. But did it, really, seriously? Are these words not gliding over an unvoiced thought? And is not that thought a double one— the same thought, in fact, that lurks, unvoiced, beneath Hain's equally smooth words to an Israeli interviewer: that the fate of the Jews will be a terrible one—and that the Jews will thoroughly deserve it.

We are getting very close now, I think, to the heart of the frustrated sense common among Jews that a great part of the criticism of Israel heard from many Western public intellectuals, and from the Western press and electronic media is, in some profound way not easy to define or formulate, seriously, even murderously, anti–Semitic. That impression arises in part, it seems to me, from two very widespread tendencies in left-wing commentary.

The first is the tendency for commentators to do everything in their power to smuggle out of sight the most glaringly obvious feature of the situation; that no political nostrum, no political ideology or narrative, can lead to an equitable and peaceful settlement in the Middle East, which fails to take account of the special historical and political circumstances of the Jews. The other is the closely related tendency, when backs are against the wall on this issue, to take refuge in the pretense that those circumstances are, if not simply invented by the Jews as a sob story to cover their dastardly behavior, in some way the fault of the Jews themselves. One wearisomely traditional form taken by anti–Semitism is the refusal to admit its own existence. Another, still more wearisome, tradition is to admit its existence, but to insist that the fact that it exists is the fault of the Jews themselves.

Both these saving delusions can be detected threading their way through the Derridian margins of the remarks by Hain and Said which we have been considering. The first shows itself in Hain's cheerfully Panglossian belief that peace, and not a second Holocaust, would follow the "negotiated" abandonment of Jewish self-government in Israel. The second lurks beneath the politely unforthcoming tone of Said's "The question of what is to be the fate of the Jews . . . is difficult for me . . . I worry about it." Said, after all, was a writer and critic, with a writer's sense of the measure and weight of words. The word "fate" is a strange and ominous one. Said might, after all, in answer to the question, have addressed the problem of how to secure minority rights in a viable single state.

He did no such thing. Instead he took the question to concern, not *the rights* of the Jews, but *the fate* of the Jews. And so interpreting it, he answered, in effect, that it was a question he found "difficult," which "worried him." We "worry," in that sort of way, over questions which are out of our hands. And why should that particular question, the question of Jewish minority rights, be out of the hands of people like Said, who, had he lived, would, in the unlikely event of such a state coming to pass, very likely have found himself among its chief sponsors and architects?

It is difficult to envisage any answer save the one suggested by the whole stance of the current pro-Palestinian lobby on the Left, with its easy equation of Zionism with Nazism, its dominant presumption that atrocities lose the character of atrocities when directed against Israeli Jews, that actions taken in self-defense against terrorism are themselves terrorism, and all the rest of it. There would be no use in discussing Jewish minority rights, Said is implicitly suggesting, because at that point the Jews, a nation accursed among the nations of the earth, would by their own actions have placed themselves beyond salvation.

Peter Hain is if anything more explicit about the nature of the fate awaiting Jewish Israelis if they fail to surrender meekly, by "negotiation," the political autonomy demanded by the Peel Commission, conferred in 1947 by the United Nations, and defended by the courage and military prowess of Israelis against repeated attempts to deprive them of it by armed aggression. Such conduct will "invite a bloodbath." Again there is the suggestion, delicately introduced by Hain's choice of the word "invite," that responsibility for a bloodbath in those circumstances would lie entirely with the Jewish population of Israel. Israelis might reasonably retort that in that case a bloodbath awaits them either way, whether they retain political sovereignty or lose it.

It would be quite reasonable, I think, to take Hain's evident failure to pick up on the possibility of that obvious retort as reflecting simple anti-Semitism on his part. But I think that would be unfair to Hain, and unfair also to the ideological complexities of the situation. As one can discover from his website, Hain is by birth and family connection a South African. His parents were deeply involved in the political opposition to apartheid; so deeply that they found it necessary to leave South Africa, to which they were prevented from returning by banning orders. The young Hain was brought up in Britain, where he remained a staunch foe of apartheid, making a name for himself in the 1970s by digging up cricket pitches with the aim of preventing a British cricket tour to South Africa.

The political goal for which Hain and his family fought was the one finally achieved a decade ago by Nelson Mandela and F. W. de Klerk: full democracy across racial boundaries on the basis of one man, one vote. And, after all, *that* surrender of power has not led to "a bloodbath." The white population of South Africa remains four million, and though they have suffered from increasing levels of crime, and though there have been disturbing signs of Mugabeism crossing the border with Zimbabwe, there has been neither mass killing nor mass expulsion of whites. No doubt this is because black and white South Africans have much in common and, despite everything, very largely get on with one another. A South African anthropologist I met a few years ago over dinner in All Souls College, Oxford, told me how, when her car broke down in a rather dangerous black area, she was picked up and taken to safety by a carload of black gangsters, all wearing gold rings and dark glasses, who were genuinely shocked at her situation and gave her a sound talking to for being such a silly girl as to drive through the area in the first place.

So far so good, then, at least for the time being. And I can well believe that this is the kind of future which the current leader of the House of Commons imagines can be envisaged for an Israel under majority Arab control. To understand both the internal logic and the illusory character of the apparent anti-Semitism of Hain's remarks to the *Jerusalem Post*, in short, one need grasp only one thing: Hain sees no important political or moral difference between the case of Israel and the case of South Africa. He takes account neither of the case for seeing the situation, not in terms of colonialism, but in terms of Wilsonian self-determination, nor of the peculiar, and quite exceptionally virulent, character of anti-Semitic hatred as opposed to the run of intercommunal hatreds we call "racial," nor of the inherent strangeness of a self-confessed "libertarian socialist" advocating the surrender, to regimes whose leaders could hardly by any stretch of the imagination be considered either socialist or libertarian, of the freedom and autonomy of a nation which those very regimes have repeatedly attempted to extinguish by armed aggression. Very likely he cannot focus on such matters. For him South Africa is an infallible moral and political template, a simple blueprint for understanding all situations of conflict between people of different "races," even when, as in Israel, the supposed "races" are not, except to the confirmed anti-Semite, all that different.

I have talked at odd moments over the past half century to a fair number of anti-Semites, some passionate, some covert, and I would give reasonable odds that Hain himself is not one. What gives his remarks an appearance of anti-Semitism is something almost worse in its potential consequences than anti-Semitism itself: his willingness to ignore crucial features of the Middle East conflict in the interests of fitting it to the procrustean bed of a reach-me-down political analogy. Of this we shall have more to say in the final chapter.

NOTES

1. The flag of the Croatian Fascist Party which allied itself with the Nazi occupying forces during World War II.

2. "Where Life's a Struggle for a Footballer's Wife," London *Daily Telegraph*, September 30, 2004, p. 19.

3. Phyllis Chesler, *The New Anti-Semitism: The Current Crisis and What We Must Do About It* (New York: Jossey-Bass, 2003), pp. 165–66.

4. Cited in Alan Dershowitz, *The Case for Israel* (Hoboken, N.J.: John Wiley, 2003), p. 157.

5. Ibid., p. 156.

6. *The New Yorker*, March 24, 2003, p. 55.

7. Dershowitz, *The Case for Israel*, p. 176.

8. Cited in James Bennet, "Mideast Sides Maneuver, Expecting Peace Effort," *New York Times*, April 14, 2003.

9. Thomas Hobbes, *Leviathan*, part II, chapter 17, para. 2.

10. Cited in Paul Iganski and Barry Kosmin, *A New Anti-Semitism? Debating Judeophobia in the 21st Century* (London: Profile Books, 2003), p. 140, from an article by Douglas Davis, "Peter Hain, Man of Principle," *Jerusalem Post*, August 6, 1999.

11. Jean-Paul Sartre, *Antisemite and Jew* (New York: Grove Press, 1962).

12. Linda Grant, "Inside the Bubble," *Guardian*, April 8, 2004, G2, p. 4.

8

WHO IS TO BLAME?

POLITICS AND MORALITY

Le public ne pardonne plus aujourd'hui que l'auteur, après
l'action qu'il peint, ne se déclare pas pour ou contre.

—André Gide, preface to L'immoraliste[1]

For reasons which I shall try to unravel in the concluding part of this
book, we live in an age in which the Left in Europe and America has
largely abandoned the territory of economics and history for that of morality. That shift goes with an altogether new dependence of "progressive" politics on the notion of guilt. Marxists of an older breed would have laughed,
at least officially, at the idea that capitalism should be replaced because it was
a system run by morally wicked men, as distinct from a class order historically progressive in its time with respect to feudalism, but historically retro-
gressive with respect to the classless order which must succeed it according
to the laws of historical determinism. The New Left, in contrast, has shown
itself as profligate in moral condemnation and accusation as any noncon-
formist preacher.

   Two of the more evident characteristics of the new moralism in radical politics are, on the one hand, a tendency to see things, morally, in black
and white; to divide humanity without reminder between the threatened
community of the Saints, who can do no wrong, and the rampaging hordes
of the Reprobate, who can do little else; and, on the other, a tendency to
imagine that the concepts of guilt and moral responsibility can be intelligibly applied to any body of human beings, however socially, intellectually, and
morally amorphous, which some faction of the Left, for reasons internal to
one of the many increasingly private and sectarian representations of reality

151

current from moment to moment in left-wing circles, happens to have assigned to the category of the Reprobate.

One of the things, indeed, which led me to attempt writing this book was rising exasperation at the unending representation, by people in the British media of the type of Orla Guerin at the BBC, or Robert Fisk at the London *Independent,* or by such stalwarts of the literary and academic left as Tom Paulin, of Jewish Israelis as, one and all, Guilty Men, simply in virtue of being Israeli and Jewish. The tendency has reached grotesque and nationally shaming depths of absurdity and low comedy on several occasions in Britain over the past few years. There was, for example, the case of Andrew Wilkie, the Nuffield Professor of Pathology at Oxford, who wrote to Amit Duvshani, an Israeli Ph.D. student hoping to pursue research in Professor Wilkie's laboratory, to inform him that that he, the writer, speaking *in propria persona,* had "a huge problem" with Israel, and would not consider offering a place to anyone who had served in the Israeli Defence Forces,[2] as if a man could place himself beyond the moral pale simply by serving his country, or a university tutor be allowed by any decent society to take nakedly political decisions concerning the acceptability or otherwise of candidates. Again there was the dismissal, by Mona Baker of the Centre for Translation and Intercultural Studies of the University of Manchester Institute of Science and Technology, of two Israeli members of the international advisory boards of two academic journals she edits, both of whom happened to be pillars of the Israeli Left, accustomed to working tirelessly for reconciliation between Arabs and Jews.[3] Nor are these by any means the only instances of this tendency.

These attitudes are in line with the tendency to see things in black and white; a tendency particularly in evidence with respect to Israel. Israel is daily represented by large parts of the British media, particularly television, as a nation incapable of acting otherwise than abominably, and as the nation uniquely and entirely responsible for the existence of conflict in the Middle East. The Palestinians, by contrast, are represented as a people *wholly without responsibility for the situation in which they find themselves,* and therefore as a people whose leaders can, literally, do no wrong, make no mistakes.

This is doubtless the sort of thing Jonathan Sacks, the chief rabbi of the United Hebrew Congregations of Great Britain, has in mind in a passage which deserves to be quoted at length:

> What, then, is anti-Semitism? This is so emotive a subject that it is best approached by way of a thought experiment. Let us suppose that someone claimed to have discovered a phenomenon he called anti-Kiwism, a patho-

logical hatred of New Zealanders. What would have to be the case to convince us that he was right and that there really is such a phenomenon?

The fact that the government of New Zealand is criticized? Clearly not. The publicly voiced claim that New Zealand has no right to exist? Perhaps. The fact that in the past twelve months—February 2001 to February 2002—there have been 7,732 terrorist attacks on New Zealand's citizens, almost one every hour of every day for 365 days. Maybe. But in truth, not yet. What all these facts would amount to would simply be a tragedy, a human tragedy, a political tragedy, but not yet *anti-Kiwism*.

Now, though, suppose that, at a United Nations Conference against racism in Durban, New Zealand, because of its treatment of Maoris, is, alone among the nations of the world, singled out and accused of apartheid, ethnic cleansing and crimes against humanity; and that those making those charges carry posters inspired by *Der Sturmer*, the paper published in Nazi Germany. Suppose that there are calls to murder all those with New Zealand loyalties, even though they were born elsewhere and live elsewhere. Suppose, on al-Jazeera television earlier this month, an official spokesman of the government of Saudi Arabia said: "The media of America is in the hands of New Zealanders." And then adds: "I am surprised that the Christian United States allows the brothers of apes and pigs [his way of describing New Zealanders] to corrupt it. The new Zealanders are the most despicable people who walk the land and are the worms of the entire world."

Suppose that New Zealand was accused of inventing AIDS to decimate the population of Africa. Suppose that, simultaneously, New Zealand was held, not merely to control the United States, but also to have engineered the attack on the World Trade Center and the Pentagon on September 11, 2001. Suppose that this claim—that it was not Osama bin Laden, but New Zealand who carried out this outrage—was not confined to fringe groups but was believed by 48 per cent of people questioned in Pakistan, 71 per cent of the population holding it to be at least possible.

Suppose Arab radio and television over the past year had broadcast a thirty-part series dedicated to proving the truth of *The Protocols of the Elders of New Zealand*; that Kuwaiti television had shown a satire in which the Prime Minister of New Zealand was shown drinking the blood of Maori children, or that the current Syrian defence minister had written a book to prove that this was true.

Suppose you discovered that in country after country, The Protocols of the Elders of New Zealand, along with Hitler's Mein Kampf, were best-sellers, and that the claim was commonplace that New Zealand is a satanic force, the embodiment of evil, against which a holy war must be fought. Then, I think, you might be reasonably convinced that there was such a thing as anti-Kiwism about, that it was alive and well, disturbing and dangerous.[4]

The British media seldom, of course, go to the lengths of the Arab sources quoted by Sacks. The unspoken barriers to overt anti-Semitism in public discourse in Britain, deriving from World War II, remain largely in place, though the episode of the *New Statesman* cover reveals how paper-thin, in some quarters, they have grown. But by representing Israel as carrying total responsibility, and the entire guilt, for the existence of the "Middle East Problem," and the Palestinians and the wider Arab world none at all, they certainly do convey with some success, to very large numbers of people whose sources of information, as is common in Britain, do not extend much beyond television and the resources of a single daily newspaper, whose coverage may be equally slanted, the impression that Israel, when it comes down to it, is indeed "a satanic force" and "the embodiment of evil."

THE LIMITS OF RESPONSIBILITY

For all these reasons it may be useful to summarize the results of the preceding chapters by addressing the questions: Who is to blame, who bears the responsibility, and who the guilt, for the current situation in the Middle East: Israel or the Arabs? The Jews, or the Muslims? America? American corporate interests? Or who, precisely?

I have chosen that way of stating the question because I have the impression that those are the terms in which it in fact presents itself to a great many people. There seems to me, however, to be serious flaws, not to say serious absurdities, in the thinking of anyone seriously tempted to put the issue in that way. One problem, which I have already touched on briefly, concerns the difficulty of intelligibly deploying such central moral concepts as *guilt* and *responsibility* to characterize partly culturally individuated entities such as nations, and even more so such wholly culturally individualized, and thus even more politically amorphous groups such as "the Jews" or "the Muslims," not to mention the cloudier constructions of political conspiracy theory, such as "American corporate interests." A second problem arises from the implied presumption that responsibility, and guilt, in a matter as complex as the Israeli–Arab conflict can be apportioned wholly to one side or the other: that there is, or could be, a single culprit, either "Israel" (or "the Jews") or "the Arabs." This is the black-and-white mindset character-istic of the liberal-left climate of opinion to which I referred earlier. A third difficulty concerns the presumption that the existence of such "problems" as the one presently affecting Israel and its neighbors is the sort of thing it makes sense to discuss in terms of moral responsibility at all. One might as well ask whose "fault" the Thirty Years' War or the collapse of feudalism was. Causally speaking, such vast fissures in human affairs are grossly, and manifestly, overdetermined. They arise from the coming together of many factors. Many of these are human acts, performed by responsible agents, but by agents possessing limited foresight, and in any case acting independently of one another in ways which permit none of them to acquire a clear grasp of the developing situation produced by, among other things, their various responses to specific challenges, until that situation is upon them. At the time of acting, it may well be, the majority of the agents concerned could deploy sound moral reasons for acting as they did. Further, they may have acted in ways actually determined by those reasons. It is only in retrospect that we, or some of us, armed with the power of hindsight, find ourselves wanting to say that they acted wrongly. That, of course, is a privilege which the present always enjoys over the past, but equally it is one which any given generation, reflecting upon the brevity of its enjoyment of its present van-tage point and upon its own nakedness before the judgment of those yet to come, would do well to employ sparingly.

First, then, the question of whether there can be such a thing as—whether it is intelligible to speak of—a *guilty nation*: Israel, for instance. The trouble with such talk, to a philosopher like myself, is that the notion of guilt, with its correlative of (moral) "fault," is conceptually "at home," "finds a foothold," to employ a phrase of Wittgenstein's, primarily in judgments con-cerning the conduct of individuals. In ordinary discourse, and leaving out a good many complexities of interest to philosophers and jurists, an individual who performs an act which, in its consequences, contravenes the law or harms another in some way not proscribed by law, is guilty of that contravention or of causing that harm if he or she planned the act, did so to secure certain per-sonal advantages arising from it, and saw it as no obstacle to securing those advantages in that way or that the act would harm others or contravene the law. One can extend the notions of guilt and responsibility to corporate per-sons, provided the corporation concerned disposes of formal means of deter-mining collective responsibility for corporate decisions, as does the board of directors of a limited company, or a governmental body such as the Cabinet. A nation, however, even a nation governed by representative democracy, is not, pace a certain tradition in classical political theory including both Hobbes and Rousseau, in that sense a corporate person. The machinery of representative democracy is designed to legitimate the exercise of power by a duly elected authority, not to transmit responsibility for each and every act of that authority to each and every citizen of the nation. Even more is that conclusion true, as I suggested earlier, of collectivities such as "the Jews," or "the Arabs," or "the Muslims," whose principle of individuation is cultural or religious, rather than political.

I conclude that talk of *nations*, let alone diffuse religio-cultural communities, as subjects of guilt or moral responsibility, is void of sense, unless a speaker can give some further explanation, not contained in the ordinary meanings of guilty or responsibility what he or she means by it. Israel is not, in fact, the only nation to be spoken of in this way: Germany is another. In World War II German citizens did many things upon which "guilty" would surely be an appropriate verdict in any court of law responsive to the German legal tradition as that existed before the Nazi era. But was *Germany* guilty? Was Germany a *guilty nation*, and every German citizen who remained loyal to his country throughout World War II a *guilty person* simply in virtue of that loyalty? I confess I do not know, and my agnosticism is a function, not of some special liking for Germans—though I have nothing whatsoever against liking Germans—but of my failure to grasp what is supposed to be *meant by* these claims, what their legal or moral implications are supposed to be, how one is supposed to set about determining their truth or falsity, and so on. Nevertheless, the idea that Germany under Nazi rule was not merely a calamitously misled and suicidal nation, in the grip of a form of murderous political hysteria which would subject it to long-lasting mutilations, not least by the loss of virtually all its Jews, but also a guilty nation, is well entrenched in the popular and not-so-popular mind and serves to give the concept of the "guilty nation" a certain fictive currency. It is, of course, because it does, and because it is almost the only thing that does, and because the notion of national guilt is so attractive to political hysterics that such efforts are made on the farther reaches of the left to accustom the easily led to an equation of the Magen David with the swastika.

So far as it makes sense to ascribe responsibility for acts bearing upon the origins of the present conflict between Israel and its Arab neighbors to assignable individuals or corporate persons, and so far as it makes sense to speak of such responsibilities entailing guilt upon those responsible for them, is it the case, as media reporting is so frequently inclined to suggest or imply, that all the guilt for the creation of the present conflict lies with Israeli, or with Jewish individuals, or corporate persons, and none with Arab or Palestinian ones? And is the "guilt," in each case—Arab or Palestinian as much as Israeli or Jewish—as implausibly unrelieved as is implied by so many commentators of the Chomsky–Fisk–Pilger persuasion, or for that matter by some of their equally apocalyptic right-wing counterparts? Are there no mitigating circumstances—for Arabs, certainly; but also for Jews, and not *solely* for Arabs, as so much pro-Palestinian coverage is sedulously structured to suggest? The best way to address these questions is no doubt to review some of the main stages in the development of the present situation.

Were, for instance, the early Zionists collectively guilty, or at least culpably self-deceived, as non-Zionist Jews occasionally suggest, in adopting the slogan "a land without a people for a people without a land"? It is not clear. Certainly, the land *was* peopled at the time, but very thinly, and by no means exclusively, as we saw earlier, by Muslim Arabs: substantial numbers of Arab, Sephardic, and Ashkenazic Jews, as well as many Christian Arabs, were also present. The Zionist settlers were, moreover, for the most part purchasing poor or marginal land from Arab landlords who were more than willing to sell.

Then were "the Jews," in the shape of the early settlers who gave body to the Zionist program, guilty *as individuals* of emigrating to settle on "somebody else's" land? Rather less so, one would have thought, than the American settlers who conquered Native American tribesmen or the Tasmanian settlers who hunted the indigenous aboriginals to extinction in their own forests.[5] There were no white Americans on the North American continent before 1500, and no Europeans in Tasmania before 1800, but there had always, immemorially, been Jews in Palestine, and always, immemorially, Jews fleeing from European persecutions into the lands of the Seljuk and Ottoman Empires.

Were, then, the Great Powers after World War I, collectively guilty in admitting the principle that a national home for the Jews should be sought in Palestine? The Ottoman Empire had ended on the losing side in that war. Its remaining territory was now restricted to Asia Minor. Some sort of political future had to be sought for the remaining lands of the former empire. How could that be done except by dividing up those lands between their very diverse inhabitants to form self-governing entities, in a way calculated to minimize intercommunal conflict? And why should not that process include the Jews, as one reasonably coherent and reasonably localized community among others in the area? Must it not, indeed, include the Jews, given the already existing history of persecution, the prevalence of the kind of Arab anti-Semitism which expressed itself in the removal of Jews from the newly created Hashemite kingdom of Jordan with the agreed prohibition of Jewish resettlement and the probability of further Arab persecution of Jews if the latter were not afforded some form of self-government within a limited enclave? The same considerations motivated the Peel Commission in 1937 and the United Nations a decade later.

Is one, then, to brand "the Arabs" or "the Muslims" as morally guilty for steadfastly resisting the idea of a self-governing Jewish enclave, however small, on former Ottoman soil? Are "the Arabs" or "the Muslims," as distinct from the actual, individual, or corporate, circulators of anti-Semitic libels, guilty of anti-Semitism? Certainly a great many Israelis and Diaspora Jews, and a lot of non-Jews besides, see it that way, and after so much hatred and so many deaths, not to mention the current tide of anti-Semitic propaganda on the Arab media and on Arab websites, that is hardly surprising. However, it is no more rational than anti-Semitism itself. The expression "the Arabs" is not—any more than are "the Jews" or "the Israelis" when the latter is understood as a collective noun signifying, not the Israeli government of the moment, but all Jewish citizens of Israel—the name of a corporate person; hence, not the name of a possible bearer of either responsibility or guilt. Not all Arabs resisted the idea of a self-governing Jewish enclave on part of the ruins of the Ottoman Empire. By no means all do now, although, as the frequent killings of Palestinian "collaborators" by armed groups testify, it has become unsafe to promote, or even to argue for, cooperation and peace with Israel within many parts of the Arab world. The tragedy for the forces of moderation and reconciliation within Arab society lies in the fact that Arab countries, since the collapse of the Ottoman Empire, have for the most part been ruled either by highly conservative monarchies or by regimes, such as the Ba'ath Party in Iraq and Syria, drawing their inspiration from European totalitarianism of both Left and Right; regimes conducted with a gloss of "socialism," but effectively operating as machines for advancing the interests of a ruling group surrounding a despot. Regimes of both types have proved even more brutal and bloodthirsty in dealing with internal Muslim opposition, whether it has come from Arabs, such as the Palestinians, from other ethnic groups such as Kurds or Iranians, or from religious groups within Islam, such as the Shia in Iraq, than they have in fighting the Jews. The Palestinians themselves have more or less fragmented into a chaos of armed groups, some Islamist, some Marxist, all of them committed to mass murder and to subverting children and young people to be used as living bombs. Israel, having been criticized for decades for occupying the West Bank and Gaza Strip, recently found itself facing a new wave of criticism on the basis of fears that if, as has now come to pass, it were to withdraw from Gaza, the Gaza Strip would be engulfed by internecine civil war between competing armed groups, a development which has indeed, at time of writing, taken place. Such are the forces into whose hands "left-liberals" of the stamp of Peter Hain, and many others on the European Left, wish to see democratic, multicultural Israel delivered. But, granting all that, it is still absurd to suggest that *blame* in any clear sense of the term, attaches to Islam, or to "the Arabs," for these developments. It can be argued, to be sure, that there are features endemic to Arab society which smoothed the way for totalitarian regimes to rise to power. But surely the same can be said of European societies, which were, after all, the original inventors and breeding grounds of totalitarianism, and which were soon in a position to learn, the hard way, over many decades, how very difficult it is to dislodge a totalitarian regime, once installed. Men are very prone, however, to forget or ignore the lessons of experience, however hard. So it is not uncommon to hear the suggestion that little better than totalitarianism and self-defeating violence is to be expected of Arab society, or of Islam, given the "backwardness" and manifest inferiority of both to European cultures imbued with the values of the Enlightenment. This is simple racism and the exact parallel of much anti-Semitic nonsense. What makes it particularly poisonous in the present context is that it is chiefly Arabs, both Christian and Muslim, who have suffered and continue to suffer from the dominance of Arab totalitarianism and from the rise of an Arab anti-Semitism based upon such European models as the *Protocols*. Had the welcome extended, as fellow Semites, to the early Zionist settlers by Emir Feisal in 1919, struck an answering chord in the heart of the Arab world, we would now be in a very different situation. There are, after all, solid historical bases for an alliance between the Arabs and the Jews of Palestine, in the common interests of both, if one were to wish to promote such a thing. In 1099 and 1100 Jews fought beside Arabs in the defense of Jerusalem and Haifa by the Crusaders and were slaughtered beside them in the sack of Jerusalem. Had Jews fleeing from persecution elsewhere been welcomed by the Arabs, the Arab world would have profited, as America did during World War II, by a large influx of highly educated and technically qualified citizens whose work would have immensely augmented both the economic and the political power of the Arab world against Europe and America. Moreover, if Jews had been welcomed and free to live in peace, and without episodes such as the Hebron massacres of 1929, which undoubtedly played a part in determining the stance adopted by the Peel Commission, throughout the Arab world, it is very likely that Zionism, which was never a popular, let alone a majority position among Jews until World War II, would not have succeeded in marshalling support for a self-governing Jewish enclave in Palestine, with the result that Israel would never have existed.

To return to the actual world, in which Israel was founded and did survive Arab attempts to destroy her by force of arms, were the "Brooklyn Jews" of Tom Paulin's murderous fulminations, the numerous Diaspora Jews, Russian, Lithuanian, American, many of them fleeing persecution, who have settled in Israel since the foundation of the state, "guilty" for so doing? I do not see how, if a national territory exists, persons of that nation can be morally at fault for choosing to take up residence there. One can reply that they are, if the territory in question should not have existed in the first place; but that move simply begs the question, by returning us to an earlier point in the discussion and to arguments which we have already found reason to reject, not least as founded not on any generally agreed principle of law or morals, but wholly upon a sectarian political ideology.

Again, is the Israeli government "guilty" for adopting the methods it adopts in its resistance against terrorism? Here again, as with the treatment of Israeli Arabs, one is getting into an area in which rational debate, which may be critical of one or another Israeli policy without being in any way anti-Semitic, is not only possible, but conducted with some ferocity within Israel itself. Media reportage outside Israel, however, particularly in the European left-of-center press is apt, here as elsewhere, to be selective in its presentation of context in ways which prejudge the argument, not against a particular policy, but against Israel per se. An example is the construction of the so-called security fence to protect Israel proper from terrorist attacks originating in the West Bank. One can argue that the hardships and losses which this project imposes on Palestinian farms and communities situated close to the fence create grievances on the Arab side which damage the peace process, and that the real aim of the whole process is not to protect Israel from terror but to prepare for the wholesale annexation of land surrounding Israeli settlements on the western fringe of the Occupied Territories; and these are the two claims mainly aired in the European media when the topic comes up. On the side of Israel it can be said, however, that any government has an overriding duty to protect its citizens from harm, that terror in Israel is, as it is not in any other Western country, a daily fact of life rather than an occasional nuisance, that terror attacks have greatly diminished in number in parts of Israel protected by the wall, and that the wall could easily be removed as part of an eventual peace settlement. Linda Grant, the novelist whose article in the left-of-center *Guardian* was mentioned in Chapter 7, provides a rare example of even-handedness on this topic: "Suicide bombings built the fence."[6] That is too bald for most left-of-center commentators, who prefer a quick fix of synthetic moral outrage to Grant's appalled but honest attempt to get to the bottom of the problem.

But there is the heart of the problem: when one gets to the bottom of it one finds, as Grant, to her distress, does, that there is no quick moral fix. The idea that the present government of Israel is, or could be, wholly and uniquely responsible for the conflict in the Middle East, besides being deeply anti-Semitic, for the reasons which Jonathan Sacks adduces and which we have explored further here, is also, considered simply as a piece of political analysis, deeply fatuous. It carries within it the assumption that *somebody* is "responsible" for the situation, and within that the further assumption that all that is necessary, in order for the situation to be satisfactorily resolved and for peace and security to reign, is for that *somebody*, on most accounts Israel, to change its ways. One passes from moral delusion to factual delusion in one easy step, almost without moving at all. In reality, nobody presently alive is "responsible" for the situation at all, in the finger-wagging, guilt-entailing sense beloved of "engaged" intellectuals, journalists, and media "commentators" who like to name a culprit. Everybody within the situation is responding to an immense variety of considerations, some of them moral in character, others merely prudential, the desire to go on living, to protect what one has, in a situation largely bequeathed by the past and maintained in existence in the present by powerful, built-in, disincentives to take any step which might lead to a way out, but which might equally well make an already difficult situation dreadfully worse for one side or the other. In one loose and superficial sense, both sides are responsible, equally. But in a more profound sense, neither is. Both are prisoners of a history made for them by preceding generations who were, in their turn, for the most part, acting for the best, as they saw things, under the appalling political and ideological pressures of the nineteenth and twentieth centuries. As Grant states it, concluding her article, "The most important word in Hebrew is *balagan* [*sic*: the word is, I am told, actually a Turkish loan-word]: oy, a *balagan*! What a mess!" True enough. But no reason to despair. There often turns out to be, in the end, a way out of such messes. But it does not often turn out to lead by way of ignorant, partial, and implicitly racist moral hectoring.

NOTES

1. "Nowadays the public is no longer prepared to pardon the author who will not take sides for or against the action he depicts" (my translation). André Gide, Preface to *L'immoraliste* (Paris: Mercure de France, 1902), p. 10.

2. Julie Henry, "Outrage as Oxford Bans Student for Being Israeli," *Telegraph*, June 29, 2003.

3. For more on this discreditable episode, see John D. A. Levy, "The Academic Boycott and Anti-Semitism," in Paul Iganski and Barry Kosmin, eds., *A New Anti-Semitism? Debating Judeophobia in the 21st Century* (London: Profile Books, 2003), pp. 249–57; and Alvin H. Rosenberg, "Anti-Zionism in Great Britain and Beyond," American Jewish Committee (2004), p. 16, available at www.ajc.com.

4. Jonathan Sacks, "A New Anti-Semitism?," in Iganski and Kosmin, eds., *A New Anti-Semitism?*, pp. 42–44.

5. Western Australian aboriginals survived, just barely. But the last recorded massacre (uncovered, through the agency of a clergyman who had been trying to convert the band in question, and subsequently punished, though not heavily) took place in that part of Australia in 1929.

6. Linda Grant, "Inside the Bubble," *Guardian*, April 8, 2004, p. 3.

9

THE USES OF ANTI-SEMITISM

ANTI-SEMITISM AS A CULTURAL PHENOMENON

> The chief joy of Satan is when he succeeds in persuading a man that an evil deed is a Mitzva. For when a man is weak and commits an offence, knowing it to be a sin, he is likely to repent of it. But when he believes it to be a good deed, does it stand to reason that he will repent of performing a Mitzva?
>
> —attributed to the Baal Shem-Tov (Israel ben Eliezer, 1700–1760)

> Durant la vie, j'ai vu la vie dans sa nudité, sans fard. Le bien et le mal, le beau et le laid se sont révélés à moi mêlés. Cela ne m'a pas transformé, grace au ciel, en moraliste. Au contraire, j'ai appris à respecter la faiblesse et à l'aimer, la faiblesse est notre essence et notre humanité. Un homme qui connaît sa faiblesse sait parfois la surmonter. Le moraliste ignore ses faiblesses et, au lieu de s'en prendre à lui -même, il s'en prend à son prochain.
>
> —Aharon Appelfeld, Histore d'une vie[1]

I want to return now briefly to my beginnings, and ask, finally: How has it come about that the "anti-racist" liberal Left finds itself currently up to its neck in the oldest form of racism? Phyllis Chesler's book on the new anti-Semitism is a particularly poignant document, so far as the phenomenon itself is concerned.[2] Chesler, who has spent her life as a leading feminist on the American liberal Left, catalogs with rising horror the invasion of the American campus by anti-Semitism of a very traditional, often violent, always rancorous kind, coming, this time round, not only from the usual suspects on the neo-Nazi right, but from the liberal Left itself. All of us who frequent campuses know that she is right. But the matter has gone beyond the campus and its generally small, though vociferous and perennial, minority of student revolutionaries and politically engaged academics. As the *New Statesman* editorial staff were incautious enough to make plain, even if one did not know it already from the conversational openings one encounters at dinner parties, the new anti-Semitism has spread to infect "left liberal" discourse at all levels.

What is to be done? "Fight the Big Lies" is part of Chesler's answer, and that is part of what I have being trying to do here. But there is also the question of why the old lies should be making a reappearance just now and from such an apparently unlikely segment of the Western political spectrum.

Earlier I suggested that political anti-Semitism, the myth of a secret, powerful, and infinitely malign pan-Jewish polity existing beneath the apparently diverse, disorganized, and utterly innocuous—indeed, to the host nation, generally vastly beneficent—visible surface of Jewish life, is a fantasy; and that its status as a fantasy is evident from the fact that, the moment one begins to subject any of its associated, quasi-factual claims to serious rational scrutiny, that claim turns out to be not so much empirically refutable as internally incoherent, and hence self-deconstructing: a tissue of nonsense which, when probed, implodes and vanishes, leaving behind it only a lingering odor of spiritual putrefaction.

Such fantasies are common enough among the seriously or mildly mentally disturbed: paranoid schizophrenics, egomaniacs, or depressives of one sort or another, and this no doubt accounts for the tendency—particularly among Diaspora Jews, who, living of necessity among non-Jews and not wishing to have all their non-Jewish relationships, most of them perfectly happy, vitiated by the crazy suspicion that beyond every goyisher face lurks stuff of this kind (for that way also madness lies)—to categorize anti-Semitism as "madness."

But this will not do. The really strange thing is that, despite the strong similarity between anti-Semitic fantasy and the delusions of the insane, most anti-Semites, in any age, are in no serious clinical, or even "folk," sense, mad. They are perfectly sane people who just happen to believe that "the Jews" are after them.

We therefore need to look for a cultural rather than a clinical explanation of the perennial and recurrent incidence of anti-Semitism. I propose to suggest one. Anti-Semitism is, in essence, a response, by holders of a highly moralized worldview, to situations in which that worldview appears to be seriously under threat, not in ways which the patterns of explanation intrinsic to it would lead one to expect, but in ways which cannot easily be grasped or articulated by appeal to any pattern of explanation internal to the worldview in question, and which are thus, precisely to the extent that their minds continue to be dominated by it, necessarily and intrinsically mysterious to its adherents.

MORALITY AND PUTATIVELY FACTUAL BELIEF

That in itself, of course, is merely an oracular remark. Let me now try to make it a little clearer. Philosophers have very often taken for granted—Kant is an obvious instance—that the demands of morality form a self-consistent set, in the sense that any moral demand can be satisfied without prejudice to the satisfaction of any other moral demand. That thesis has been persuasively questioned by the philosopher and historian of ideas Isaiah Berlin. Berlin's counterclaim is that the basic considerations which we find morally compelling are a very mixed bag, arising from such diverse concerns and aspects of human life that there must constantly arise situations in which moral demands of one type can only be satisfied at the expense of a less than perfect satisfaction of moral demands of another type. It is not hard to think of examples of such conflicts: the preservation of liberty of one sort or another for individuals cannot always be easily squared with the pursuit of social welfare; the rights of the fetus cannot always be honored without infringing on those of the mother, and vice versa; the demands of loyalty to friends or family sometimes conflict with those of loyalty to the nation or simply to people in general outside the charmed circles of personal relationship. What Berlin suggests is that there is no trick philosophical wheeze which will either equip us with a rule or algorithm for settling such conflicts or show them to be merely apparent. They are, sadly, quite real, and quite unavoidable.

I think Berlin was right about this, and I want to try to build a little further on his ideas. Such moral dilemmas can only be addressed if one can find good reason for giving one set of moral demands greater weight than competing demands in a given type of situation. And this, I think, is what people in fact attempt to do. But in attempting it they seldom approach the question with a perfectly blank mind. Minds like blank slates are seldom to be found outside the pages of Locke. People, even "simple" or "ordinary" people, commonly entertain very complex general views about how the world, meaning by that not merely the natural or human world but also the transcendent world of religion, works and is structured; and such world-views cannot but affect the manner in which particular people are inclined to resolve specific moral dilemmas. Not uncommonly, difference of world-view will lead to differences in the way different people are inclined to re-solve specific dilemmas. And in time, through the development of world-views in the direction of greater complexity of internal organization, this may lead to differences, between holders of competing worldviews, con-cerning the content of morality itself.

AN EXAMPLE

An example may clarify what I have in mind. During the Cold War a great many people in Britain supported the Campaign for Nuclear Disarmament (CND), a loosely organized political group, broadly on the left, but with many Christian and a few conservative adherents, which advocated unilateral nuclear disarmament by Great Britain. In arguments with CND people, which could get pretty fiery, one was apt to be told that withholding support for CND showed one to be a wicked, even an evil, person. When one asked how that could be so, one often got a reply along the lines of "Well, you just don't give a damn whether your children are vaporized in a nuclear holo-caust." One felt inclined to reply to this that it was precisely because one did not care to have one's children vaporized in a nuclear holocaust that one did not support CND, since unilateral nuclear disarmament by a major European power seemed, on the whole, more likely to invite a nuclear holocaust than to prevent one. Such a reply seldom served to placate one's interlocutor. Usu-ally he or she, changing his or her ground, would reply that such an answer showed one to be the sort of person who, possessing a mind insensible to the moral demand that people trust and reach out to one another, can only think of human relationships in terms of threat and counterthreat, and therefore a person even more wicked than someone who *did* wish to see his children consumed in a nuclear holocaust. Warming to his theme, one's interlocutor would conclude that unless people in the West—*even people like you!*—were at some point prepared to trust in the good intentions of the Soviet Union, it was difficult to see how nuclear war could be avoided. One might weakly reply that, really, one *was* prepared to trust people, provided one had good reason to suppose them trustworthy; but one might as well have saved one's breath. One had already been blown out of the water, and a withering look generally concluded the conversation.

Let us now look more closely, in the light of my earlier remarks about Berlin, at what is going on in, and behind, the above exchange. Both parties agree that certain considerations have what one might call *prima facie moral force*, namely, the thought that war should be avoided if possible, that children should, if possible, be protected from the ravages of war, and that there is a general duty for people to be willing, as far as possible, to trust one another. These considerations correspond roughly to Berlin's kit of basic moral intuitions which, diverse as they are, have somehow to be squared with one another in concrete situations, in some, if not all, of which the satisfaction of one will to some extent threaten the satisfaction of others. They are accepted, as possessing *intrinsic moral force*, by both parties to the dispute. In this they differ from the goal of unilateral nuclear disarmament. One party to the dispute indeed takes this goal to possess, like the other three, intrinsic moral force, so much so that he is prepared to regard anyone who takes a different view as ipso facto immoral. The other party to the dispute regards unilateral nuclear disarmament, not only as *not* an intrinsically morally compelling goal, but as a piece of political folly likely to invite rather than prevent nuclear war, and thus itself to be resisted on moral grounds.

What, then, accounts for the difference between the two parties over which considerations possess intrinsic moral force? I suggest, differences in their overall political worldviews. The supporter of CND (I think this is a fairly accurate account of an actual outlook current at the time, based on many conversations and much reading during the period concerned) believes that the Cold War is largely the fault of the West. He sees the Soviet Union as a peace-loving nation based on collectivist, socialist values, not unlike his own, forced into a costly and socially ruinous arms race by the suspicions of a Western world, led by America, whose moral atmosphere, by contrast, is that of a rampant commercial individualism, in which everybody is trying to get ahead and nobody trusts anyone else. He tends also to see relationships between nations as relationships not between governments but between "peoples." The worldview of the opponent of CND, on the other hand, differs, let us suppose, in that he holds international relations to be largely determined by relations between governments, not peoples. He therefore takes the question of whether people at large in a given country are, or are not, "peace-loving" to be largely irrelevant to the issue of whether that country is, or is not, going to be prepared to wage aggressive war if the chance of doing so presents itself. His estimate of the nature and intentions of the Soviet government, in particular, is darker and bleaker than that of his adversary's estimate of those of "the Soviet people," and his estimate of the moral character of Western societies is less bleak. He, therefore, unlike his adversary, holds that the prima facie duty to trust others must give way, being largely irrelevant in the circumstances, to the duty to do what one can to prevent war.

The CND supporter and his opponent hold opposing examples of what I earlier labeled *highly moralized worldviews*. They agree on certain fundamental, or basic, moral principles, but disagree about certain less fundamental ones. This is because the interior workings of highly moralized worldviews operate to transfer moral force from the agreed, basic principles to a small set of logically derivative ones, while the internal workings of the other worldview operate in such a way as to frustrate precisely that transfer. One could put the point more concretely by saying that, while the CND supporter's worldview supplies factual premises from which, in combination with the evaluative premises supplied by the basic, agreed moral principles, it follows logically that it is morally wrong not to support unilateral moral disarmament, his opponent's worldview fails to supply factual minor premises licensing that particular logical transition.

However, it is unlikely that an actual CND supporter would recognize that the moral demands dearest to his heart are not "basic" moral intuitions capable of eliciting assent from anyone, no matter what his worldview, but derivative principles whose very standing *as* moral principles depends on assent to factual claims internal to his own worldview. On the whole people are disinclined to distinguish critically between different components of their systems of moral belief from the standpoint of what they would regard as hair-splitting philosophical distinctions. They simply take whatever seems to them a valid moral demand to be a demand universally valid for all mankind, or "for all rational beings," as Kant would say. Normally, therefore, they are very far from taking themselves to be responding, some of the time to moral demands which *anyone* would agree to possess moral weight, and the rest of the time to a second, derivative set, possessing moral force only by inference from the first set, by a logical transition valid only given the support of certain factual minor premises accepted as true only within the cultural or political circle to which they happen to belong. They simply take themselves to be responding to the demands of *morality, tout court.*

Moreover, a political worldview is not, in general, entertained, by those who hold it, as a mere hypothesis, instrumentally useful, insofar as the view of reality it offers proves accurate enough to serve primary, noninstrumental goals defined externally to it, but freely open to modification or abandonment should it prove seriously astray from reality and thus ineffectual as a guide to the origination and direction of strategies aimed at achieving those goals. On the contrary, the value of a highly moralized worldview, to someone who holds it, is that it allows him to define and articulate, internally to it, primary goals of a type which he or she would not otherwise have been able to conceive. Since a person's primary, noninstrumental goals are by definition those which direct the overall course of his life, determining the company in which he feels happiest, as well as the content of the intermediate, instrumental goals he finds himself pursuing, they are felt by that person both as defining his or her selfhood—the "sort of person" he or she is—and as providing a large part of what "gives meaning to life."

A highly moralized worldview is thus not something one easily gives up. For that reason, the attempt by argument to compel someone to give up one central to his whole view both of himself and of his "values"—his beliefs concerning what things in life are, morally speaking, most to be sought and most to be shunned, most to be praised and most to be condemned—will generally be vigorously resisted; which is why political or religious arguments are commonly so much more bitter and acrimonious than arguments about things to which the disputants are merely instrumentally related: disputes about the best way to prune roses, say, or to get from London to Stansted by train.

Nevertheless, highly moralized worldviews are very seldom secured against the ravages of rational debate by being hermetically sealed off from all contact with reality in the sort of way often envisaged by anthropological relativists. That they are not, indeed, constitutes one of the most obvious of the many differences between holding a highly moralized worldview and being subject to paranoid delusions. Highly moralized worldviews, by their nature, give hostages to experience. That follows from the fact that, by definition, some moral claims central to such a worldview depend for their status as *moral* claims on the concurrence of certain factual beliefs equally central to the worldview in question. And, in the nature of things, any such belief may turn out to conflict with ascertainable facts in ways which may raise difficulties for the internal coherence of the worldview in question, or even prove fatal to it.

A highly moralized worldview exists, therefore, under the shadow of the permanent threat that reality will fail to live up to expectations whose satisfaction is essential to its internal coherence. If this threat materializes in the guise of an articulate and argumentative opponent, as in the above dialogue, the holder of the threatened worldview very often has an obvious line of defense, which he will very often follow: that of concluding that his opponent is simply a bad man, deaf to at least some of the demands of morality. That hypothesis will enable him to explain the fact of the adversary's existence; to site it in terms of the structure of reality, as that is represented by his worldview. Thus, in the exemplary dispute set out above, the worldview of the CND supporter leads him to suppose that the Cold War is largely the result of a failure by Western conservatives to trust sufficiently in the good intentions of the USSR. Very well, here is just such a conservative, actually confronting him; and displaying precisely the sort of moral blindness which the worldview would lead one to expect in such a person.

Here the worldview sees off a challenge by appeal to explanatory principles internal and intrinsic to it. But suppose a sharper challenge arises from reality itself, one which cannot be dismissed by appeal to explanatory principles internal to the worldview? Suppose, in the CND case, the Soviet Union undertakes some military adventure, along the lines of the Soviet invasion of Czechoslovakia but rather worse, which makes it difficult to continue believing in the pacific intentions of the USSR; something, in short, which is just not to be expected, given the putative truth of central tenets of the CND outlook, from the peace-loving, collectivist Soviet people, and which cannot be explained on any grounds internal to that outlook?

The events of 1968 in Czechoslovakia in fact produced a great many personal crises among people I knew then who belonged to the British Communist Party, and these led to some considerable thinning of the ranks of the party. Let us suppose that the same thing happens, under our imaginary circumstances, to the ranks of CND, with the usual accompaniments of acrimonious debates, storming out of rooms, and the breaking off of long-held and previously cordial friendships. Anything which enables people to maintain their faith in the worldview characteristic of CND members at this moment of crisis will, in other words, be welcome. Now suppose that at this juncture a significant, even dominant, fraction of the Politburo happens to consist of persons of Jewish descent. A saving possibility now opens before us: the possibility that the Politburo has ceased to represent the interests of the peace-loving Soviet people, because it has been infiltrated and taken over by the Jews. Admittedly it may be obscure at first sight why this takeover by persons putatively loyal to Jewish rather than Russian interests should have resulted in armed belligerence. But on the one hand it is well known that the Jews are a commercially minded people, always on the make: subject, in fact, to just those vices which our CND supporter sees as characteristic of a morally corrupt Western society. And on the other hand, there is no reason, is there, why anyone should be in a position to know the secret purposes of a people so much given to keeping itself to itself, keeping its real goals, in other words, well out of the public view. All one can say for sure is that if it were not for having been taken over by the Jews the Soviet Union *could not* be behaving in this way, since we know the Soviet people themselves to be essentially peace-loving.

No such move was, of course, ever made by supporters of CND in the 1960s. At that time the entire British Left was, or at least seemed, refreshingly free from overt anti-Semitism. But the example, contrived and artificial as it is, may serve to introduce the main features of the explanation I have in mind for its present recrudescence. The thought is that a political worldview tends to project "ordinary" moral convictions—those to which most people would assent irrespective of political standpoint—into new forms which depend for their *moral* validity on the support of highly complex factual-cum-theoretical beliefs which allegedly represent reality, but whose claim to do so may come under threat from events. Simple jettisoning of the threatened factual-theoretical beliefs will be rendered difficult for many by the extent to which their lives and social relationships have become intertwined with a political worldview. Moreover, because derivative moral convictions swiftly come to be felt as exercising the same moral force as primary ones, many will feel it to be morally unacceptable to admit that the factual-theoretical beliefs which led them to embrace those convictions in the first place may, in their power to represent reality accurately, leave anything to be desired. Yet there remains an uncomfortable feeling that *something* is impeding the neat rendering of political reality into terms of those convictions and their underlying factual-cum-theoretical supports. What precisely that *something* is will remain difficult to apprehend without to some extent calling both into question. Hence, there arises a need, in the thinking of those who wish very much to call neither into question, for it to be a thing external to the entire fabric of their political thinking: a thing, in other words, in the nature of a political *deus ex machina*. For some, under certain circumstances, that *deus ex machina* will prove readily identifiable— as some new manifestation of the eternal machinations of "the Jews." And any moral qualms which those who make this choice may feel about succumbing to anti-Semitic ways of thinking will, in the case of many, in one sense at least, perfectly "honest," perfectly "well-meaning" people, be entirely submerged by a sense of the overriding moral rectitude of the "sane," "progressive" political values which they have come to see "the Jews" as working ceaselessly behind the scenes to subvert.

This possibility, that certain types of anti-Semitism may be motivated by the desire to save the credit of a threatened worldview, perhaps offers an explanation for two quite puzzling things about political anti-Semitism. The first is the improbable, not to say superhuman, degree of wickedness with which political anti-Semites credit the Jews. The quality of nightmare which exudes from the cartoons in the prewar *Der Sturmer* will give one a rough idea of what I mean, but the same atmosphere of near-hysterical threat can be encountered, only a little more hedged and politely expressed, in the bizarrely one-sided and obsessive coverage of Israel currently aired by parts of the media in Britain and elsewhere. The second is the essential *mysteriousness* of the Jews, on the political anti-Semite's account of them. Why *are* these people *so* wicked, *so* monomaniacally devoted to the destruction of everything "we" hold dear? It is simply a datum, something taken for granted, that Jews are just simply like that. The explanation offered by the suggestion we are exploring is that these are features, not of the Jews, but of the *predicament*, the sense of threat to a highly moralized worldview, a threat which may, of course have in reality nothing whatsoever to do with the Jews, which the appeal to the supposed machinations of Jewry serves to defuse. They are, in short, as the psychiatrists say, phenomena of transference. The holder of a threatened worldview will in the nature of things find it difficult, if not impossible, to focus upon the precise nature and causes of the threat, because, given that what makes the threat a threat is precisely that it cannot be explained and sited within the general picture of reality offered by the worldview, to do so would already require one to move some way across the boundaries of that view, and thus to weaken one's attachment to it: in other words, to begin the task of revising one's picture of him- or herself and of the world. The whole point of blaming the problem, whatever it may be, on the Jews is that they are *so* mysterious that *their* machinations can explain anything at all, without any need to risk the uncomfortable consequences which might arise from an examination of the relationship of the threatened worldview to the everyday world; a world, unfortunately, too little shrouded in mystery to be always entirely sympathetic to the fantasies we entertain concerning it. In the same way, once the Jews have been fixed on as the real source of whatever problem it may be that threatens a worldview, their absolute, *total* wickedness follows as a simple reflection of the fact that the threatened worldview provides its holder with the totality of his values. Anyone, or anything, who works against that worldview is thus *totally* bad because he, she or it works against the *totality* of what constitutes, for the holder of the threatened worldview, the Good.

MESSIANISM VERSUS MELIORISM

Let us now examine how far these ideas can be made to shed light on the second main issue of this book, the causes behind the current recrudescence of a new left liberal version of anti-Semitism; a version, like earlier versions, deeply rooted in moral ideas and feelings, but with the supporting morality coming this time from sources diametrically opposed to those of earlier versions; not, this time from essentially right-wing ideas of nationalism and national salvation, but from essentially left-wing ideas of internationalism and humanitarianism.

So far I have been using the term Left in a very broad-brush sort of way, relying, largely for reasons of space, on context to do the work of analysis. A little more in the way of the latter is now needed, at the cost, perhaps, of a little belaboring of the obvious, simply because, while certain of the sorts of outlook and accompanying general worldview which we loosely label "left-wing" or "liberal" have been placed under threat by events over the past quarter century, others have not. One can make a rough distinction between *meliorist* and *messianic* versions of liberalism. The former owes its origin and intellectual allegiance to the tradition of philosophic liberalism whose founding luminaries include Hume, Adam Smith, Bentham, and John Stuart Mill. It accepts the general superiority of a "civil" society based on the individual and corporate ownership of property, with accompanying economic and social pluralism based on some form of representative democracy, but divides (into what are nowadays termed conservative and liberal wings) over the issue of the extent to which the remedy for specific social ills arising in such societies is best left to the operations of the market, or, on the contrary, necessitates some form of state intervention. The latter, messianic liberalism, though it stems from a great variety of intellectual sources, traces its main line of descent from the tradition of broadly rationalist moral and political theory which proceeds from Leibniz, by way of Rousseau, Kant, and Hegel, to Marx.

The central thesis of messianic liberalism is that the "civil society" promoted by the tradition of meliorist liberalism from Adam Smith onward is irredeemably corrupt; is, as Hegel put it, "a mere battlefield of private interests," in which the "universal" interests proper to humanity in general must go to the wall. Hegel believed that universal interests could be served by a state bureaucracy, but the actual experience of Prussian bureaucracy disappointed both him and the Young Hegelians, who sought a more radical solution. This was supplied, for many, by Marx's "materialist" rewriting of Hegel in terms of economics and class conflict. Hegel had already proposed a "spiritual history" (*Geistesgeschichte*), according to which history becomes, not a mere accumulation of historical accident, but a rational process proceeding through the resolution of "contradictions" within a world mind, or soul, and leading to the final self-realization, or self-understanding, of that mind. Marx retained the Hegelian notion of a rational motor of historical change powered by the resolution of conflict, or "contradiction," but reinterpreted the contradictions as conflicts arising within successive social orders based upon the exploitation, by some dominant class, of the surplus production of the working-class; production "surplus" in the sense of production over and above that required for the subsistence of the working class. Conflict arises, according to Marx, when new technological advances open opportunities for increased production which can only be exploited by a new ruling class that therefore displaces the previous one. The most advanced class to emerge from this dialectical process is the one which rules the society under which we live, namely, the capitalist class. But it, according to Marx, is destined to be replaced by the working class itself, as a result of a "Communist revolution" which will overthrow civil society and return the entire product of the "alienated labor" of the working class, in the shape of the entire, vast industrial machine accumulated by the era of exploitation in all its historical stages, up to and including capitalism, to its rightful owners.

What organization of society, precisely, is to follow the revolution? Here there is a gap in Marx's own writings. In practice, however, there is only one answer, one which has been adopted by every subsequent writer in the tradition of the messianic Left, and which comes to us directly from the pages of Hegel: namely, *socialism*.[3] The socially owned industrial machine created by the labor of all must be controlled by a "universal" class, that is to say, by a wise and public-spirited state bureaucracy which will plan its operation for the benefit of all. State control, exercised through bureaucracy and central planning, is central to the socialist program, because control must be exercised, and the only other conceivable form of control, control by private owners, has been excluded as morally and politically unacceptable.

We can now begin to lay in some of the planks of the worldview shared by believers in the hopes articulated, since the late eighteenth century, by the messianic Left. It would be a great mistake to identify the class of adherents of that worldview with the membership of organized political parties, whether Communist or social democratic in character. The vein of Left messianism arising from the Marxist–Hegelian tradition has put down very deep roots in Western society. In particular it has come, over the past century, to constitute part of the framework within which very large numbers of well-meaning middle-class people of generous moral instincts view the world. The aspirations of such people go beyond personal and family success to embrace society and mankind in general; they wish to believe not only that life is capable of improvement, not only for themselves but for the poorest, but that improvement of the desired kind is somehow guaranteed by impersonal historical forces. Left messianism of the sort I have in mind, usually divorced from any specific commitment to party politics, has come to provide, for many such people, the worldview in terms of which they find it easiest to articulate such beliefs and their accompanying values.

The most basic, and amiable, of these values is the desire to promote what one might term human flourishing. That desire includes the wish to see people well rather than sick, comfortably off rather than grindingly poor, thoughtful and well educated rather than unkind and ignorant; children kindly and wisely treated rather than starved, beaten, and abused; women allowed to become independent, self-directing persons rather than unpaid domestic drudges; to see people at peace rather than at war, gaining their living by pursuits chosen and enjoyed rather than by one or another form of hated wage slavery, and so on. These are, of course, desires, "values," if you will, very widely shared by meliorist liberals and conservatives across a wide political spectrum. They are the sort of thing we earlier labeled basic, or primary, values, values very generally shared and pursued, though not, of course, without conflicts between certain among them arising in certain specific contexts.

The messianic Left combines these basic values with a variable set of putatively factual beliefs including at least the following:

1. That "civil society," a society governed by economic liberalism, founded upon private and corporate ownership of property, competition conducted within a framework of law, and a considerable measure of individual freedom guaranteed by law, is inherently incapable of realizing the basic values for any but a small class of privileged, wealthy people.

2. That a far better, indeed on many accounts a perfect, realization of those values could be achieved by a socialist society, that is, one in which all economic resources are owned by the state and directed for the general good by a corps of bureaucratic planners.

3. That the transition from civil society to socialist forms of government is both historically inevitable and necessary for any sort of morally tolerable future for mankind, even though steps to achieve it may be endlessly opposed, and for a time frustrated, by those who profit from their position within civil society. To these core beliefs, which mainly concern the politics of the advanced world, we may add two more, which concern the general state of the world at large.

4. That the exercise of economic power, either by direct colonial rule or by less direct forms of economic control (which nevertheless equally deserve the name of colonialism), by the governments and corporate interests of technologically advanced civil societies, is directly and solely responsible for the impoverishment of the third world.

5. That the overthrow of civil society, and with it of colonialism, and the establishment of socialist regimes throughout the world, can be relied upon to lead to an era of planned economic development, resulting in the general realization of the basic values of human flourishing. That era will have as one of its main features the ending of racial animosity and the coming together of all the workers of the world, of all races, in the common task of building socialism.

Taking the basic values, or moral beliefs, in combination with the above set of factual beliefs yields a set of secondary or inferred moral beliefs. These have a certain tendency, like the strands in Protestant (or, in Catholicism, Jansenist) Christianity which constitute the second main source, along with the tradition of Hegel and Marx, for the moral thought of the messianic Left, to divide humanity between the Saints and the Reprobate. The latter, as might be expected, include most believers in the values of civil society. To the believer in Left messianism, civil society, by comparison with the socialist society to come, is on several counts morally corrupt. It encourages its citizens to pursue greed, through the naked pursuit of wealth and personal power, rather than public service and the good of others. It uses the economic and military power generated by its technological success to hinder and stave off for as long as possible the eventual triumph of socialism, thus setting its face against the basic values of human flourishing. It impoverishes the third world, causing untold harm and suffering, through its unending attempt to enrich itself at the expense of the poor through (overt or covert) colonial exploitation.

The Saints, by contrast, are all those who oppose the continued reign of civil society and work to bring on the socialist future. Because they are working to bring in the only form of society which can permit the realization of the basic values of human flourishing, all the moral virtue invested in those values invests them also. They may do wrong by the standards of bourgeois society, but their fidelity to the cause of the poor and oppressed against those who would exploit them for profit turns their moral dross to gold and justifies them by the light of the messianic order to come.

This summary of the basic tenets of left messianism is no doubt too bare and schematic to represent the outlook of any actual believer. But I do not think it describes a straw man. The worldview whose outlines it captures remains a recognizable part of the political landscape we at present inhabit.

MESSIANISM AND ITS DISCONTENTS

It is a worldview which has come under serious and increasing threat from world events in the years since World War II, and particularly over the past twenty years. First, there has been the collapse of the Soviet Union, a collapse not only incomprehensible to, but entirely unforeseen by, many on the messianic wing of the Left. The problems exposed by that collapse call into question, by their nature, not merely the totalitarian organization of Soviet communism, but the entire program of socialism: the belief in the power of centralized planning, administered by a wise and incorruptible bureaucracy, to direct the operations of an entirely state-owned industrial machine for the good of all.

There are three unanswered questions haunting this program. In order of increasing gravity they are: (1) Is it really possible for central planners, working at some remove not only from the consumers, but also from the day-to-day operations of the industries they are attempting to control, to know what way of conducting those industries will best serve public needs, now and in the future? (2) Is it not likely that the operations of any centrally devised plan will become progressively distorted, as its implementation progresses outward through the various levels of a very intricately organized technological society, by the need of subordinate managers in the system to advance their own careers and secure themselves against a perceived failure on their part to implement the plan? (3) Is it not highly likely that the entire bureaucratic apparatus, the *Apparat*, as it came to be called in the Soviet Union, situated as it is, as both the originator of all decisions required in the running of society and the final court of appeal on the success of those decisions, will transform itself into a species of self-renewing collective oligarchy, running things not for the benefit of society at large, but primarily for the benefit of those within its ranks?

All of these pigeons came home to roost in the seventy-year lifespan of the Soviet regime, and it is largely because they came home to roost that socialism in the Soviet Union collapsed in 1989. In the 1970s it was fashionable among "liberal communists" to argue that what was wrong, and "reactionary" about the Soviet Union was merely its authoritarian, quasi-czarist political system. The Soviet mode of economic organization, such people thought, was "progressive" in just the way socialists had always envisaged, and once freed from its authoritarian political matrix could be relied upon to deliver economic plenty and social progress in the manner promised by Marx. This analysis turned out to be at exactly 180 degrees to the truth. What kept the Soviet Union going for seventy years was the fact that it was a police state. What eventually brought about its collapse was that neither the efforts of "liberalizing" communists like Mikhail Gorbachov, nor those of the KGB, were able to hold back the vast tide of public discontent against the *Apparat* and all its works arising from the innumerable absurdities, inefficiencies, and recurrent shortages of goods created by the state and its bureaucratic systems of planning and control.

The collapse of the Soviet Union, in short, was hence not, or not only, an indictment of totalitarianism. It was an indictment of the idea that the political ideal of socialism, given its intimate conceptual dependence on the idea of state ownership, bureaucracy, and central planning, will, or can, deliver on its supposed promises. Moreover, that message has, in quiet ways, been absorbed and accepted by the more centrist sections of the European Left, at least when it comes to practical politics. In Britain, for example, the past two decades have witnessed the progressive ditching of the language and ideology of "socialism" by the Labour Party. The latter, having finally reinvented itself, under Tony Blair, as "New Labour," is now, in a somewhat Gorbachev-like fashion, and in the face of stiff resistance from the hard left of the party, attempting to "reform" the health service, the education system, and parts of the rail transport system, the three departments of British life which still, to a greater or lesser degree, retain the stamp of state ownership and centralized planning conferred upon them by the first postwar Labour government of Clement Attlee. The general strategy of these reforms, one originally introduced under the conservative government of Margaret Thatcher, is, essentially, to preserve the structural characteristics of state ownership and centralized control over these segments of the British economy by introducing, within that structure, certain features of a market economy. It remains to be seen whether the very modest measures of "liberalization" contemplated will prove sufficient to arrest the gradual slide of systems strategically indistinguishable from a Soviet-style command economy toward a degree of inefficiency and failure sufficiently alarming to the general public to force the dismantling of centralized bureaucratic control.

Second, and still worse, both in its material and its ideological consequences than the collapse of state socialism in the Soviet Union, has come the appalling debacle of the same political philosophy in the third world. Many ex-colonial countries whose postcolonial leaders had for the most part been trained in Western universities and infected to some extent with

Western "progressive" ideas, dutifully opted for "socialism," but the "socialism" they opted for, though buttressed with all the latest rhetoric from Vincennes and the London School of Economics, either turned out to be, or evolved in a majority of cases, as power changed hands, into the merest fig leaf for abuses running from genocide in the case of Pol Pot in Cambodia or the leaders of the Hutu in Rwanda, to ruthless exploitation of the peasantry in the cause of the enrichment and self-aggrandizement of a host of "leaders" from Colonel Mengistu Haile Mariam in Ethiopia to the ex-Marxist turned tribal dictator Robert Mugabe in Zimbabwe. In a sense, one should hardly be surprised. That regions of the world having little cultural or historical connection with the West should turn out to obey "laws of historical development" conceived on the parochially European model favored by the founders of political historicism would have been surprising. But the bloody political chaos of the world set free from the influence of the Western model of civil society briefly and patchily imposed between, say, 1760 and 1960 is, to say the least, hardly a testimony to the predictive power of historical materialism. In sum, the socialist millennium failed to arrive on schedule. Worse still, the promise of historical materialism has not merely been delayed but reversed: authoritarian socialism in the Soviet Union, and increasingly in China, has given way to authoritarian capitalism as the new wave of the future. In the Middle East the secular nationalism and socialism of the first postwar regimes has increasingly given way to regimes based on despotic forms of religious obscurantism. These developments have in turn eroded the hope of a single world, purged of ethnic and religious hatreds, in which all peoples would unite in building socialism.

The result of these setbacks, which have been fully reported by the Western media and are thus fully open to view in the West, has been a sharp loss of influence by the parties of the messianic Left, coming about either by simple collapse at the polls, as in the case of most Western European communist parties, or, as has happened in recent years in the British Labour Party, by takeover by an essentially meliorist-liberal leadership of powers formerly exercised by messianic socialists further to the left of the party.

The political losses have proved impossible to ignore. What has proved possible to ignore, at least to a considerable extent, has been the damage to the derivative values of the messianic Left, the values, in other words, most directly constitutive of the moral self-image specific to that wing of politics, occasioned by the collapse of the factual minor premises required to license the inference of those values from more general, and generally shared, ones. Whatever may be corrupt, and corrupting, about excessive greed, or competitiveness, in individuals, it is difficult to see how moral charges of that description can intelligibly be leveled against a given mode of economic organization of society per se unless there is some other mode of economic organization manifestly lacking in the forms of corruption complained of. That was, precisely, the role assigned to socialism in the worldview of the messianic Left. But if socialism merely brings in the rule of a self-interested and corrupt bureaucracy, managing the economic instruments committed to it with a degree of inefficiency and consequent suffering, equal, if not worse than, that which can be alleged of capitalism, and at worst maintaining its control through the medium of oppressive police power, what remains of the case against civil society, which at least disposes of the legal and political means of mitigating whatever abuses may be endemic to its constitution? Again, if the ending of Western colonial rule in large parts of the world has resulted, not in the inauguration of a messianic age of socialism, but, as has happened in much of Africa, in the replacement of civilized and modestly economically progressive regimes with a state of endemic war, poverty, and terror, dominated by murderous private armies loyal to ruling cliques which, for all their occasional mouthing of "progressive" sentiments operate in practice as gangsters and kleptocrats, what becomes of the case against colonialism? And ultimately, of course, what becomes of the moral credentials of those whose idea of the "moral high ground" remains framed in terms of some version of the worldview of Left messianism as set out above? Don't the categories of the Saints and the Reprobates begin to display an unnerving tendency to switch their moral polarities?

Such thoughts are not comfortable ones. A great many people's lives and self-images continue to be built upon the conviction that the derivative moral beliefs of socialist messianism are valid: that civil society is inherently and per se corrupt; that the present sufferings of vast numbers of people in the third world are uniquely the fault of "Western capitalism"; that the direction of economic life by the state is always, both morally and practically, preferable to its remaining in private hands; that any armed movement which presents itself as opposed to the West and as the "authentic representative" of a non-Western "people" is ipso facto on the side of progress, and also ipso facto operating in the interests of the people it claims to "represent," however thin its claim to represent anything but its own delusions and the personal cupidity of its leaders.

Considered as moral convictions, all of the above are clearly secondary, or derivative, ones, in the sense we have been exploring. That is, they are moral convictions which could only have attained the status of *moral* convictions within the context of a highly complex, highly elaborated worldview;

in the present case the fabric of "socialist" economics, social criticism, and philosophy of history which gradually, over the past two and a half centuries, came to constitute the intellectual stock-in-trade of the messianic Left.

That fabric of factual-cum-theoretical beliefs, we have been arguing, has come over the past half century to seem, even to many former believers, increasingly out of step with reality. But there is, evidently, a way of saving the *moral outlook* associated with the Left messianism from going down in a common ruin with the body of factual-cum-theoretical beliefs which formerly motivated it; one which succeeds in maintaining the distinction between political Saints and political Reprobates; a distinction as attractive to the mainly middle-class consumers of liberal Left journalism and ideas in Western countries today as it was to the sternly Protestant—or Jansenist—ancestors of most of them a century or two ago. It is to treat the main moral contentions comprising it—that is to say, at least those listed in the previous paragraph but one—as free-standing moral convictions: as moral convictions, that is to say, needing no support from any body of factual-cum-theoretical beliefs to establish their moral credentials; credentials held now, by those who accept them as valid, to be *intuitively* compelling, evident to inspection.

THE MORALIZING OF PROGRESSIVE POLITICS

This, I think, is very much what has happened, over large swathes of left-wing opinion, since the 1970s. It is the source of the tendency I mentioned earlier, for indignant moral hectoring to replace sectarian forms of economic and historical analysis in left-wing journalism and conversation. Some adjustment in the content of the moral outlook of the Left has, admittedly, been necessitated by this shift to a political *Weltanschauung* founded purely in moral conviction. Thus, the evils of capitalism are now more frequently represented in terms of moral notions—those of "greed," of "unfairness," of an "individualism" which supposedly tramples upon the values of "community," of a "dog-in-the-manger" attitude to the distribution of natural resources, and so on—than in terms of that older, Marxist theory of history and class conflict which would expressly have condemned such moralizing as politically ignorant and "utopian." Similarly, what is wrong in the relationship of technically advanced civil societies to less advanced ones is often, and increasingly, represented not in economic terms—that is, in terms of exploitation, markets, terms of trade, and so forth, but in terms of such moral notions as "power," "respect," "the arrogance of wealth," "racism," and so on. There are indeed voices to be heard at the moment protesting, rightly, against the damage done to third world *economies* by Western protectionism, particularly in agriculture and the garment trade, but they tend to be voices from the libertarian Right or center Right of politics; in other words, from those who wish to emphasize the advantages to the third world of free trade and the economic globalization that goes with it. On the left, broadly opposed to globalization as it largely is, the objection to Western capitalist societies often appears no longer to be that the economic practices necessary to their survival prevent the achievement of the universally high standards of living which would, it used to be supposed, follow the transition to socialism on a world scale, but simply that those societies remain, for the moment, very much richer in terms of gross national product than most non-Western societies, and in consequence, again for the moment, exercise more influence in world affairs. One consequence of this is that, in many left-wing circles, the peoples of the third world have come to be seen, in moral terms, primarily as *victims*: victims of the greed, the economic and cultural aggressiveness, the racism of Western countries; in particular, and most grossly, America. This stands, of course, in sharp contrast to the earlier Marxist view, according to which third-world proletariats were no *more* victims of capitalist exploitation than Western proletariats. That rather more egalitarian view of things also motivated a considerably more politically discriminating view of armed revolutionary movements in the third world than is commonly encountered today. To a Marxist, what constituted the moral credentials of a revolutionary movement, in any part of the world, was that it could plausibly be construed as a "progressive" movement: one aiming at the establishment of socialism. On the other hand, armed movements of a reactionary or fascist nature, aimed at the establishment of either a secular or theocratic tyranny as hostile to the interests of the working class as the most unreconstructed forms of capitalism, were also possible, *and equally deserving of rejection and resistance in any part of the world.* To the new, "moralized" version of Left messianism, on the other hand, *any* armed revolutionary movement whatsoever, of whatever political complexion, in any country which can be represented as a victim of "colonialism" (including such evidently first-world countries as Ireland) counts as "progressive" simply in virtue of being a revolt of the victims against the wielders of power. There is thus no need to develop, for a given movement, any even remotely plausible argument establishing the capacity of that movement to further economic or social progress should it succeed in establishing itself in power. Its moral credentials derive simply from its self-announced status as "authentically" representing a "victimized" people or culture against the "greed" and "arrogance" of "capitalism," the latter term increasingly used without any serious Marxist reference, simply as a convenient label for what is thought of on the Left as American world hegemony.

WHY ANTI-SEMITISM?

But now, it might be asked, what bearing has all this on anti-Semitism? The transformation of the once rather majestic theoretical edifice of messianic socialism into the hasty and ill-digested collection of indignant, "politically correct"[4] moral knee-jerk reactions which form the basis of so much left-wing comment and journalism in Western countries today, may well be depressing; but why should it have led to the emergence of a new anti-Semitism on the Left?

There is, of course, no reason why it *need* have done so. For "the Jews" to appear, to holders of a foundering worldview, to bear the main responsibility for the difficulties in which that worldview finds itself, events must have so shaped themselves as to acquire *in reality* some sort of Jewish dimension. At the present time this has come about as a result of the transformation of the politics of the Muslim world, by the Islamist revolutionary movements which have emerged over the past three decades, beginning with the Iranian revolution. The politics and ideology of these movements is complex and motivated by factors to a great extent internal to the Islamic world. Moreover, the ferment and the range of conflicts they have engendered at the boundaries of the Islamic world have been worldwide in scope. Radical Islamists are deeply hostile to Western societies, and in particular to America. But they are equally as hostile to Hindus and Buddhists and indeed to any non-Muslim religious group. There are at present in the world a remarkable diversity of conflicts between Muslims and other groups: Thai Buddhists or Christian Filipinos in the Far East, Hindus in Kashmir, Assyrian Christians in Iraq, Coptic Christians in Egypt, Christian and animist tribes in the southern Sudan, Russians in Chechnya, Jews in Israel, Europeans intermittently, and Americans whenever possible.

What is left of the old European messianic Left no longer has at its disposal, if it ever had, a theoretical apparatus either sufficiently complex or sufficiently grounded in reality to allow it to make sense of these developments in its own terms. With a degree of Eurocentrism surprising in people ostensibly committed to shaking off the assumptions of the colonial era, people on the liberal Left tend to leave entirely out of account the hostilities between radical Islamists and other third-world cultures and peoples, and to see in these developments a movement *purely* of opposition to "the West" or to "Capitalism."

To abstract the issues in that way is, of course, to present radical Islamism as *solely* a movement of protest against forces in the world—those represented by the group of economically liberal civil societies of which the United States is at present the most globally active and influential—which the entire history of the messianic Left has conditioned its present representatives to perceive both as intrinsically corrupt and as hostile to the messianic mission of the Left. Presenting matters in that way assimilates the problem to the worldview of the messianic Left, while, simultaneously, restructuring the issues in terms of the essentially *moral* polarities now central to that worldview. Those polarities, as we have seen, when seriously entertained as valid, force one, in a manner reminiscent of certain forms of religious fundamentalism, to see matters in stark black and white. Not only must there be heroes and villains, there can be only one way in which those roles can be distributed. If Islamism has a grievance against the West, that grievance must be a just and reasonable one, since, coming as it does from (at least some of) the inheritors of a non-Western culture, it can only be construed, in terms of the residual moral convictions which now constitute the sole analytic resource of the Left, as a protest of the victimized and powerless against the powerful. Moreover, in terms of those convictions, there can only be one "morally appropriate" response from the West: to admit its guilt and to do whatever is required to rectify the grievances advanced by those for whom it is, no doubt rightly, seen as an oppressor.

But in what, in the present case, does the guilt of the West, and in particular America, consist? Radical Islamist movements identify a variety of grievances relative to their dealings with the West. They include the loss, in the late Middle Ages, of el-Andalus, the Muslim possesions in Spain, and the presence of Western armed forces, particularly American ones, on Muslim soil. But the one to which radical Muslim, and indeed moderate Muslim, opinion, returns incessantly, is the existence of Israel, its military success in the three wars of aggression waged since 1948 with the object of destroying the Jewish state, and America's support for it.

The messianic Left thus stands compelled by the logic of its own position to accept all these as just grievances, ones that is, which deserve to be rectified. But neither the return of el-Andalus—that is to say of large parts of present-day Spain and Portugal—to Muslim control, nor the unilateral abandonment of the option of armed response on the part of Western nations, are not projects which the Left in Europe and America can espouse with any hope of political gain. The one Muslim grievance which it can make its own, with some hope of securing substantial domestic support and propaganda gains, is the existence of Israel. That alone is sufficient to explain the centrality which Israel, and in general the Middle East conflict, has assumed in the political worldview of the Left since the fall of communism.

The Left stands here, from the point of view of the sustainability of its worldview, in a last-ditch redoubt. If it admits that there might be anything to be said against the legitimacy of the Islamist denial of the very right of Israel to exist, its whole moral position begins to unravel, and with it its entire worldview, given the pivotal role now occupied in developing that worldview by moral *prises de position*. But there are grave difficulties to be encountered in defending that redoubt. The first is that the conflict, between Israel and the Arabs, in ordinary moral terms, terms, that is, which most people would grant to possess moral force irrespective of political standpoint, is, as I have argued at length here, as ambiguous as most such conflicts tend to be. Once one discards the special moral vision which animates the Left considered as a specific, sectarian body of opinion, relying instead upon the more basic—and more varied—moral considerations which most people, irrespective of political allegiance, would grant to possess moral weight, there appears, as I argued in the preceding chapter, as much to be said morally for one side as for the other, and very little scope indeed for assigning overriding, *ultimate* blame for the situation to either. It is just a mess, of a kind in which human history abounds, which one simply has to try to resolve, and for which the first requisite for resolution is a withdrawal by both sides from absolute, black-and-white, *prises de position*.

The messianic Left, however, for reasons that we have begun to explore, cannot grant that without denying the power of its sectarian worldview, and the moral convictions associated with it, to illuminate the problem. It must, therefore, argue that the Arab side is *absolutely* in the right, morally speaking, and the Israelis *absolutely* in the wrong. In defending that position, it must have some answer to those who point out the inherent savagery, and the inherent fascism, of the terrorist methods consistently adopted by Arab anti-Semites in their long war against Israel and—as they, if not their Western sympathizers, are entirely happy to admit—against "the Jews." The only answer that can possibly be advanced is that such atrocities are justified because no atrocity committed by anyone, including the Nazis (since one might as well proceed at once to the logical terminus of the argument), can be imagined which approaches that of the crimes committed by the Israelis. And so that answer *is* advanced, by at least some on the Left. It is, for reasons we have examined here at length, an overtly anti-Semitic answer: one entirely in tune with the most traditionally and virulent forms of political anti-Semitism. But advanced it must be, if the alternative is, as it can only be, to question the continuing adequacy of the moral assumptions which not only underlie, but to a great extent constitute, the entire intellectual stock-in-trade of what remains of the messianic Left.

A further difficulty confronting those who pursue this line is that of explaining why America should support Israel. One obvious reason that might be advanced is that the United States, for the greater part of the twentieth century, has, commendably, perceived its national advantage to lie in supporting open, economically and politically liberal societies, wherever they may be found in the world; a decision which, given its momentous consequences during, and in the aftermath to, World War II, and despite occasional disastrous aberrations since, has had a determining, and on balance overwhelmingly positive, influence in shaping the world in which we live today. For evident reasons, however, this explanation is not open to people who regard the political culture of the United States as dominated by rabidly anti-communitarian forms of self-interest, and the United States itself, as a left-wing American acquaintance once put it to me, as a "bandit nation." An explanation in terms of the grosser forms of national self-interest on the part of the United States must therefore be found, but it is difficult to think of any very significant economic advantage which the United States draws from its connection with Israel, and certainly not one which could outweigh the hatred, in large parts of the Islamic world, whose consequences it has had to endure as a result of that connection.

At this point again, Jewish-conspiracy theory presents itself as a means of resolving a theoretical impasse and saving the credit of a worldview at odds with reality. "The Jews" are at their old work of subverting the politics of the host nation to their own nefarious advantage, in this case the advantage of the Nazi-apartheid State of Israel. It is not American self-interest, reprehensible though that may be, but *Jewish* self-interest which explains the foreign policy of the most powerful nation on earth. In this vein it is a claim constantly rehearsed on the Left, in Britain as well as more widely in Europe, that all American administrations, particularly republican ones like the Bush administration, are in thrall to "the Jewish vote." The facts of the matter, which can easily be ascertained, are that Jews account for approximately 3 percent of the population of the United States, and that the Jewish vote, such as it is, numerically divides between the republican and democratic parties, with a considerable edge to the latter. That these facts, as evident and anodyne as they manifestly are, fail utterly to disturb the conviction of many on the Left, not to mention what would appear to be majority opinion in Muslim countries, that the actions of the U.S. government are entirely dictated by "the Jews" does rather tend to demonstrate the extent of the power exerted over otherwise sane minds by the ideological structures which we have been uncovering here.

Similarly, people on the messianic wing of radical politics, not wishing to confront the possibility that the current influence of American neo-conservatism may be due to the perceived strength of some neo-conservative arguments, or even wishing seriously to examine those arguments, very frequently attempt to explain that influence away as an instance of the malign influence of a Jewish cabal, loyal to the interests of Israel rather than to those of the United States, and moved by inveterate hostility to Muslims. Of course this won't hold up either. Many of those generally fingered as within the neo-conservative fold are not Jews (Condoleezza Rice, Dick Cheney, Donald Rumsfeld, George Tenet, for instance), while others, who are Jewish (Bill Kristol and Richard Perle, for instance) were in the forefront of efforts to induce the Clinton administration to intervene in Kosovo to stop the slaughter of Muslims there.[5] And of course such suggestions are overtly anti-Semitic—or "racist" to put it in the preferred language of the confirmed "anti-racists" who advance this kind of nonsense at present with most gusto. But who cares, since it serves to "explain" what would otherwise, given the limited explanatory machinery available to the current worldview of the messianic Left, be inexplicable.

Jewish-conspiracy theorizing of this type has also made an appearance in British politics. Many on the left of the British Labour Party, for instance, find it impossible to understand how their party could have fallen into the hands of a centrist meliorist like Tony Blair. From their point of view, the problem is to explain how any Labour leader as dominant within the party as Blair can hold many of the views which Blair and his New Labour circle manifestly hold without confronting the obvious explanation; namely, that the ideas of "Old" Labour, having outlived their day, can no longer serve as the basis for a practicable, electorally successful politics.

Here, once again, the Left stands in urgent need of a *deus ex machina*, and "the Jews" stand ready, as ever, to serve in that role. The accusation that the prime minister was "being unduly influenced by a cabal of Jewish advisers" was publicly leveled, on schedule, as it were, by the Scottish MP Tam Dalyell, at that time a leading parliamentary figure on the Left of the Labour Party, as part of his contribution to a profile of Tony Blair in *Vanity Fair*.[6] Evidence for a less public, but doubtless more widespread, currency in private conversation, shows itself in the articles by John Pilger and Dennis Sewell, from the January 14, 2003, issue of the *New Statesman* which we analyzed in Chapter 2. It displays itself, for instance, in John

Pilger's rumblings concerning the alleged Jewish sympathies of Lord Levy and Ben Bradshaw, and plenty of other instances could no doubt be found by trawling other recent publications from the left of British politics. Dennis Sewell, after all, admits as much when he notes the current fear on the left of the bogey-figure of the "Big Jew" (see Chapter 2).

In all these suggestions we encounter the claim, typical of anti-Semitism, that the Jews, a small, deeply politically divided people, many of whom staunchly support, as Walter Rathenau did German nationalism, the very values Jews are accused of conspiring against, exercise a mysterious but nonetheless determining influence over political entities overwhelmingly populated, and wholly politically dominated, by non-Jews. A mind capable of giving a moment's credence to this sort of nonsense is, I want to say, a mind in desperation. But we live in times in which desperation of just the required sort is not uncommon: a desperation, namely, born of the sense that the present reality of world politics is slipping inexorably out of the grasp of a worldview to which vast numbers of, on the whole, good, intelligent, well-meaning people have committed their powers as thinking adults.

These problems for the largely residual, but nevertheless deeply held, version of the old messianic Left worldview still espoused by very large numbers of educated, middle-class people, offer a considerable part of the explanation for the obsessive concentration of the more left-oriented sections of the Western press and electronic media on Israel and for the extraordinary unfairness of much of the resulting coverage. Messianic socialism, as we noted earlier, has formed, for more than a century, an important constituent in the worldview of very large sections of the European middle classes, as well as a smaller, but still influential, section of the American middle classes, particularly intellectuals, artists, and those in occupations connected with the acquisition and diffusion of knowledge and culture generally—scientists, medical workers, people in the universities, the media, the education system, and so on. Few of these people have ever, unlike their counterparts in eastern Europe, actually experienced life in a fully socialist economy and state. Nor do they expect to do so in their lifetime, since it is manifest that the political will to establish such a state, having exhausted itself in the wars and revolutions of the past century, no longer exists, except in a few quarters entirely marginal to the political process. What has happened, however, as I have suggested here, is not that the messianic socialist ideal has been consciously criticized and abandoned, but that it has been regretfully relinquished as a practical proposition while at the same time being rarefied and etherialized by processes which began with the "New Left" of the 1960s, into a system of "values." In other words, many of the moral beliefs and attitudes rendered intelligible by a serious belief in the factual adequacy of the traditional worldview of messianic socialism have been retained as unquestionable in the absence of any such belief, as if they still made any sense, were even intelligible, without it.

As we have seen, it is not easy to assimilate the Middle East conflict to the terms dictated by the resulting outlook. The disanalogies are immense and fundamental. But with a sufficiently sedulous attention to the exclusion of inconvenient details, those disanalogies can be eased out of the picture, at least the fuzzy but exciting sort of picture which is all that press and television are required to provide. Making those exclusions requires one to present all Israelis without exception as insensate, utterly morally blunted servants of American corporate interests, people who are prepared, for their own narrow, sectarian interests, to delay forever the arrival of peace and racial harmony, and correlatively to present all those Diaspora Jews and others who support Israel as, simply, evil: people whose acts and outlook have no redeeming features, as people no better than the Nazis, in fact.

This move, from an elite Left consciousness seeing itself as founded primarily in a superior understanding of economics, history, and class conflict, to one seeing itself as founded primarily in a superior moral outlook, carries with it, as we have seen, two consequences which assist the reception of such a vision of things. The first is the erosion of the distinction between "ordinary" morality and the special, political moralities which we distill out of it by combining its principles with structures of theoretically motivated belief. Once that distinction is lost sight of, derivative moral convictions are felt by those who share them to possess the same moral force as the most evident tenets of everyday morality. Every moral commitment now comes to appear as invulnerable to reasoned criticism, as much a matter of intuitive conviction as any other. The "immorality" of Israel's occupying lands which at any former point were in Arab hands becomes as unshakeable a moral datum as the immorality of the deliberate murder of noncombatants. The second is that the enthusiasm, the moral certainty with which these convictions are held, altogether conceals from the holder that the comforting certainty of political rectitude which he derives from them, itself exacts a moral price: that of becoming the worst kind of anti-Semite; the kind for whom anti-Semitism masquerades as a moral virtue.

And so that price is paid: the threshold which opens before those willing to pay it is passed. And once again the cloudy, bloated lay-figure of "the Jew" is on its feet and shambling along the horizon of a tormented world which awaits nothing but the destruction of Jewish arrogance and greed to return to a condition of perfect peace. Of course this is nonsense, and murderous nonsense. But when the alternative is to face up to the failure of a worldview in which one has invested everything, many will choose murderous nonsense.

Bearing all this in mind, let us return, finally, to the concrete and local issue from which we started: the appearance of a respected mainstream organ of the British Left with a cover redolent of *Der Sturmer* and contents to match. What can explain the extraordinary morass of confusion, moral incoherence, and aporia to which we found it possible, by the application of really quite modest resources of textual analysis, to reduce the considered statements of serious, leading, left-wing journalists? The suggestions we have been pursuing, concerning the functions of political anti-Semitism in the thought of those attracted by it, offer us, I think, some help here as well.

From the perspective we have been exploring, one can see, for instance, why, from the point of view of a writers like Sewell, it is immaterial that there are certain facts, about the history of the Israel/Arab conflict, about the precise wording of UN resolutions, and so on, which might be adduced as part of a case in favor of Israel. For Sewell, and others who think like him, there cannot *be* such a thing as a case for Israel, because Israel is *self-evidently* a "colonial" state, its Jewish citizens *colons* who live by exploiting "native" people. Its very existence is a stench in the nostrils of all right-thinking people, because the existence of such a state is, simply and unarguably, *because* morally, wrong.

Plainly, if this is the proposition to which one is going to nail one's flag, then the possibility that there might be *anything*—anything at all—to be said in favor, either of the right of Israel to exist or of Israeli institutions, the conduct of its legal system, its press, its armed forces, for that matter the conduct of the Israeli Left, or of Diaspora Jews, becomes a threatening one; one, that is, capable of disturbing the black-and-white absoluteness of a sectarian morality which is now all that stands between the worldview of messianic socialism and its final dissolution. And so any such suggestion must be contested by all means, from sweeping the facts under the carpet, to moral hyperbole, to the grossest ridicule, as in the case of Sewell's comparison of the Jewish Left to a comic Jewish family in a Woody Allen film. It must also be made to appear that the only people who see anything wrong with this view of things are people with a vested interest in opposing it, namely, Jews. So we are led, by a succession of easy steps, none of which seem individually, to those taking them, anything but sound and in line with the highest morality (the "moral high ground" in the cant phrase of the present day) to the proposition that Israel is an evil society, foisted on the world, with their usual devotion to self-interest at the expense of everybody else, by the Jews: a Jewish conspiracy, in fact.

That proposition expresses, of course, as we have been at pains to show, a deeply traditional anti-Semitism of the worst, the political, kind. But messianic socialism and left-wing views in general are understood by their adherents as opposed root and branch to "racism." This is the problem with which we found the editor of the *New Statesman* wrestling in his "apology" for the cover. Part of the strategy of that article was, as we saw, to reconstitute the concept of racial prejudice in terms of the worldview of the messianic Left, in its current redaction as a species of moral drama. In terms of that reconstitution, and its accompanying political dramaturgy, "racism" becomes, in effect, indistinguishable from "colonialism," that is, from the putative exercise of "power" by "Western" civil societies, led by the United States, over "non-Western" peoples. On this view of things, while there is, of course, or at least has been in the past, such a thing as anti-Semitism, it was brought to an end by the overthrow of the Third Reich and need no longer concern us, except insofar as the sufferings endured at that time have left memories which demand "sensitive" handling. But sensitivity, however morally desirable, cannot excuse the Left from the superior moral duty to continue pointing out the manifest racism implicit in the mere existence of Israel . . . and so on, and so forth.

There is something almost impressive about the capacity on the part of some highly intelligent people, to which this kind of writing so expressively bears witness, to avoid confronting even the bare existence of anti-Semitism, let alone any serious inquiry into its nature and origins, even when their own thoughts are manifestly rotten with it. One of the things aiding this type of blindness is the perennial attempt to transform the long, bloody struggle, first of Christianity, then of the Enlightenment, with the obstinate otherness of the Jews, from the intense culturally and historically complex phenomenon that it has been and is, into a theoretical counter to be freely exchanged against other counters in one or another more or less abstract game of political theorizing. There is a certain family resemblance, is there not, between Marx's assertion that Judaism "is" no more than universalized egoism, and Sartre's suggestion that "the Jew" is entirely the creation of anti-Semitism, and will vanish, as an existential possibility, with the coming of socialism? Both are, in a strange way, attempts to cause Jews and Judaism to vanish from the world, to deny their very existence, except as products of processes capable of being pellucidly grasped in terms of the conceptual framework offered by a favored, and entirely non-Jewish, political philosophy. In a similar way, the editor of the *New Statesman* wants, as it were, and by exactly the same means, to move the Jews, and their eternal complaints, out of the path of "progressive" politics. They were persecuted, they are no longer persecuted, why are they still there, with their ridiculous, racist state and their obstinate refusal to admit what should be obvious, that we are right and they are wrong? Why can't we have our cover? Do we have to go on apologizing forever? And why should we apologize at all, when we are so transparently the good people, occupying the high moral ground? Of course these questions are not easily silenced. They go on asking themselves, at wakeful moments in the night, when people's forces are at their lowest ebb. I suspect, as I suggested earlier, that it is these nocturnal, sibilant, spectral voices of unsilenced self-doubt, rather than the bodily ones of angry Jews, which actually whisper "Anti-Semite!" in the ear of certain enemies of Israel.

We have to deal, in short, with a new version of a once familiar type of politico-moral hysteria, once again operating on the crumbling edge of the pit which led Europe into its last, and bloodiest, bout of anti-Semitism. The new version is prevented from collapsing wholeheartedly into it by the fact that, this time, it is the hysteria of people deeply committed to "antiracism," who, because of that, constantly lurch over the edge of the pit and then draw nervously back, in the manner of Wilby making his "apology." But the source of the hysteria is the same: the will to keep afloat, at all costs, for reasons combining generous sentiments, venal compromise, and intellectual muddle in almost inextricable confusion, a worldview seriously and increasingly at variance with reality: a worldview, whatever form of generous, "liberal" thinking may ultimately replace it, which has, however sadly, however tragically even, outlasted its time.

DOES IT MATTER?

Does the new anti-Semitism actually matter all that much? It is possible to argue that it does not, on the grounds that, in Britain, it affects a rather narrow segment of society. Richard Bolchover, noting that "The business world is a friendlier environment for British Jews and other minorities now than it has ever been," observes that "as a colleague remarked to me recently, 'In the city no-one reads the *Guardian*.'"[7]

To the limited extent that I am in touch with the business milieu, my impression is the same. Unfortunately, the *Guardian* is widely read among groups, including teachers and academics, people in the arts and media, civil servants of one sort and another, whose political and media influence is probably greater than that of the city. The same thing is true in Continental Europe, where the kind of views that we have been attacking are also widespread among those groups, aided, in this case, by an equally wide-spread and often virulent anti-Americanism. We are not, it seems to me, on the brink of anything resembling the murderous anti-Semitism of the first half of the twentieth century, not least because since the brief explosion of 1968, the elite groups in question have not shown themselves capable of organized extra-parliamentary political action.

Nevertheless, there can be no question that attacks on Jews and Jewish institutions, both in Britain and Europe, have increased greatly of late years. It is difficult to imagine that the sustained campaign of demonization, of both Israel and the Jews, conducted in certain parts of the media, has no tendency, on the one hand, to reduce public opposition to these attacks, by planting in many people's minds the suggestion that the situation in the Middle East renders them "natural," or even "deserved"; and, on the other hand, to encourage the perpetrators by giving them the impression that quite a lot of "decent," "respectable" people agree with them.

At the same time, the political courting of the terrorist wing of Arab politics by European politicians with one eye on sections of the media, a phenomenon most recently visible in the almost royal state send-off given by the French government to the remains of Yasser Arafat, and demonstrated recently by the determination of the European Union to find ways of continuing to fund the Palestinian Authority despite its having fallen under the control of Hamas, does nothing whatsoever to further the cause of a peaceful settlement between the Palestinians and Israel.

What can be done about it? In the longer run, no doubt, there is the permanent fact of generational change to reckon with. The generation dominant in European politics, media, and academic life at present is, broadly speaking, the one whose ideas were formed in 1968 and the decade or so that followed. There is no reason to suppose that it will have any more success than previous ones in ensuring the transmission of its views to future generations, and every reason to predict, given the extreme artificiality and fragility of many of its most characteristic *prises de position*, that it will not.

There can be no harm, however, in doing what can be done to move that process along: not least by bringing to the attention of "decent," "progressive" people, as I have been trying to do here, the many reasons why the consensus on Israel currently dominant among them deserves neither of those epithets. I would in particular ask people in academic life, in my own field and others, to consider seriously whether it is at all likely that the constant slanted reporting of the Middle East conflict, by every device of misrepresentation, selection of evidence, and omission of relevant context, and the parroting of these reports over the dinner table, in such a way as to suggest that there is nothing whatsoever to be said on the side of the Israelis, can, on the one hand, be without effect, in the present disturbed political climate in Europe, in encouraging attacks, some of them murderous, on Jews; or, on the other hand, be of any service in securing the peace and progress for the Palestinian people that they claim to desire, given that these things can only conceivably be secured through some advance by the Palestinians beyond the politics of terror. Beyond that, I would ask them to consider whether academics, and for that matter people in the media, should not feel bound by a duty to truth itself: to openness to the facts, however inconvenient those facts may be for the coherence and plausibility of any mere worldview, however central that worldview may seem to the self-construal of "nice" people.

One can, after all, live perfectly well without the support of a large political or religious metaphysic capable, at least putatively, of comprehending and mastering the entire course of human affairs. One can live, for that matter, without the slightest pretence of understanding world affairs: many simple people do. One cannot, though, live perfectly well on a diet of murderous lies. Europe tried that in the 1930s. It would do well not to try it again.

POSTSCRIPT: THE MEARSHEIMER/WALT CONTROVERSY

In March 2006, while this book was in production, but still open to revision, an article titled "The Israel Lobby," by two leading figures in the American academic establishment, John Mearsheimer and Stephen Walt, appeared in the *London Review of Books*.[8] Mearsheimer is the Wendell Harrison Professor of Political Science at the University of Chicago. Walt is Robert and Renee Belfer Professor of International Affairs at the Kennedy School of Government at Harvard University. A longer version of the article had appeared, and remains available, on the Kennedy School of Government website.[9]

The article roused a storm of controversy, in the correspondence columns of the *London Review of Books*[10] and elsewhere, and Mearsheimer and Walt contributed a lengthy reply to their critics in the May 11 issue of the magazine. It is a measure of the interest attracted by the article that the *New York Review of Books*, in its June 8, 2003, issue[11] published a lengthy retrospective of the debate, by Michael Massing, titled "The Storm over the Israel Lobby."

In the course of these exchanges, Mearsheimer and Walt were widely accused of anti–Semitism and responded forcefully that, in their opinion, such accusations were baseless and were being leveled purely in order to suppress legitimate criticism of Israel and its supporters. It seems worth inserting a brief discussion of the arguments here, for two reasons. The first is that the controversy offers a further test-bed—this time an American one—for the criteria developed in this book for distinguishing between anti-Semitism—intentional or otherwise—and "legitimate" criticism of Israel in current political debate. The second is that it offers an equally good opportunity to test the suggestions offered in this chapter about why a version of anti-Semitism, this time one singularly unwilling to admit and embrace its own nature, should have surfaced in public debate at this particular point in time.

Mearsheimer and Walt's article advances two related theses. One might describe them, respectively, as the "core thesis" and the "framing thesis." The core thesis is (1) that the support given by the United States to Israel, particularly the support given since 1967, has always been, and remains, contrary to the national interest of the United States; and (2) that the dysfunctionality, in terms of national self-interest, of American support for Israel, is so extreme and so evident to reason that some special circumstance, over and above the ordinary workings of politics and opinion-forming in America, must be sought, if it is to be possible to explain, causally, how successive U.S. administrations could have been led to overlook it.

The framing thesis is that the special circumstance in question is to be found in the activities of what Mearsheimer and Walt term "the Israel Lobby," a collection of organizations of which the American–Israel Public Affairs Committee (AIPAC) is a leading example.

Various minor claims which deserve mention are advanced in connection with the core and the framing thesis. It is, for example, an essential part of the core thesis that Israel is in a morally considerably weaker position than the Palestinians. Israel has "perpetrated crimes" against the Palestinians;[12] by contrast, the Palestinian recourse to terrorism is described as "wrong, but it isn't surprising."[13] The framing thesis includes as a subordinate contention the claim that the Israel lobby uses the accusation of anti-Semitism purely as a tool to suppress criticism of Israel. All talk of a "new anti-Semitism" is asserted to be part of a deliberate strategy: "Israel's advocates, when pressed to go beyond mere assertion, claim that there is a 'new anti-semitism,' which they equate with criticism of Israel. In other words, criticise Israeli policy, and you are by definition an anti-semite."[14] That contention in turn is supported by the assertion, reminiscent of the *New Statesman* in 2002, that talk of a new anti-Semitism must be a fraud, motivated purely by the desire to exercise political influence, because anti-Semitism is in fact on the decline. "Measuring anti-semitism is a complicated matter, but the weight of the evidence points in the opposite direction."[15]

A further point of contact with the *New Statesman* articles discussed in Chapter 2 is that neither Mearsheimer and Walt nor the editors of the *London Review of Books* are at all anxious to be branded as anti-Semites. "It's a very effective tactic," say the former, speaking of the supposed Jewish willingness to dismiss all critics of Israel as anti-Semitic: "anti-semitism is something no-one wants to be accused of."[16] The latter suggest that "the letters accusing Mearsheimer and Walt of having written an 'anti-semitic rant', and those congratulating them for having exposed a 'secret Jewish . . .conspiracy' have something in common: they come from people who appear not to have read the piece, and who seem incapable of distinguishing between criticism of Israeli or US government policy and anti-semitism."[17]

Is it reasonable, now, to criticize any part of Mearsheimer and Walt's essay as—no doubt unintentionally—anti-Semitic? And if so, which parts? And do the arguments developed earlier in this book afford any means of providing clear and definitive answers to those questions?

For a start, if we have argued correctly, there is nothing intrinsically anti-Semitic about Mearsheimer and Walt's core thesis. The issue of whether or not specific policies pursued by a state serve its national interest is surely a legitimate subject of academic inquiry; and the mere fact that such an inquiry concerns the question of American support for Israel cannot possibly make it *anti-Semitic* to arrive, on the basis of dispassionate inquiry, at a negative answer. Nor, if our arguments are to stand, is their anything anti-Semitic about the supporting arguments of the core thesis. It is not *anti-Semitic*, that is, to criticize, on moral grounds, specific policies of Israeli governments, from the building of settlements on land in the Occupied Territories to the use of truncheons by the IDF in the first intifada to "break the bones of Palestinian protesters."[18] Provided such criticisms are verifiable and properly documented, advancing them no more argues prejudice against Jews than criticism of the French, say, for sinking the Greenpeace vessel *Rainbow Warrior* in the Pacific, argues Francophobia. The only thing that might conceivably motivate a charge of anti-Semitism relative to Mearsheimer and Walt's development of their core thesis is their relative unwillingness to find fault with the Palestinians. But even there it might be argued that the worst they assert is moral equivalence between Israel and the Palestinians. "The Arabs are said to have acted with great wickedness. Yet on the ground, Israel's record is not distinguishable from that of its opponents."[19] And that falls far short of what we distinguished earlier as the unquestionable and overt anti-Semitism of asserting moral equivalence between Israel and the Nazis.

Matters become considerably less clear, however, when we turn our attention to the framing thesis and its associated claims, and to the relationship between the framing thesis and the core thesis. The central contention of political anti-Semitism has always been, as we argued earlier, that "the Jews" operate in conspiratorial ways to subvert the national interest of any nation that harbours them. And the framing thesis of Mearsheimer and Walt's essay would certainly appear, on the face of it, to be that that is what is taking place in America today, and has been taking place for at least the past forty years. In their reply to their critics, Mearsheimer and Walt argue that that is not what they said: "we described the lobby as a loose coalition of individuals and organizations without a central headquarters. It includes gentiles as well as Jews, and many Jewish–Americans do not endorse its positions on some or all issues. More importantly, the Israel lobby is not a secret, clandestine cabal; on the contrary, it is openly engaged in interest-group politics, and there is nothing conspiratorial or illicit about its behavior."[20]

These admissions are indeed what is needed to rebut the accusation of anti-Semitism. The overall impression given by the original essay, however, is rather different. It is entirely true that Mearsheimer and Walt admit certain gentile groupings to the Israel lobby; specifically, Christian evangelicals and gentile neo-Conservatives.[21] But the choice of these two relatively marginal groups, neither of which could seriously be called representative of the mainstream of American life and opinion, can surely only serve in context to suggest to the reader that very few "normal" gentiles, gentiles other than religious fundamentalists and neo-Conservatives, support Israel. And at many other points they describe the lobby in terms which make it clear that they see it as a primarily Jewish operation ("Jewish Americans have set up an impressive array of organizations to influence American foreign policy"),[22] while at one point they expressly describe AIPAC as a "de facto agent for a foreign government."[23] This is sailing very close indeed to the traditional language of political anti-Semitism. The impression it gives is mitigated, to be sure, by the admission that 36 percent of American Jews confess themselves either "not" or "not very" emotionally attached to Israel, but the effect of this is immediately contradicted by the assertion that although "Jewish Americans . . . differ on specific Israeli policies . . . moderates and hardliners both favour giving steadfast support to Israel."[24] With all due respect to the authors, the impression the reader is left with is that a very substantial majority of American Jews are de facto agents for a foreign power. If that is not an anti-Semitic libel I fail to see what is. It was, after all, the nerve of the charges brought against Dreyfus. That association might be considered unfair in the context, given that Dreyfus was, after all, accused, albeit falsely, of a crime. Mearsheimer and Walt are careful to avoid any such accusation. In "The Israel Lobby" they write, "There is nothing improper about American Jews and their Christian allies attempting to sway US policy: the Lobby's activities are not a conspiracy of the sort depicted in tracts like the protocols of the elders of Zion."[25] But if this is so, and the activities of the Israel lobby are, as they are, perfectly legal, what is the point of publishing a long article denouncing the lobby and its activities? Plainly, Mearsheimer and Walt have only one answer available to them: the activities of the lobby threaten the national interest. Jews, and others who support it, are acting, as Mearsheimer and Walt explicitly phrase it, as de facto agents for a foreign government. If you accuse a man of being a traitor to his country, it matters little if you add that what he is up to is perfectly legal! Indeed, it makes things worse: it suggests to the reader that what we have before us is not merely a traitor, but a traitor cunning enough to stay on the right side of the law! I submit that the authors wish to deploy the traditional language of anti-Semitism while simultaneously washing their hands of it. But they need to find a stronger soap: the stuff they are using merely deepens the dye.

The framing thesis also conforms to the traditional pattern of political anti-Semitism in the formidable power, in this case an absolute power to determine events, overriding all other causal considerations, with which it credits the lobby. And as it turns out, the power of the Israel lobby, according to Mearsheimer and Walt, goes far beyond merely engineering financial support for Israel. They credit it at length with largely determining, through "an unrelenting public relations campaign to win support for an invasion of Iraq, a crucial part of which was the manipulation of intelligence in such a way as to make it seem as if Saddam proposed an imminent threat,"[26] the American decision to go to war a second time with Iraq. Once again, what one hand gives rhetorically another endeavors to take away by means of a tactical qualification, one which seeks to evade the accusation of anti-Semitism while not quite blunting the force of the original accusation. In the present case we find the following: "Although neo-conservatives and other Lobby leaders were eager to invade Iraq, the broader American Jewish community was not. . . . Clearly, it would be wrong to blame the war in Iraq on 'Jewish influence'. Rather it was due in large part to the Lobby's influence, especially that of the neo-conservatives within it."[27] But if the lobby, as Mearsheimer and Walt elsewhere claim, consists of a network of organizations, however lacking in central control, largely originated, financed, and manned by Jews, how can anyone who thinks that the lobby played a determining part in taking America to war possibly *avoid* blaming the war on "Jewish influence"? Logic, after all, is not mocked: one claim either entails the other or it does not, and if it does, no amount of verbal hand-washing can alter the fact.

Slice it any way you like, in short, this is still salami. Michael Manning, in his survey of the controversy in the June 8, 2006, issue of the *New York Review of Books,*[28] observes that "The Israel Lobby" has some serious short-comings, citing factual errors, quotes out of context, thin documentation, and a general tendency to ignore contending explanations. It must be admitted, in that connection, that the general tone of the paper, in its combination of vast, but unfocused, threat and cloudy innuendo, mirrors leading characteristics of much consciously and intentionally anti-Semitic writing. One has the impression that a myth is being created, as argued earlier in this chapter, which explains what is felt to be otherwise politically inexplicable—in this case the extraordinary recent collapse in the perceived power of the Democratic Party to influence political developments in the United States which its adherents, particularly on the academic left of the party, for the most part regard with appalled horror—by appeal to a familiar political *deus ex machina*: Jews at work behind the scenes. The worst of it is that the creation of such a myth seems quite unnecessary. There is, after all, nothing particularly puzzling about the processes by which American policy has come, over the past four years, to take the directions it has. One powerfully determining factor was, surely, the attack on the World Trade Center in 2001, which persuaded vast numbers of Americans, Jewish and non-Jewish, that the comparative military invulnerability conferred by the continental size and geographical location of the country was at an end, and that, therefore, something "had to be done." And surely no one who has known America, as I have, for fifty years, can suppose that the present eclipse of Democratic influence can be anything other than temporary: may, indeed, already be coming to an end.

The plausibility of the claim of unique and titanic causal efficacy ascribed by the framing thesis to the lobby depends to a very great extent, of course, on the plausibility of the core thesis. What has to be shown in support of the core thesis, if the framing thesis is to follow from it, is that the costs to America of supporting Israel are so great, the gains to be anticipated from ending or substantially weakening that support so overwhelming, and both so evident to inspection, that it is simply inconceivable that successive U.S. administrations, both republican and democratic, would have continued to support Israel *had it not been for the machinations of the lobby*. This claim, as several correspondents to the *London Review of Books* pointed out, is not easily believable. Defending it would seem to require so great an expenditure of argument and scholarship that one might have expected Mearsheimer and Walt's essay to have been mainly occupied with advocacy of the core thesis; and its title to have been something along the lines of "Does America's Support of Israel Serve the National Interest?" In point of fact, the defense of the core thesis is perfunctory, conducted entirely in terms of generalities entirely familiar from commonplace partisan debate on the issue, and occupies little more than the opening 20 percent of the essay, the remainder being entirely devoted to exposing the machinations of the lobby.

Suppose, however, that the core thesis could be successfully demonstrated. Would not the result be, while giving essential support to the framing thesis on one level, to raise insuperable difficulties for it on another? To whatever extent we succeed in showing it to be *beyond reasonable doubt* that America's support for Israel betrays the national interest, that is, do we not make it, to precisely that extent, hard to understand how responsible American politicians and officials, very few of them Jewish, can have failed to notice the fact, and act appropriately? Do we not put ourselves, dialectically speaking, in the position of having to argue for a greater degree of stupidity or venality on the part of large numbers of eminent, patriotic, and unimpeachably non-Jewish people than is either acceptable or plausible? No doubt the Jews are, as Churchill thought, a remarkable people. But a people capable of setting up a lobbying organization which for forty years succeeds in reducing the entire American political establishment to a state of bemused sleepwalking are more than remarkable; such a people is a creature of fantasy; to be found no doubt in computer games or the products of the Hollywood dream factory, but not in the prosaic world we actually inhabit. In Chapter 1 I argued that it is a feature of anti-Semitic conspiracy theory to be self-defeating, self-undercutting. I submit that that is the case in the present instance also.

Finally, if the framing thesis is not to risk being dismissed as a new version of traditional kinds of anti-Semitic fantasy, the issue of anti-Semitism must somehow be neutralized, in such a way as to prevent it from obtruding itself into the discussion. Here Mearsheimer and Walt avail themselves of the familiar accusation that it is impossible to voice any criticism of Israel without being accused of anti-Semitism. Two of the claims they put forward in this connection demand particular attention.

The first is that anti-Semitism in Europe and elsewhere has shown no increase in recent years. They defend this assertion by appeal to two surveys of European public opinion, one by the Anti-Defamation League, the other by the Pew Research Center for the Press and the People, and they note that, if these surveys are to be believed, the situation differs greatly from that of the 1930s, when "anti-semitism was not only widespread among Europeans of all classes, but considered quite acceptable."[29]

With this I would be inclined to agree, though very cautiously indeed, given the slenderness of the evidence cited and the methodological pitfalls attending public opinion surveys on this kind of issue. But it fails to address the issue. What is claimed by people worried about "the new anti-Semitism" is not that there has been an increase in popular, or as one might say, "folk" anti-Semitism, but that there has been, over the past decade, a very considerable, and well-documented, increase in attacks on Jews and Jewish institutions coming largely from a variety of right-wing or Islamist groupuscules, together with a parallel rise in the type of elite, or "salon," hostility to Jews which it has been the chief business of this book to examine.

The second claim is that concern about "the new anti-Semitism" represents an entirely dishonest attempt by Jews supportive of the aims of the Israel lobby to smear pro-Palestinian journalists and intellectuals, including the authors: "Israel's advocates, when pressed, claim that there is a 'new antisemitism' *which they equate with criticism of Israel.*"[30] Speaking as a non-Jew, I have read most of what has been published so far on "the new anti-Semitism," most of it, as I said in the Preface, by Jews. None of this writing, to my knowledge, asserts equivalence between anti-Semitism and criticism of Israel. How one might set about justifying such an equation I have no idea, not least given the fact that the Jewish community itself, as I noted in some detail in Chapter 3, is alive with vociferous critics of Israel. In this book I myself have argued, in line with the overwhelming majority of Jewish commentators of all political viewpoints, that there is nothing in the least anti-Semitic about the vast bulk of specific criticisms directed at acts of various Israeli governments. It is no more anti-Semitic to suggest, say, that Israel ought not, in 1967 and subsequently, to have occupied the West Bank and the Gaza Strip, than it is anti-American to suggest that the invasion of Iraq was illegal under international law, or that the financing of health care in America is inadequate and socially divisive. What *is* anti-Semitic, I have argued, are two specific sorts of claim. The first is the claim that "the Jews" constitute an organized political force, or conspiracy, of immense and terrifying power, working to serve interests different from, and hostile to, the interests of whatever country gives Jews shelter. The second is the claim that the ends served by this supposed conspiracy are, in some absolute sense, evil. I have argued (1) that the second type of delusion has effectively been revived by those who wish to brand Israel as a "Nazi state," to put it beyond "the pale of world opinion," and so on; and (2) that the first, and more basic type, belief in the existence of a "Jewish conspiracy," has recently begun to find a home again, this time serving as a support to a left-liberal and humanitarian worldview rather than to a right-wing and nationalist one, in much left-liberal journalism and debate about the Middle East conflict. I am afraid I do find more than a trace of the first sort of anti-Semitic fantasy, Jewish-conspiracy theory, in "The Israel Lobby." Possibly it is intentional, possibly not. Either way, the supposed "equation" of anti-Semitism with criticism of Israel has nothing to do with the matter.

The proposition that "the Jews" try to represent all criticism of Israel as anti-Semitic is, of course, itself—in its own right, as it were—an anti-Semitic calumny. It is a variant of the ancient anti-Semitic canard that "the Jews" always try to make some sort of dishonest capital out of their famous sufferings, for which, in consequence, they deserve little sympathy. Matters here, of course, are complicated (a little, but not much) by the fact that Jews on the Right often do, in the heat of the moment, accuse Jews on the Left, of being anti-Semites, or worse than anti-Semites. One thinks of Jonathan Freedland's account, in the *Jewish Quarterly*, of his encounter with "Mr. M.," which I mentioned in Chapter 3. A Jewish correspondent to the *London Review of Books,* Marion Woolfson, gives a similar account. "More than thirty years ago, I was one of the first British Jewish writers to write about the harsh behaviour of the Israeli authorities towards the Palestinians living under a cruel and illegal occupation. Although I did not write about anything which I had not witnessed, I was accused of lying, of being 'paid by the Arabs', and even of having 'sex intercourse with the Arab gangsters.'. . . One man wrote to say he considered it his duty 'to prevent a Jewess from damaging the cause of Israel.'. . . As far back as 1980, the May/June issue of *Yiton* (a Hebrew literary monthly) published an article by the Israeli writer Boaz Evron on the use of accusations of anti-semitism and reminders of the Holocaust to silence critics."[31]

So far as one can judge from its position in a page of correspondence for and against "The Israel Lobby," this letter was written in support of Mearsheimer and Walt. But in fact it does not support them. What it shows is that people who have been appallingly traumatized, as so many Jews have been by the Holocaust, are apt to respond with violent and hurtful invective to anyone whom they take to be sympathizing with their enemies. That is a general characteristic of human beings, by no means confined to Jews. Many of my father's generation, who had been grievously harmed in World War I and could never subsequently be persuaded to look on Germans as fellow members of the human species, were wont to display a similar reaction to any remark that might be interpreted as pro-German: for example, to the suggestion that the terms imposed on Germany by the Versailles Treaty might have had something to do with the subsequent rise of Hitler. What

Mearsheimer and Walt are saying, though, is not that some Jews occasionally respond to people, including other Jews, who express pro–Palestinian sympathies, with fierce and bitter accusations of anti–Semitism. What they are saying, in effect, is that, *in current public debate with non-Jews, Jews supportive of Israel invariably, and dishonestly, attempt to represent any criticism of Israel whatsoever as anti-Semitic, and that this is particularly true of all those who have contributed to the current debate on "the new anti-Semitism," a nonexistent phenomenon invented by Jews in pursuit of precisely this, disreputable, political strategy.* On the one hand, this charge is massively, and demonstrably, false; on the other hand, it revives, in a new form, a very old type of anti-Semitic calumny, namely, the calumny that Jews are always ready to use, in dishonest ways, their real or pretended sufferings to gain advantage over non-Jews.

I conclude with another letter to the *London Review of Books*, this time from Michael Taylor, of Old Maldon, North Yorkshire, that is, from someone whom one would take by his name to be, like me, a non-Jewish Englishman. Taylor writes:

> Perhaps you know, perhaps you don't, that the longer, unedited version of John Mearsheimer and Stephen Walt's essay . . . is being distributed by the PLO in Washington, and is being hailed by Abdul-Moneim Abul-Fotouh, a senior member of the Egyptian Muslim Brotherhood, and by David Duke, the former Ku Klux Klan leader. He had this to say about it: "I have read about the report and read one summary already, and I am surprised how excellent it is. It is quite satisfying to see a body in the premier American University essentially come out and validate every major point I have been making since before the war even started. . . ." I don't want to be in such company, and neither should you. Please cancel my subscription.[32]

Michael Massing, in his review of the controversy in the *New York Review of Books*, notes that "*The Washington Post*'s Richard Cohen called the citing of David Duke's support for the paper a McCarthyite tactic, and a form of 'rank guilt by association' that 'does not in any way rebut the argument made in their paper.'"[33]

On the level of knock–about political polemic this misses its mark by getting things back to front. Senator Joseph McCarthy made his name by accusing people of un-American activities. That is, in effect, precisely the stance adopted by Mearsheimer and Walt. It is Alan Dershowitz and the other pro-Israel American Jews who have protested against this treatment who now occupy the role of the beleaguered Hollywood stars and East Coast intellectuals who bore the brunt of McCarthyism.

On a more serious level, Cohen's retort entirely misses the point of Taylor's penultimate sentence. The point he is making is surely the one I also make earlier on in this book, in Chapter 2; that flirting with the traditional formulas, and in the case of the *New Statesman* with the traditional iconography, of anti-Semitism, however temptingly they may present themselves to people on the liberal-left of politics, whose own intentions and motives may be of the purest, is to be avoided, if on no other grounds, on the grounds that it gives aid, comfort, and encouragement to groups and individuals in whose company none of us should wish to find ourselves. On that note, I shall stop.

NOTES

1. "During my life I have seen life naked, without makeup. Good and evil, the beautiful and the ugly, have been revealed to me mingled inextricably together. That, thank God, has failed to make a moralist of me. On the contrary, I have learned to respect, to love, weakness, that weakness which constitutes our essence and our humanity. A man acquainted with his own weakness will sometimes know how to surmount it. The moralist is unaware of his weakness, and instead of turning upon himself, turns upon his fellow-man." Aharon Appelfeld, *Histore d'une vie* (Paris, Editions de l'Olivier, 2004), p. 128 (my translation).

2. Phyllis Chesler, *The New Anti-Semitism: The Current Crisis and What We Must Do About It* (San Francisco: Jossey-Bass, 2003).

3. Georg Wilhelm Friedrich Hegel, *Philosophy of Right*, trans. T. M. Knox (Oxford: Clarendon Press, 1942), esp. sections 287–89 (pp. 188–89).

4. "Politically correct" is, of course, a term of Marxist theory which once had a substantial—if ultimately, and tragically, ill-founded—intellectual content. To contemplate the sad collection of reach-me-down moral clichés comprehended under the term today is to recognize the truth of Marx's own observation that history has a way of repeating itself, the first time around as tragedy, the second as farce.

5. On this, see Irwin Seltzer, ed., *Neoconservatism* (New York and London: Atlantic Books, 2004).

6. *Vanity Fair*, May 2003.

7. Richard Bolchover, "The Absence of Anti-Semitism in the Marketplace," in Paul Iganski and Barry Kosmin, eds., *A New Anti-Semitism? Debating Judeophobia in the 21st Century* (London: Profile Books, 2003), pp. 267–75.

8. *London Review of Books*, 29, no. 6 (March 23, 2006), pp. 3–12.

9. Available at www.ksg.harvard.edu/research.working_papers/index.htm.

10. See especially the issues of April 6, April 20, and May 11, 2006.

11. *New York Review of Books*, 53, no. 10 (June 8, 2006).

12. *London Review of Books*, 29, no. 6 (March 23, 2006), p. 12.

13. Ibid., p. 5.

14. Ibid., p. 8.

15. Ibid., p. 8.

16. Ibid., p. 8.

17. *London Review of Books*, 29, no. 8 (April 20, 2006), p. 4.

18. *London Review of Books*, 29, no. 6 (March 23, 2006), p. 5.

19. Ibid., p. 5.

20. *London Review of Books*, 29, no. 8 (April 11, 2006), p. 4.

21. *London Review of Books*, 29, no. 6 (March 23, 2006), p. 6.

22. Ibid., p. 6.

23. Ibid., p. 6.

24. Ibid., p. 5.

25. Ibid., p. 6.

26. Ibid., p. 10.

27. Ibid., p. 10.

28. *New York Review of Books*, 53, no. 10 (June 8, 2006).

29. *London Review of Books*, 29, no. 6 (March 23, 2006), p. 8.

30. Ibid., p. 8.

31. *London Review of Books*, 29, no. 8 (April 20, 2006), p. 5.

32. *London Review of Books*, 29, no. 7 (April 6, 2006), p. 5.

33. *New York Review of Books*, 53, no. 10 (June 8, 2006).

APPENDIX: SOURCES FOR ILLUSTRATIVE MATERIAL

One reader of an earlier draft of this book, for whose work in the area I have the greatest respect, urged me to include considerably more in the way of illustrative material. In the end I decided against this, for the reasons briefly noted in the Preface. My target is not particular "anti-Semitic" individuals or groups, but the latent, unacknowledged anti-Semitism lurking in the silences and internal incoherence of a particular, rather widespread outlook. The main role of illustrative material in such an enterprise is merely to establish that the outlook under scrutiny is not a straw man, but one shared and propagated by real people. More than the minimum of illustration necessary to establish this would, it seemed to me, simply serve to hold up the progress of the argument and obscure its structure and articulations. In addition there are a number of well-researched books and articles already available which offer abundant carefully documented instances of the new anti-Semitism. The following is a selection only, but one which may be of service in directing further reading.

An excellent French study of the revived anti-Semitism I have been examining here, in France, but also worldwide, is Pierre-André Taguieff, *La nouvelle judéophobie* (Paris: Mille et une Nuits, 2002), available in English translation under the unfortunate title *Rising from the Muck, The New Anti-Semitism in Europe* (Chicago: Ivan R. Dee, 2004). Gabriel Schoenfeld, *The Return of Antisemitism* (New York: Encounter Books, 2004) undertakes a wider survey, including the Muslim world.

For an account of the relationship between European anti-Semitism and its equivalent in the Muslim world, see Ian Buruma and Avishai Margalit, *Occidentalism: The West in the Eyes of its Enemies* (New York: Penguin Press, 2004).

A good collection of articles, covering mainly the British situation, is Paul Iganski and Barry Kosmin, eds., *A New Anti-Semitism? Debating Judeophobia in the 21st Century* (London: Profile Books, 2003). A further extensive and extremely well-documented study is "Anti-Zionism in Great Britain and Beyond: A 'Respectable' Anti-Semitism" (2004), by Alvin H. Rosenfeld, professor of English and Jewish studies and director of the Institute for Jewish Culture and the Arts at Indiana University. This is published by the American Jewish Committee, and can be downloaded from their website [http://www.ajc.org].

For a history of Jewish opposition to Israel, utterly destructive of the idea, central to all versions of anti-Semitism, that "the Jews" are united either in their defense of Jewish interests or in their perception of what those interests consist in, see Edward Alexander and Paul Bogdanor, eds., *The Jewish Divide over Israel* (New Brunswick and London: Transaction Publishers, 2006).

Recent books on the new anti-Semitism in the United States include Phyllis Chesler, *The New Anti-Semitism: The Current Crisis and What We Must Do About It* (New York: Jossey-Bass, 2003); and a good collection of essays, *Those Who Forget the Past: The Question of Anti-Semitism*, edited by Ron Rosenbaum, with an Afterword by Cynthia Ozick (New York: Random House, 2004).

An index of current disquiet in British government circles concerning the rise of the new anti-Semitism is offered by a memorandum, dated January 7, 2005, submitted by the Parliamentary Committee Against Anti-Semitism (a cross-party body whose—mostly non-Jewish—officers include such distinguished Labour parliamentarians as the Rt. Hon. Stephen Byers MP and Lord Merlyn-Rees) to the Select Committee on Home Affairs. The analysis of the situation it offers is very much in agreement with the one pursued here. For instance it recognizes the January 14, 2002, issue of the *New Statesman* as having represented the crossing of a "watershed," and describes the imagery of the cover as "unmistakably anti-Semitic." A copy of this document can be found at: http://www.publications.parliament.uk/pa/cm200405/cmselect/cmhaff/165ii/165we32.htm.

Other non-Jewish expressions of concern at the present recrudescence of an anti-Semitism, no less real for being rooted in what are felt to be humanitarian political concerns, are to be found on the websites of Anglicans for Israel (http://www.anglicansforisrael.com/), and at the websites of the Israel friendship organizations of two of the main British political parties, Labour Friends of Israel and Conservative Friends of Israel. The URLs of these are respectively, http://lfi.org.uk/, and http://www.cfoi.co.uk/index.html. (The third main party, the Liberal Democratic Party, has a similar group, but I have been unable to locate a web address for it.)

INDEX

ABOUT THE AUTHOR

Bernard Harrison is currently E. E. Ericksen Professor of Philosophy Emeritus at the University of Utah. His books include *Meaning and Structure* (Harper & Row, 1972), *Form and Content* (Blackwell, 1973), *Fielding's 'Tom Jones': The Novelist as Moral Philosopher* (Chatto/University of Sussex Press, 1975), *An Introduction to the Philosophy of Language* (Macmillan, 1979), *Inconvenient Fictions: Literature and the Limits of Theory* (Yale University Press, 1991), and most recently (with Patricia Hanna), *Word and World: Practice and the Foundations of Language* (Cambridge University Press, 2004).